Sexual Harassment Awareness Training

60 Practical Activities for Trainers

Andrea P. Baridon

David R. Eyler

McGraw-Hill

New York   San Francisco   Washington, D.C.   Auckland   Bogotá
Caracas   Lisbon   London   Madrid   Mexico City   Milan
Montreal   New Delhi   San Juan   Singapore
Sydney   Tokyo   Toronto

2 3 4 5 6 7 8 9 0   MAL/MAL   9 0 0 9 8 7

ISBN 0-07-005429-0

The sponsoring editor for this book was Phillip Ruppel, the editing supervisor was Fred Dahl, and the production supervisor was Donald Schmidt. It was set in New Caledonia by Inkwell Publishing Services.

Printed and bound by Malloy Litho.

Library of Congress Cataloging-in-Publication Data
Baridon, Andrea P.
    Sexual harassment awareness training : 60 practical activities for
trainers / Andrea P. Baridon, David R. Eyler.
      p. cm.
    Includes index.
    ISBN 0-07-005429-0 (pbk.)
    1. Sexual harassment—Prevention—Study and teaching.
2. Employees—Training of—Handbooks, manuals, etc. 3. Employee
training personnel—Handbooks, manuals, etc. I. Eyler, David R.
II. Title.
HF5549.5.S45B37 1996
658.3´1244—dc20
                                  95-23785
                                  CIP

CONTENTS

Section 3 Judging When Workplace Behavior Becomes Sexual Harassment   **121**

Section 4 Applying the Reasonable Person Standard to Sexual Harassment   **163**

Section 5 Determining Employer Liability in Sexual Harassment Cases   **207**

Conclusion   **249**

PREFACE

Sexual harassment is an ugly reality of the business world—the meanest of power struggles between a working woman and man. Its consequences can be painful—even destructive—for the individuals and the company involved. Some types of borderline behavior that may be precursors of the harassment to come, on the other hand, can be managed and changed:

- Words or actions that result from honest misunderstandings arising between a man and woman who haven't established necessary boundaries

- Playful remarks or actions that are OK for a man and woman in a social setting but are out of place among colleagues at work

- Spontaneous words or actions that, like spent arrows, cannot be retrieved before they cause harm that may not have been intended

- Actions taken or things said with disregard for the realities of the new rules governing working relationships among women and men

- Words or behavior that attach disproportionate value to perceived differences between the sexes relative to their ability to do a job

- Actions or words taken down paths that must be cut off immediately if minor irritations are not to become major offenses whose resolution slips from the personal problem-solving prerogatives of the woman and man involved to third-party intervention or litigation.

In our many years of working together, we have learned to deal with one another as colleagues and as gender opposites, observing other women and men in the workplace, then commenting on our experiences and observations in our two previous books, *More Than Friends, Less Than Lovers: Managing Sexual Attraction in Working Relationships* and *Working Together: The New Rules and Realities for Managing Men and Women at Work.* In *More Than Friends,* we dealt with sexual attraction in the workplace, focusing mostly on the individuals involved; in *Working Together,* we considered the overall challenges posed by a work environment composed of almost equal numbers of women and men. And in each of these books, we addressed sexual harassment as one issue among many. As we researched to write, we read a great deal of material on sexual harassment, most of which focuses on extreme behavior that begs for litigation—actions that are grossly offensive, illegal, and subject to court remedies.

But that isn't the only kind of relationship found in the workplace. Some men and women, when the conditions and their chemistries are right, find romance at work. When they are free to pursue it, healthy relationships can develop; when they are not, relationships disruptive to productivity and workplace harmony may occur. When a mismatched attraction is pursued without encouragement or becomes coercive, sexual harassment happens. But what about everyday working people who aren't sure just what the rules are? How can they keep out of trouble without virtually ignoring their opposite sex colleagues for fear of making a mistake? We have concluded that there is a real need to address the less dramatic, lower threshold sexual harassment challenges for normal men and women who occupy the vast middle of the workplace relationship continuum—those who would not intentionally engage in behavior that may be defined as harassing, but at the same time, are confused about what they see as blurry lines between appropriate social and workplace behavior.

Since it is safe to assume that sexuality will never be checked at the office door, leaving an androgynous work group free of attractions and the need to cope with them, it is reasonable to have protocols to deal with what individuals can themselves manage—their behavior. At the center of the continuum are company and societal policies that set the boundaries of acceptable behavior. To one side of the center is the growing license allowed those who choose to form consenting personal relationships—the unwritten rule of most companies today is that these relationships must not interfere with work. To the other side are messy affairs and sexual harassment that bring into the arena the disciplinary mechanisms of the company, the Equal Employment Opportunity Commission, and the courts.

Most workers, gratefully, fall near the center and have only to deal with the complexities of being normal in the problematic environs of the mixed-gender workplace. The goal of this book is to take its users beyond their comfortable intellectualization of gender fairness and have them experience its complexity directly. In our own work we have come to appreciate the need to reduce issues to illustrative experiences that lend themselves to the "ah ha!" test. We may "know" a problem and its solution, but we may not have experienced it, but once we do (ah ha!), the likelihood of gaining insight that will alter our future dealing with the opposite sex at work increases. Whether they are audibly expressed or kept quietly inside, these "ah ha!" moments of insight move us nearer our goal of helping men and women better understand each other as they share the exciting potential and the demanding responsibilities of working together in mixed-gender teams.

It is toward this end that the exercises here are dedicated. Enter into them freely in the spirit in which they are offered—not to condemn or embarrass, but to inform, enlighten, and stimulate the self-evaluation of what you think and do. The activities can prompt the examination of values, but judging their merits and deciding to adopt them is ultimately a private choice.

Absorb the messages addressing values, make your personal accommodations to them at your own pace, but understand the necessity to immediately change your *behavior* enough to function legally and effectively in the mixed-gender workforce. Laws and regulations can dictate overt behavior, but they will not change internal beliefs. While we think the values underpinning the exercises represent positions most reasonable people can comfortably make their own, they are offered with the understanding that outward behavior can be changed more readily than internal beliefs. The latter process is a more personal and time-consuming task that each person must undertake in his or her own way, but while *behaving* according to accepted standards.

INTRODUCTION

This book has five parts. It is designed and written to provide men and women, who share the workplace in almost equal numbers, with training experiences that sensitize them to problem areas surrounding the issue of sexual harassment. To modern workers and their companies most problems fall into one or more of these clusters:

1. *Myths and Realities of Gender*—Assumptions about the other sex drives the way men and women behave toward one another; making accurate assumptions is an important factor in their ability to interact reasonably.

2. *Illustrating the Kinds of Sexual Harassment*—As the issue became litigious and the subject of regulation, sexual harassment offenses were sorted into categories that are key to understanding the boundaries of acceptable behavior.

3. *Judging When Workplace Behavior Becomes Sexual Harassment*—Although definitions are not carved in stone and evolve over time, continual testing in the courts is yielding the criteria against which offending behavior is judged. Workers need to be familiar with the emerging guidelines.

4. *Applying the Reasonable Person Standard to Sexual Harassment*—Since most workers are, at least at the outset of a problem, left to judge for themselves what offends and what does not, the perspective of the reasonable person becomes the benchmark for individual decisions.

5. *Determining Employer Liability in Sexual Harassment Cases*—Courts are providing guidance on the measure of when the consequences of personal behavior assume broader ramifications and the misdeeds of the individual become the responsibility of the company.

Before going on to the exercises, you will find three additional items in the introduction useful: (1) some suggestions on how to conduct training on the sensitive issues of sexual harassment; (2) how to use this book; and (3) an overview of male/female working relationships, including a brief history and discussion of the major sources of misunderstandings between the sexes at work, some demographic facts of life, the essential myths and realities of man-woman differences and their significance in modern work, landmark legal points to assist in understanding the issues of sexual harassment, and the inevitability of change.

TRAINING SUGGESTIONS

It isn't just on the job that sexual harassment is reaching the courts—workers are coming forward with charges that they are being discriminated against by the very training sessions billed as solutions to the problem. Prominent cases at the moment include the Seattle ferry boat authority and the Federal Aviation Administration. Although actual legal challenges are few, their message is worth hearing. People resent attempts to stuff even seemingly righteous change down their throats. To enhance rather than obstruct progress in sexual harassment training, which is now required by many companies, we encourage a pragmatic approach that says you will do more good faster by respecting the sensibilities of the audience you address.

How? People come to group experiences with different levels of willingness to participate openly, not to mention with deep-seated and sometimes very private beliefs on the issue of proper relationships between the sexes. Respecting individual sensibilities does not mean you must dilute your message or pander to intransigence, but it does mean that you may gain more by designing and implementing sexual harassment sensitivity training with these points in mind:

✓ Enough substantive material exists on the issues that you do not need to sensationalize or graphically demonstrate that demeaning behavior cuts both ways.

✓ You can evaluate your audience in advance or early in the session and identify participants who will actively help you implement the exercises.

✓ Encourage active participation but do not demand it of everyone. Let individuals warm to the task with the passage of time, accept the probability that some will be passive participators, and design your workshop to ensure that even those on the sidelines receive the message.

✓ Expect to be a facilitator and accept that your own participation, and that of your training associates, may be required to make an exercise work.

✓ Always leave the participant a face-saving way out. Your ability to command the respect of the group and nudge it toward your desired outcome depends on providing a safe training environment in which people can maintain privacy or take risks, learn from them, and walk away whole and unembarrassed.

✓ Without shaming those who miss the point or advocate a different view, steer the exercise to the "school solution" when that is the goal and explain, when it is true, that your outcome represents the company's perspective on the problem and its expectations for workers' behavior.

✓ Cultivate an attitude that demands behavioral change, but accepts different personal beliefs. Insist that workers must learn to practice the correct behavior, encourage the development of compatible attitudes and beliefs, but stop short of chastising or condemning personal values. In the final analysis, you and the company you represent can demand compliance with standards of behavior, but you cannot and should not demand that employees change the way they think.

✓ Protect individuals from embarrassment by filtering publicly expressed thoughts through group consensus (e.g., if a spontaneous reaction turns out to have an awkward connotation, the laugh is on the group, not an individual or the group's spokesperson). Encourage confident risk taking by individuals, but make it clear that it is not expected of everyone.

✓ Acknowledge at the outset that the topics are potentially sensitive and that everyone is entering into an unwritten contract to be considerate of others in the group. Candor is encouraged, but deliberate embarrassment will be avoided. The objective is to learn from one another, not to win or lose a contest.

✓ Finally, not every point addressed has a definitively correct answer. Mention that we're still refining our knowledge, offer the best judgment for the times, but leave the door open to further developments that could alter today's thinking. The point of the exercises is to stimulate thought and to better sort accepted from questionable practices—not to solve every problem with certainty.

HOW TO USE THIS BOOK

The table of contents is an outline of the book and provides a complete list of the exercises and where to find them. For a more thorough introduction to the substantive content of each section, turn to its first pages, which begin with a brief statement of rationale followed by its selection of exercises. The exercises of the section are presented in an annotated list that identifies the methodology employed and the subject matter covered and describes how the exercise works. The 10 methodologies used are: agree/disagree, demonstration, make the case, match the items, multiple choice, rate the accuracy, solve the riddle, sort the lists, true/false, and spontaneous reaction. Finally, an optional cross-reference to the companion volume, *Working Together: The New Rules and Realities for Managing Men and Women at Work,* is provided so that those using it can increase their personal knowledge of the topics.

AN OVERVIEW OF WORKING RELATIONSHIPS

While our companion volume, *Working Together: The New Rules and Realities for Managing Men and Women at Work,* develops these points fully, this summary will give you a useful orientation for implementing the exercises that follow. Context will help you orient and motivate yourself and those you train toward the goal of achieving gender fairness in the workplace. Begin with some basic knowledge that sheds light on unraveling the mysteries of problematic workplace relationships.

History

Depending on your view of creation, man and woman either emerged from the primordial ooze together and evolved to their present state or a single rib turned into a gender opposite in an early apple orchard. Either way, men and women go back to the beginning together and traditionally have had different roles and status in their homes and workplaces.

When we regress very far from modern times, we find that survival of the species depended on a division of labor. Underwriting all gender differences is *the* difference in reproductive roles—women and men are, at least in that regard, indisputably different. Childbearing and nurturing have always colored man-woman relationships and influenced both the opportunities available to individuals and their ability to pursue them.

As women and men evolved physically and culturally, gender roles became so distorted by a mixture of real and imposed differences that they are perhaps eternally riddled with never-to-be-resolved arguments of nature and nurture. What matters is that the sexes shared their early years in ways that allowed them to continue as a species—whether hunting and gathering eons ago or fighting and surviving a great world war only half a century ago.

Today, as the beneficiaries of that evolutionary success story, men and women face problems which are comparatively pleasant as they attempt to share work and opportunities equitably. Frontier culture no longer dictates that men ride the range and women tend the home or the saloon; the economy isn't that of the mid-1940s when women were expected to abdicate their new careers to men returning from war. The women of today expect to have the same kinds of opportunities enjoyed by men, and society has signaled its concurrence by passing laws guaranteeing those rights. All that remains is day-to-day acceptance of this reality by the men and women who populate the work environment. This book is a means of helping you to implement one of the great ideas of modern history—real gender equity in the workplace.

Misunderstandings

A number of erroneous assumptions that have been around so long they've assumed an aura of truth are serious obstacles to achieving gender equality at work. The first of these is that if women and men are to share work equitably it must be established that men and women are the same. How foolish! Take one look and you realize that women and men will *never* be the same. The arguments of women's advocates who insist that their success rides on proving their sameness with men are self-defeating. Likewise, men who verbally profess a willingness to change, but block the way until women prove they are the same as men, create an unwarranted impasse to progress.

A second wrong assumption is that separate-but-equal approaches will solve the problem: keep women and men away from each other, and there's nothing to fight about—right? Wrong! Blatantly separate jobs and work situations are no longer common, but decision makers can still deny full opportunity by *mentally* segregating women and men as they make management decisions. The damage is done by managers or coworkers who think they "know" a woman could or couldn't, would or wouldn't, should or shouldn't be hired for a particular position or perform a particular job assignment simply because of her gender. These are examples of the thinking that is at the heart of the glass ceiling problem.

"Different but equal" should be the catch phrase, and it is a perspective that embodies an age of technology-assisted work in which man-woman differences are not justifiable obstacles to pursuing virtually all occupations. The cure is to cultivate a management mindset in which hiring and assignment decisions are based only on merits. The misunderstanding to conquer is the one that whispers in management's ear: "Use human resources wearing heels differently than those wearing wing tips." It is the last vestige of unfairness and it resides almost invisibly in the habits and thinking of managers who bear few outward signs of the old thinking—and it is the hardest to overcome.

Demographics

No significant measure of the working population or those waiting in the wings to replace it denies the emergence of women as equal players in the economy. *Working Together* includes 18 tables and graphs based on Census Bureau, Department of Labor, and other reliable data that chart the ascending path of women. A sampling of the trends shows:

✓ From the early 1980s to the early 1990s women increased as a proportion of almost every job classification used in labor statistics.

✓ Women made dramatic gains in categories such as executive, administrative and managerial; engineer; mathematician and computer scientist; natural scientist; health diagnosing occupation; and lawyer and judge.

✓ In the federal work force, women went from populating only the lower grades to significantly increased numbers in the senior grades between 1970 and 1989.

✓ From 1869 until the late 1970s more men than women enrolled in college; the trend since then continues to favor women.

✓ Since about 1980, more women than men earned associate, bachelor's and master's degrees, and the trend lines became parallel or reversed in favor of women for first professional and doctor's degrees. Again, this trend is projected to continue.

✓ Changes in the percentage of women earning first professional degrees jumped dramatically between 1960 and 1988—5.5 percent to 33 percent for M.D., 0.8 percent to 26.1 percent for D.D.S. or D.M.D. and 2.5 percent to 40.4 percent for LL.B. or J.D.

✓ Women as a percentage of the labor force grew from 38 percent in 1970 to 45 percent in 1990 and the expectation is for a continued upward trend.

The gist of it all? Women have entered the mainstream of American work, and the demographics show their place solidifying and expanding. They now make up about half the work force, and they are in the workplace to stay. The roles they play increasingly include those traditionally held by men. The workplace is thoroughly mixed by gender, and it is destined to become more so. Learning to live and prosper in this changed environment is a necessity for all its inhabitants.

Myths and Realities

Gender differences are many and real. They are discussed fully in *Working Together*, where the best of scientific knowledge is cited to place these differences in an accurate context. However, the bottom line is straightforward in nearly every instance—women and men are quite different in important ways, but none of the differences are significant when it comes to performing modern work.

Here are some examples:

✓ Overall, men are larger and stronger than women.

✓ Men and women have different hormonal chemistries; the differences are large enough to measure and they can make the sexes behave differently, but not uniformly or dramatically so.

✓ Men's and women's brains are structurally different; connecting paths and regional activities vary; the male brain is larger. In terms of intellect or the ability to perform in the modern workplace, however, the differences are trivial, found mostly at the extremes of a large overlapping center where men's and women's abilities are much the same.

✓ As sociolinguist Deborah Tannen and others have demonstrated, men and women communicate differently and their approaches to managing people can vary, but there is tremendous overlap and reason to believe these differences will diminish as men and women become the product of more common life experiences. In addition, their differences in approach often are complementary rather than conflicting.

The conclusion is that, taken as groups, women and men are much more alike than different. There are more differences between *individuals* than between the *sexes*. The differences of nature are indisputably true, but relatively insignificant in the context of modern work. Occupational differences are largely the result of nurture, i.e., they are cultural rather than genetic—so that both genders have essentially the same occupational capabilities. This is true for most of what we know about sex differences, whether they are the measurable differences in the human body and its chemistry or the unmeasurable differences in style between men and women. The differences are observable and sometimes fascinating, but a convincing case cannot be made for using them to predict someone's capability to do a job successfully or to prevent a person from having a chance.

Legal Landmarks

There is a time line of social progress on gender issues that dates back to the Fourteenth Amendment to the Constitution (July 28, 1868), which established equal protection under law. The Voting Rights Amendment, Article XIX of the Constitution, was next (August 26, 1920), and it gave women the vote.

Although many early statutory landmarks did not have gender as their focus, they laid important groundwork for the future. Modern legislation that set the rules of gender equity began with the Equal Pay Act of 1963, followed by the Civil Rights Act of 1964; Executive Orders 11246 and 11375, which banned discrimination by federal contractors; the 1972 Equal Employment Opportunity Act; the 1978 Pregnancy Discrimination Act; the 1980 Sexual Harassment Guidelines; and the Civil Rights Act of 1991.

The public impact of these laws has been interesting, sometimes unexpected. In *Working Together* we reviewed case law in which the principals included everyone from bank employees to mill workers who asked the courts to help them right the wrongs of gender discrimination. Public figures such as Supreme Court Justice Clarence Thomas, once head of the

Equal Employment Opportunity Commission, and Senator Robert Packwood of Oregon, a vocal advocate of women's rights, have become entangled in this relatively new form of social regulation.

Times have changed, and managers need to understand how to operate intelligently and sensitively in a workplace where a 50:50 mix of women and men interacts on a daily basis. The ultimate arbiter of whether they succeed is the courts. Demonstrating the practical side of the law may be justifying which behaviors are acceptable and which are not—is the purpose of this book.

Inevitable Change

A paradigm shift of major proportions has taken place—the ways women and men live and work have changed forever. A look at the current work force, college enrollments, or college graduates yields the same message—women do and will increasingly constitute a major part of the trained work force.

Women who accounted for 1 percent of business travelers in 1970 constituted 30 percent of them in 1991 and are projected by the hospitality industry to make up 50 percent of that market by the year 2000. Change is already in the pipeline in so many fundamental ways that there is no doubt about its magnitude or direction. Work force projections remove any doubt that women and men will be spending more time together professionally. Therefore, as the sexes find themselves working side by side for the indefinite future, they must learn to get along as coworkers, not merely to tolerate each other. To this end, they need to:

✓ Increase their understanding of one another

✓ Acknowledge their differences, appreciate their underlying similarities, and then capitalize on the uniqueness they each bring to accomplishing a task

✓ Accept that there are alternative ways of reaching professional objectives together—often more efficiently and enjoyably as mixed-gender teams

✓ Agree to accept the obligation to act in good faith to change what negative behaviors and attitudes they can and to effectively manage the rest

We hope the exercises in this book will help you and your coworkers make these ideals realities.

Section 1

MYTHS AND REALITIES OF GENDER

Rationale

The overarching thought behind the exercises of Section 1 is: Assumptions about the other sex drive the way men and women behave toward one another; making accurate assumptions is an important factor in their ability to interact reasonably.

Selection of Exercises

Use these thumbnail sketches of the exercises in Section 1 to choose those best suited to your purposes.

AGREE/DISAGREE

1. *Women's Work vs. Men's Work*—Participants anonymously score statements on tasks with traditional gender-linked connotations on an agree/disagree scale. Identifying themselves only as male or female raters, they mark the statements once with their candid opinion and once as what they believe is "politically correct." Trainers calculate averages, note extremes, and help participants separate myth from reality in a guided discussion of their differences.

2. *Gender Really Does Matter*—Participants anonymously score statements about likely differences between women and men on an agree/disagree scale. Identifying themselves only as male or female raters, they mark the statements once with their candid opinion and once as what they believe is "politically correct." Trainers calculate averages, note extremes, and help participants separate myth from reality in a guided discussion of their differences.

DEMONSTRATION

3. *Sorting Laundry*—An actual or simulated sorting of home laundry by randomly chosen or volunteer men and women lets participants witness a task "superiority" born of cultural experience. The resulting sorted batches of clothes are critiqued to show the likely superiority of women at the task, taking into consideration color vs. whites, delicate vs. hearty fabrics, etc.

4. *Contact Lenses*—Observing a man and a woman insert a pair of contact lenses lets participants witness a task "superiority" born of cultural experience, i.e., applying eye makeup. The experience is critiqued to show why most women will likely be superior at the task.

MAKE THE CASE

5. *Who Gets the Job?*—A group of men is tasked with defending a woman's right to a nontraditional job assignment, while a group of

women assumes the traditional male role and debunks the woman's assignment. Participants experience the feel of stereotyped limitations in job assignments from the perspective of their gender opposites.

6. *Doing It My Way*—A group of men is tasked with defending a woman's way of doing her job, while a group of women assume the traditional male role and debunk her approach. Participants experience the feel of the different-but-equal reality from the perspective of their gender opposites.

MATCH THE ITEMS

7. *Men Better/Women Better*—Participants are given a list of terms and are asked to select using the letters M, W, and N (Men, Women, No difference) who, if anyone, is better in the category. Again, they are asked for their first thought, not one that is the result of deciding what is politically correct. The results are computed and trainers help participants confront stereotyped thinking and modify each other's positions in guided discussion.

8. *What Women and Men Want*—Participants are given a list of questions and are asked to choose one of three answers [Want, Don't want, Neutral] based on what they think women or men want. The results are computed and participants confront stereotyped thinking and modify each other's positions in guided discussion.

MULTIPLE CHOICE

9. *Male Superiority*—Participants judge the validity of a number of male-superiority assumptions by selecting multiple-choice answers. Trainers tabulate and compare the results, then, during a guided discussion, aid participants in examining the strengths and weaknesses of commonly held stereotypes.

10. *Reaction Differences*—Participants judge the validity of a number of "how would a man/woman react?" assumptions by selecting multiple-choice answers. Trainers tabulate and compare the results, then, during a guided discussion, aid participants in examining the strengths and weaknesses of commonly held stereotypes.

RATE THE ACCURACY

11. *Different Drummers*—Individuals are asked to score several statements anonymously on an accurate/inaccurate scale. Identifying themselves only as male or female raters, they mark the list once with their candid opinion and once as what they believe is "politically correct." Trainers calculate averages, note extremes, and help participants separate myth from reality in a guided discussion of their differences.

12. *Typical Woman/Man*—Individuals are asked to score several statements anonymously on an accurate/inaccurate scale. Identifying themselves only as male or female raters, they mark the list once with their candid opinion and once as what they believe is "politically correct." Trainers calculate averages, note extremes, and help participants separate myth from reality in a guided discussion of their differences.

SOLVE THE RIDDLE

13. *Doctor/Parent*—Participants are asked to solve a riddle in which clinging to sexual stereotypes clouds their judgment and hinders their ability to find the solution. Trainers guide the discussion to reveal the stereotypes and their relevance to attitudes at work.

14. *Cabinet Spouse*—Participants are asked to solve a riddle in which clinging to sexual stereotypes clouds their judgment and hinders their ability to find the solution. Trainers guide the discussion to reveal the stereotypes and their relevance to attitudes at work.

SORT THE LISTS

15. *50:50 Split on Attributes*—Participants are asked to make forced choices among attributes—half must be listed under each gender. The results are tallied for men and women and they are examined during a guided discussion.

16. *50:50 Split on Aspirations*—Participants are asked to make forced choices among aspirations—half must be listed under each gender. The results are tallied for men and women and they are examined during a guided discussion.

TRUE/FALSE

17. *Nature/Nurture*—Participants take a true/false quiz based on whether nature or nurture best accounts for certain things linked to gender differences in the workplace. The results are tallied for men, women, and the total group, and the responses are examined during a guided discussion.

18. *Conventional Wisdom*—Participants take a true/false quiz based on the presumed validity of certain items of conventional wisdom about men and women that are linked to gender differences in the workplace. The results are tallied for men, women, and the total group, and the responses are examined during a guided discussion.

SPONTANEOUS REACTION

19. *News Flash*—Participants are presented with a news flash, brief headline kind of statement with workplace gender overtones and are asked to respond with an immediate reaction. The results are tallied for men, women, and the total group, and the responses are examined during a guided discussion.

20. *Office Gossip*—Participants are presented with a snippet of office gossip having workplace gender overtones and are asked to respond with an immediate reaction. The results are tallied for men, women, and the total group, and the responses are examined during a guided discussion.

Optional Cross-References—The following chapters of *Working Together: The New Rules and Realities for Managing Men and Women at Work* (Baridon and Eyler, McGraw-Hill, 1994) are recommended if you need additional information to understand the issues and support your discussions.

Chapter 2, "The Myths and Realities of Gender Differences"

Chapter 4, "Workplace Etiquette for Men and Women"

Chapter 5, "Managing Women and Men"

EXERCISE 1

WOMEN'S WORK VS. MEN'S WORK

Method

AGREE/DISAGREE

Problem

Men and women continue to express fundamental differences in what they perceive as appropriate workplace roles for the sexes. In this exercise participants indicate their opinions on whether or not women should hold various kinds of positions. The results are then tallied and discussed.

Objective

Demonstrate to the participants that equal opportunity laws and regulations have not erased many of the traditional views that certain jobs are more appropriately held by one sex or the other. Use the experience to create awareness of the sexes' differences in perception and to adjust both genders' perceptions to a more accurate view.

Procedure

✓ Due to a great deal of publicity about sexual harassment, most people know the "politically correct" responses to questions about the roles of women and men in the modern workplace. When you begin the exercise, acknowledge this and then emphasize that participants' answers will be anonymous and that the usefulness of the training relies on their candid responses. Ask them to express their gut feelings rather than those they think are "right" and to avoid extreme responses that do not express their true beliefs.

✓ Distribute the rating scales. (A sample page is provided or you may create your own.) Ask members of the group to indicate their gender and then rate each assumption candidly by circling a number on the scale. Also ask for a second rating that indicates what they *think* the politically correct (PC) answer would be. Clarify that the PC response does not have to be different from the one expressing their gut feeling. The two might be the same and they may or may not be "right." The objective is simply to react instinctively and then indicate what is perceived to be the socially acceptable response.

✓ Have the respondents fold their surveys for privacy and ask volunteers to collect and score the results. Have them calculate the average score for men, women, and the total group on each question (i.e., add up the individual scores and divide by the total number of surveys in that group for each question)—for candid and PC responses. Post the results before the group and discuss them.

Discussion Questions

1. Were you surprised at the answers of the opposite sex? your own gender? the group? Why or why not?

2. How do you account for the differences among the groups?

3. What messages do the results convey?

4. What are some possible implications for sexual harassment?

5. Why do you think there are differences between the candid and politically correct responses? Do you think they might be narrowed in the future? If so, why? How?

WHAT'S THE POINT?

It is a myth, and unrealistic, to assume that because women and men are different, they are suited or not suited to certain occupations on the basis of stereotypes that prejudge their capabilities just because a difference can be demonstrated. Men and women sometimes view each others' capabilities differently and discriminate on the basis of their perceptions. It is important to evaluate whether the perceived differences are real and whether they are significant in the context of performing specific jobs.

Materials

✓ Blackboard and chalk, or markers and board or pad to display results before the group

✓ Copies of the surveys for individual members of the group

✓ A pocket calculator

Time Required

Approximately 30 minutes

"WOMEN'S WORK VS. MEN'S WORK" SURVEY FORM

Directions:

A. Check your gender, but *do not put your name* on this anonymous survey.

☐ Male   ☐ Female

B. Read each statement and mark it twice: (1) Circle the number on the scale that best represents your candid, personal opinion; and (2) circle the number that represents what you believe to be the "politically correct" response.

1. A woman would make a perfectly good DIRECTOR OF HUMAN RESOURCES of a major newspaper.

				Candid opinion:					
1	2	3	4	5	6	7	8	9	10
Agree								Disagree	

				Politically correct opinion:					
1	2	3	4	5	6	7	8	9	10
Agree								Disagree	

2. A woman would make a perfectly good PILOT for a major airline.

				Candid opinion:					
1	2	3	4	5	6	7	8	9	10
Agree								Disagree	

				Politically correct opinion:					
1	2	3	4	5	6	7	8	9	10
Agree								Disagree	

3. A woman would make a perfectly good CHIEF EXECUTIVE OFFICER of a major automobile maker.

				Candid opinion:					
1	2	3	4	5	6	7	8	9	10
Agree								Disagree	

				Politically correct opinion:					
1	2	3	4	5	6	7	8	9	10
Agree								Disagree	

EXERCISE 2

GENDER REALLY DOES MATTER

Method	AGREE/DISAGREE
Problem	Men and women view the significance of gender differences differently. In this exercise participants indicate how important they believe real and presumed gender differences are in accomplishing particular kinds of tasks. The results are then tallied and discussed.
Objective	Demonstrate to the participants that men and women have differing views of the importance of differences between the sexes in how well they do their jobs and deal with one another at work. Use the experience to create awareness of the significance of differences and to adjust both genders to a more accurate view.

Procedure

✓ Due to a great deal of publicity about sexual harassment, most people know the "politically correct" responses to questions about the roles of women and men in the modern workplace. When you begin the exercise, acknowledge this and then emphasize that participants' answers will be anonymous and that the usefulness of the training relies on their candid responses. Ask them to express their gut feelings rather than those they think are "right" and to avoid extreme responses that do not express their true beliefs.

✓ Distribute the rating scales. (A sample page is provided or you may create your own.) Ask members of the group to indicate their gender and then rate each assumption candidly by circling a number on the scale. Also ask for a second rating that indicates what they *think* the politically correct (PC) answer would be. Clarify that the PC response does not have to be different from the one expressing their gut feeling. The two might be the same and they may or may not be "right." The objective is simply to react instinctively and then indicate what is perceived to be the socially acceptable response.

✓ Have the respondents fold their surveys for privacy and ask volunteers to collect and score the results. Have them calculate the average score for men, women, and the total group on each question (i.e., add up the individual scores and divide by the total number of surveys in that group for each question)—for candid and PC responses. Post the results before the group and discuss them.

Discussion Questions

1. Were you surprised at the answers of the opposite sex? your own gender? the group? Why or why not?

2. How do you account for the differences among the groups?

3. What messages do the results convey?

4. What are some possible implications for sexual harassment?

5. Why do you think there are differences between the candid and politically correct responses? Do you think they might be narrowed in the future? If so, why? How?

WHAT'S THE POINT?

It is a myth, and unrealistic, to assume that because women and men are different, they are suited or not suited to certain occupations on the basis of stereotypes that prejudge their capabilities just because a difference can be demonstrated. Men and women sometimes view each others' capabilities differently and discriminate on the basis of their perceptions. It is important to evaluate whether the perceived differences are real and whether they are significant in the context of performing specific jobs.

Materials

✓ Blackboard and chalk, or markers and board or pad to display results before the group

✓ Copies of the survey for individual members of the group

✓ A pocket calculator

Time Required

Approximately 30 minutes

"GENDER REALLY *DOES* MATTER" SURVEY FORM

Directions:

A. Check your gender, but *do not put your name* on this anonymous survey.

☐ Male ☐ Female

B. Read each statement and mark it twice: (1) circle the number on the scale that best represents your candid, personal opinion; and (2) circle the number that represents what you believe to be the "politically correct" response.

1. Women and men have significantly different management styles and men, being more assertive, are more effective managers.

				Candid opinion:					
1	2	3	4	5	6	7	8	9	10
Agree								Disagree	

				Politically correct opinion:					
1	2	3	4	5	6	7	8	9	10
Agree								Disagree	

2. Due to the differences in body chemistry that stem from their reproductive roles, women are less suited than men to positions of great responsibility.

				Candid opinion:					
1	2	3	4	5	6	7	8	9	10
Agree								Disagree	

				Politically correct opinion:					
1	2	3	4	5	6	7	8	9	10
Agree								Disagree	

3. Real differences such as body fat content and buoyancy explain why women might excel in tasks like swimming the English Channel, while men, who have greater upper body strength, dominate sports like baseball.

				Candid opinion:					
1	2	3	4	5	6	7	8	9	10
Agree								Disagree	

				Politically correct opinion:					
1	2	3	4	5	6	7	8	9	10
Agree								Disagree	

EXERCISE 3

SORTING LAUNDRY

Method	DEMONSTRATION
Problem	Men and women accomplish some jobs with different levels of proficiency because they bring different experiences to those jobs. In this exercise participants observe the phenomenon as volunteers perform an everyday task that one gender usually does better than the other. Trainers lead discussion of the group's observations, pointing out how "natural" superiority can be a faulty presumption based more on past experience than innate potential.
Objective	Demonstrate to the participants that culture and prior experience play major roles in some differences between the sexes. Use the experience to open the participants' thinking to the possibility that the principle demonstrated might be generalized to workplace situations in which wrongly perceived "natural" ability is used as a criterion for job discrimination.

Procedure

✓ Select an all-male team and an all-female team from the group of participants—about six members each is ideal, but the number is not critical.

✓ Separate the teams so they are unable to observe what the other team is doing. Ask the audience not to influence the outcome by commenting or providing guidance.

✓ Give each team an identical bag of laundry and detergent and bleach containers with any instructions for their use removed. (You might use labeled jars or pieces of paper to represent these items, if you prefer.)

✓ Ask the teams to sort the clothes for washing as economically, but effectively, as possible.

✓ When they have finished, ask each team to explain its approach.

✓ Explain what the appropriate sorting scheme would be.

Discussion Questions

1. To which team would you entrust your laundry?

2. Do you think either women (or men) are naturally superior or inferior at the task of sorting laundry?

3. If they weren't born with the natural ability to do laundry correctly, how would you explain the winning team's superiority at the task?

4. What might this demonstration imply about the significance of differences between the sexes in the workplace?

5. Do wrong assumptions about these kinds of differences cause gender problems at work? What kind?

6. Can these kinds of differences be overcome? How?

WHAT'S THE POINT?

Although women are more likely to be better at sorting laundry because they grew up doing it, it is a myth and unrealistic to assume that such learned superiority renders men eternally less capable at getting the job done. Men and women come to the workplace (and life) with different cultural experiences that explain their sometimes different approaches to problems and their "natural" superiority at certain tasks. By demonstrating the phenomenon using a common event with which most people can identify, you open participants' thinking to broader possibilities about presumed differences that are more the result of learned behavior than inborn abilities. In this demonstration, less experienced men are more likely than more experienced women to mix colors, fabrics, etc., inappropriately, thus showing that women are superior to men at the task of sorting laundry—a practical application of chemistry and science at which men might be expected to excel if the setting were industrial and not domestic.

Materials

✓ 2 tables on which the groups can sort their laundry

✓ Enough (clean) laundry to fill two identical bags. Depending on your own and your group's sensibilities, include washable items that would clearly belong in chlorine bleach wash and those that definitely would not. (See list for suggestions.)

✓ Containers representing chlorine bleach and laundry detergent for each group, or optional paper or other representations of laundry and cleaning materials

Time Required

Approximately 25 minutes

SUGGESTED LAUNDRY LIST

✓ pair of dark socks with elastic tops

✓ pair of white socks with elastic tops

✓ white T-shirts

✓ new navy blue, black, or red sweat shirt

✓ tan gym shorts with elastic top

✓ cotton underwear with elastic tops

✓ white handkerchiefs

✓ pair of new navy blue, black, or red towels and washcloths

✓ white cotton blouse or shirt

✓ kitchen dishcloths and towels

✓ pastel pillow cases

✓ pastel fitted bed sheet

✓ pastel top bed sheet

[A variation of this exercise substitutes home or office decorating for the laundry project. The task changes to selecting complementary decorating colors, textures, and appointments—something at which women generally excel because they have had more experience at this kind of task than men have had. The results should be similar to those found in the laundry project.]

EXERCISE 4

CONTACT LENSES

Method   DEMONSTRATION

Problem   Men and women accomplish some jobs with different levels of proficiency because they bring different experiences to those jobs. In this exercise participants observe the phenomenon as volunteers perform a common task that one gender usually does better than the other. Trainers lead discussion of the group's observations, pointing out how "natural" superiority can be a faulty presumption based more on past experience than innate potential.

Objective   Demonstrate to the participants that culture and prior experience play major roles in some differences between the sexes. Use the experience to open the participants' thinking to the possibility that the principle demonstrated might be generalized to workplace situations in which wrongly perceived "natural" ability is   ed as a criterion for job discrimination.

Procedure   ✓ Identify among the participants a woman and man who wear contact lenses—people who recently got contacts are preferred. NOTE: Be prepared for the possibility that there won't be a man and woman wearing contact lenses who are willing to participate in the exercise in your audience. Arrange before the session to have members of your staff, other employees, or acquaintances available for the demonstration. The observers can still be drawn from the audience. If the outcome isn't as expected, lead the discussion as though it were, and explain that there are sometimes exceptions to the rule—see if there's a logical reason. (Man has worn lenses longer; he usually has trouble but got lucky, etc.)

✓ Ask the volunteers to demonstrate for the group how the lenses are removed and inserted.

✓ If you have a large group, select four observers (two men and two women) to come forward with the participants and watch them closely.

✓ Provide a comfortable chair, table, clean towel, mirror, and the appropriate contact lens fluids and containers for the participants.

✓ Have the lens wearers step outside and wash their hands prior to the demonstration.

✓ Emphasize that this is not a contest, speed is unimportant; all you want is the opportunity to observe a man and a woman remove and insert their contact lenses.

✓ When both finish, discuss the differences observed by the general audience and the close observers.

Discussion Questions   1. Who got the lenses out and back in more easily, the woman or the man?

2. Why might one be better than the other at this particular task?

3. Do you think either sex is born with a natural ability to insert and remove contact lenses?

4. If they weren't born with the natural ability to use contacts, how would you explain the more proficient individual's superiority at the task?

5. What might this demonstration imply about the significance of differences between the sexes in the workplace?

6. Do wrong assumptions about these kinds of differences cause gender problems at work? What kind?

7. Can these kinds of differences be overcome? How?

WHAT'S THE POINT?

Although women are more likely to be comfortable manipulating objects near their eyes because they've learned to control their reflexes when they apply eye makeup, it is a myth and unrealistic to assume that such learned superiority renders men incapable of wearing contact lenses. Men and women come to the workplace (and life) with different cultural experiences that explain their sometimes different approaches to problems and their "natural" superiority at certain tasks. By demonstrating the phenomenon with a common task with which most people can identify, you open participants' thinking to broader possibilities regarding presumed differences that are more the result of learned behavior than inborn abilities. Men who have worn contact lenses for a while, those who have used eyedrops frequently, or actors who have applied stage makeup will be just as proficient as most women at manipulating contact lenses. Conversely, women who have never worn makeup will probably have trouble.

Materials

✓ 2 tables and 6 chairs arranged so the two contact lens wearers can face the audience and four close observers while removing and inserting their lenses

✓ a clean towel or table covering for each lens wearer

✓ a box of tissues for each lens wearer

✓ a contact lens case for each lens wearer

✓ sterile bottles of lens fluid and saline solution for each lens wearer

Time Required

Approximately 30 minutes

[A variation of this exercise substitutes over-the-counter eye drops for contact lenses. The task changes to putting drops into one's own eye, and the results are similar to those obtained with contact lenses.]

EXERCISE 5

WHO GETS THE JOB?

Method MAKE THE CASE

Problem A good trial lawyer steps back from the emotional aspects of the client's case and, using logic and reason, puts on the best defense possible. In this exercise participants are asked to defend gender equity positions with which they might adamantly disagree.

Objective Provide participants with the occasion to understand gender equity points of view that differ from their own. Have them change positions and think as would advocates for a position alien to their own. Use the experience to soften the resentment toward different, but not threatening, perspectives and, in the process, facilitate the growth of more mutually acceptable views.

Procedure
✓ Select two teams of about six each, one consisting of men, the other of women.

✓ Pass out Scenario 1 to the women's team and Scenario 2 to the men's team.

✓ Instruct the teams to read and discuss their scenarios and to come up with their strongest defense for their assigned position—whether they agree with it or not.

✓ Ask the women's team to have a spokesperson describe its scenario and summarize its defense for the position. Other team members are encouraged to contribute to the defense. (You may suggest a line of defense if necessary to get the discussion started.)

✓ Ask the men's team to challenge the women's position. (You may suggest some challenges if necessary to move the discussion forward.)

✓ Briefly note key words and phrases on a pad or blackboard—this helps people go back and elaborate on earlier points.

✓ Encourage the challenge and defense exchange until you feel the relevant points have been made.

✓ Solicit a yes or no vote from the entire audience, which serves as the jury. The question for the jury: When all things are equal, is it best to select the man and not the woman for a remote assignment?

✓ Note that the objective is to uncover points of view that participants might not have considered. The cases are deliberately ambiguous, open-ended, and subject to various interpretations and judgments (just like real life situations). Acknowledge this so you don't leave the group frustrated that a "correct" judgment was not reached.

Discussion Questions
1. Do you see legitimate arguments for each of the positions in this case? If so, what are they?

23

2. Could there be some underlying traditional thinking at work in the position advocating the male's posting to the remote location? What might that be?

3. Do you think those advocating either position intend to discriminate deliberately against the loser of the position based on gender? Why or why not?

4. Where would you place each position on a chronology of socially progressive thinking? Caveman? American frontier? Roaring 20s? World War II? 50s? 60s? 90s? etc.?

5. Do you believe that the people advocating the position different from yours sincerely feel the way they do, or do you assume that their behavior is simply meant to offend you? If so, why?

6. Is either position out of vogue with mainstream thinking in the 90s? If so, did you realize this prior to this training exercise? Does it matter to you? Do you see any practical reasons to reconsider any of your assumptions?

WHAT'S THE POINT?

It is a myth, and unrealistic, to assume that the woman should be "spared" (from the traditional male perspective) or "denied" (from the modern female perspective) the remote assignment when a man of equal qualifications is available to take it. Women in the modern workplace are entitled to equal opportunity, and should not be "protected," whether or not the protector is well-meaning. It is revealing to be forced to advocate something you don't necessarily believe. Conscientiously playing devil's advocate can give participants insights into the opposing view that they would not have voluntarily considered. Understanding (if not accepting) a position they oppose can help them deal more effectively with those who espouse it.

Materials   ✓ Blackboard and chalk, or markers and board or pad to display notes before the group

✓ Copies of the scenarios for the teams

Time Required   Approximately 35 minutes

"WHO GETS THE JOB?" SCENARIO 1 (WOMEN'S TEAM)

Directions:

Discuss the scenario as a team. Understand that *your role as a team is to defend the position whether you agree with it or not*. Think about the arguments wrong-thinking people would use to advocate such a position even if you would not. You will have a chance to say why you consider the position you articulate in this game is wrong. The team should choose a spokesperson, but everyone is encouraged to contribute to the discussion.

Situation

✓ A new operating division of the company is to be established in a rural part of the upper Midwest. The site is relatively isolated, served only by twice-daily commuter flights or a three-hour drive to the nearest major city airport. Management has two excellent candidates for heading the initiative: (1) an up-and-coming, thirty-something man in a dual-career marriage with two kids in elementary school, and (2) an up-and-coming woman in a dual-career marriage with two kids in elementary school. Their resumes are mirror images of one another's. Both are trusted, highly regarded team players with bright futures in the firm.

✓ *The nod goes to the man.*

✓ The men's team will assail your position from the woman's perspective and you are to defend the selection of the man in these circumstances.

"WHO GETS THE JOB?" SCENARIO 2 (MEN'S TEAM)

Directions:

Discuss the scenario as a team. Understand that *your role as a team is to attack the position whether you agree with it or not.* Think about the arguments wrong-thinking people would use to advocate such a position even if you would not. You will have a chance to say why you consider the position you articulate in this game is wrong. The team should choose a spokesperson, but everyone is encouraged to contribute to the discussion.

Situation

✓ A new operating division of the company is to be established in a rural part of the upper Midwest. The site is relatively isolated, served only by twice-daily commuter flights or a three-hour drive to the nearest major city airport. Management has two excellent candidates for heading the initiative: (1) an up-and-coming, thirty-something man in a dual-career marriage with two kids in elementary school, and (2) an up-and-coming woman in a dual-career marriage with two kids in elementary school. Their resumes are mirror images of one another's. Both are trusted, highly regarded team players with bright futures in the firm.

✓ *The nod goes to the man.*

✓ The women's team will defend its position from the man's perspective and you are to attack the selection of the man in these circumstances.

EXERCISE 6

DOING IT MY WAY

Method

MAKE THE CASE

Problem

A good trial lawyer steps back from the emotional aspects of the client's case and, using logic and reason, puts on the best defense possible. In this exercise participants are asked to defend gender equity positions with which they might adamantly disagree.

Objective

Provide participants with the occasion to understand gender equity points of view that differ from their own. Have them change positions and think as would advocates for a position alien to their own. Use the experience to soften the resentment toward different, but not threatening, perspectives and, in the process, facilitate the growth of more mutually acceptable views.

Procedure

✓ Select two teams of about six each, one consisting of men, the other of women.

✓ Pass out Scenario 1 to the women's team and Scenario 2 to the men's team.

✓ Instruct the teams to read and discuss their scenarios and to come up with their strongest defense for their assigned position—whether they agree with it or not.

✓ Ask the women's team to have a spokesperson describe its scenario and summarize its defense for the position. Other team members are encouraged to contribute to the defense. (You may suggest a line of defense if necessary to get the discussion started.)

✓ Ask the men's team to challenge the women's position. (You may suggest some challenges if necessary to move the discussion forward.)

✓ Briefly note key words and phrases on a pad or blackboard—this helps people go back and elaborate on earlier points.

✓ Encourage the challenge and defense exchange until you feel the relevant points have been made.

✓ Solicit a yes or no vote from the entire audience, which serves as the jury. The question for the jury: Because the woman's approach is different from that traditionally taken by male managers, will it be less effective in solving the problem?

✓ Note that the objective is to uncover points of view that participants might not have considered. The cases are deliberately ambiguous, open-ended, and subject to various interpretations and judgments (just like real life situations). Acknowledge this so you don't leave the group frustrated that a "correct" judgment was not reached.

1. Do you see legitimate arguments for each of the positions in this case? If so, what are they?

2. Could there be some underlying traditional thinking at work in advocating the male's approach? What might that be?

3. Do you think those advocating either position intend to discriminate deliberately against the other's position based on gender? Why or why not?

4. Where would you place each position on a chronology of socially progressive thinking? Caveman? American frontier? Roaring 20s? World War II? 50s? 60s? 90s? etc.?

5. Do you believe that people advocating the position different from yours sincerely feel the way they do, or do you assume that their behavior is simply meant to offend you? If so, why?

6. Is either position out of vogue with mainstream thinking in the 90s? If so, did you realize this prior to this training exercise? Does it matter to you? Do you see any practical reasons to reconsider any of your assumptions?

WHAT'S THE POINT?

It is a myth, and unrealistic, to assume that the woman's approach to solving a business problem is less effective than the traditional approach taken by most men just because it is different. Women in the modern workplace are entitled to equal opportunity, and should have the prerogative of approaching problems in their own way as long as they achieve the expected results. It is revealing to be forced to advocate something you don't necessarily believe. Conscientiously playing devil's advocate can give participants insights into the opposing view that they would not have voluntarily considered. Understanding (if not accepting) a position they oppose can help them deal more effectively with those who espouse it.

Materials

✓ Blackboard and chalk, or markers and board or pad to display notes before the group

✓ Copies of the scenarios for the teams

Time Required

Approximately 35 minutes

"DOING IT *MY WAY*" SCENARIO 1 (WOMEN'S TEAM)

Directions:

Discuss the scenario as a team. Understand that *your role as a team is to defend the position whether you agree with it or not.* Think about what arguments wrong-thinking people would use to advocate such a position even if you would not. You will have a chance to say why you consider the position you articulate in this game is wrong. The team should choose a spokesperson, but everyone is encouraged to contribute to the discussion.

Situation

✓ Resentment is growing over game playing by employees on office computers. The problem has become noticeable in part because several of the "players" sit at computer screens that are conspicuously visible to others walking by their work stations. Upper management has made it clear that playing games on office time is unacceptable. The situation is complicated by concerns that a severe crackdown will have a negative impact on employee morale, leading to a decline in work quality and productivity that would be worse than time lost to the games. Division managers will be rated in their own performance reviews on how well they solve the problem. One division is headed by a woman and another by a man. Both rank in the top 15 percent of their management class, and for all intents and purposes, their divisions are the same.

✓ Playing golf at the club one afternoon, two top managers express a preference for the man's more direct approach to the situation. One says that the offenders know their behavior is unacceptable, further discussion would be unproductive, and the time has come simply to remove the games from all computers in the office. The other is skeptical of the woman manager's plan to talk with each of the offenders individually; tell them that she understands the games can provide an occasional relief of tension, but may be played only during lunch hours and before and after work; and then give them a specific ultimatum that if they are seen playing outside those hours, the games will be removed from all the computers.

✓ The men's team will assail your position from the woman's perspective and you are to defend the two top managers' position.

29

"DOING IT *MY* WAY" SCENARIO 2 (MEN'S TEAM)

Directions:

Discuss the scenario as a team. Understand that *your role as a team is to attack the position whether you agree with it or not.* Think about the arguments wrong-thinking people would use to advocate such a position even if you would not. You will have a chance to say why you consider the position you articulate in this game is wrong. The team should choose a spokesperson, but everyone is encouraged to contribute to the discussion.

Situation

✓ Resentment is growing over game playing by employees on office computers. The problem has become noticeable in part because several of the "players" sit at computer screens that are conspicuously visible to others walking by their work stations. Upper management has made it clear that playing games on office time is unacceptable. The situation is complicated by concerns that a severe crackdown will have a negative impact on employee morale, leading to a decline in work quality and productivity that would be worse than time lost to the games. Division managers will be rated in their own performance reviews on how well they solve the problem. One division is headed by a woman and another by a man. Both rank in the top 15 percent of their management class, and for all intents and purposes, their divisions are the same.

✓ Playing golf at the club one afternoon, two top managers express a preference for the man's more direct approach to the situation. One says that the offenders know their behavior is unacceptable, further discussion would be unproductive, and the time has come simply to remove the games from all computers in the office. The other is skeptical of the woman manager's plan to talk with each of the offenders individually; tell them that she understands the games can provide an occasional relief of tension, but may be played only during lunch hours and before and after work; and then give them a specific ultimatum that if they are seen playing outside those hours, the games will be removed from all the computers.

✓ The women's team will defend top management from the man's perspective and you are to attack its position from the woman's perspective.

EXERCISE 7

MEN BETTER/WOMEN BETTER

Method   MATCH THE ITEMS

Problem   Men and women continue to express fundamental differences in what they perceive as appropriate workplace roles for the sexes. In this exercise participants indicate their opinions on whether or not women should hold various kinds of positions. The results are then tallied and discussed.

Objective   Demonstrate to the participants that equal opportunity laws and regulations have not erased many of the traditional views that certain jobs are more appropriately held by one sex or the other. Use the experience to create awareness of the sexes' differences in perception and to adjust both genders' perceptions to a more accurate view.

Procedure

✓ Due to a great deal of publicity about sexual harassment, most people know the "politically correct" responses to questions about the roles of women and men in the modern workplace. When you begin the exercise, acknowledge this and then emphasize that participants' answers will be anonymous and that the usefulness of the training relies on their candid responses. Ask them to express their gut feelings rather than those they think are "right" and to avoid extreme responses that do not express their true beliefs.

✓ Distribute the "Task-To-Gender" Matching Form. (A sample is provided or you may create your own.) Ask members of the group to indicate their own gender and then mark each entry candidly by circling the selection they feel indicates which gender would be better at the task. Also ask for a second matching that indicates what they *think* the politically correct (PC) answer would be. Clarify that the PC response does not have to be different from the one expressing their gut feeling. The two might be the same and they may or may not be "right." The objective is simply to react instinctively and then indicate what is perceived to be the socially acceptable response.

✓ Have the respondents fold their matching forms for privacy and ask two volunteers to collect the forms and tally the results. Have them tally the responses for men, women, and the total group on each item (i.e., how many men, women, and total group participants marked the item for Men, Women or No Difference)—for candid and PC responses. Post the results before the group and discuss them.

Discussion Questions

1. Were you surprised at the answers of the opposite sex? your own gender? the group? Why or why not?

2. How do you account for the differences among the groups?

3. What messages do the results convey?

4. What are some possible implications for sexual harassment?

5. Why do you think there are differences between the candid and politically correct responses? Do you think they might be narrowed in the future? If so, why? How?

WHAT'S THE POINT?

It is a myth, and unrealistic, to elevate occupationally insignificant differences between women and men into stereotypes that support contentions that one gender is better or worse than the other at doing certain things, when the issue is more one of difference than of effectiveness. Men and women sometimes view each others' capabilities differently and discriminate on the basis of their perceptions. It is important to evaluate whether the perceived differences are real and whether they are significant in the context of performing specific jobs.

Materials

✓ Blackboard and chalk, or markers and board or pad to display results before the group

✓ Copies of the matching forms for individual members of the group

Time Required

Approximately 20 minutes

"TASK-TO-GENDER" MATCHING FORM

Directions:

A. Check your gender, but *do not put your name* on this anonymous survey.

☐ Male   ☐ Female

B. Read each statement and mark it twice: (1) circle the selection on the form that best represents your candid, personal opinion of who can best perform the task; and (2) circle the selection that represents what you believe to be the "politically correct" response.

1. Landing a jumbo jet with 400 passengers in bad weather with serious engine problems

Candid opinion:		
Men	Women	No difference

Politically correct opinion:		
Men	Women	No difference

2. Planning a reception and dinner for 40 important guests

Candid opinion:		
Men	Women	No difference

Politically correct opinion:		
Men	Women	No difference

3. Serving as vice president for research and development of a major firm specializing in nuclear technology

Candid opinion:		
Men	Women	No difference

Politically correct opinion:		
Men	Women	No difference

4. Serving as a family practice physician in a large urban HMO

Candid opinion:		
Men	Women	No difference

Politically correct opinion:		
Men	Women	No difference

EXERCISE 8

WHAT WOMEN AND MEN WANT

Method	MATCH THE ITEMS
Problem	Men and women continue to have different perceptions about what the other sex wants in the workplace competition. In this exercise participants register their opinions about what motivates opposite-gender workers. The results are tallied and discussed.
Objective	Demonstrate to the participants that equal opportunity laws and regulations have not erased many of the traditional views of what women and men want from their careers. Use the experience to create awareness of the sexes' differences in perception, and to better adjust both genders' perceptions to a more accurate view.

Procedure

✓ Due to a great deal of publicity about sexual harassment, most people know the "politically correct" responses to questions about the roles of women and men in the modern workplace. When you begin the exercise, acknowledge this and then emphasize that participants' answers will be anonymous and that the usefulness of the training relies on their candid responses. Ask them to express their gut feelings rather than those they think are "right" and to avoid extreme responses that do not express their true beliefs.

✓ Distribute the "What Women and Men Want" Matching Form. (A sample is provided or you may create your own.) Ask members of the group to indicate their own gender and then mark each entry candidly by selecting the term that indicates what they believe women or men want. Also ask for a second matching that indicates what they *think* the politically correct (PC) answer would be. Clarify that the PC response does not have to be different from the one expressing their gut feeling. The two might be the same and they may or may not be "right." The objective is simply to react instinctively and then indicate what is perceived to be the socially acceptable response.

✓ Have the respondents fold their matching forms for privacy and ask volunteers to collect the forms and tally the results. Have them tally the responses for men, women, and the total group on each item (i.e., how many men, women, and total group participants marked the item Want, Don't Want or Neutral)—for candid and PC responses. Post the results before the group and discuss them.

Discussion Questions

1. Were you surprised at the answers of the opposite sex? your own gender? the group? Why or why not?

2. How do you account for the differences among the groups?

3. What messages do the results convey?

4. What are some possible implications for sexual harassment?

5. Why do you think there are differences between the candid and politically correct responses? Do you think they might be narrowed in the future? If so, why? How?

WHAT'S THE POINT?

It is a myth, and unrealistic, to deal with one another at work on the basis of what we often mistakenly perceive to be what the other sex wants from its occupational maneuvering. Men and women sometimes view each others' occupational aspirations differently and inaccurately and discriminate on the basis of those perceptions. It is important to discover an associate's real motivations before discriminating on the basis of imagined ones.

Materials

✓ Blackboard and chalk, or markers and board or pad to display results before the group

✓ Copies of the matching form for individual members of the group

Time Required

Approximately 20 minutes

"WHAT WOMEN AND MEN WANT" MATCHING FORM

Directions:

A. Check your gender, but *do not put your name* on this anonymous survey.

☐ Male   ☐ Female

B. Read each statement and mark it twice: (1) circle the selection on the form that best represents your candid, personal opinion of what women and men want; and (2) circle the selection that represents what you believe to be the "politically correct" response.

1. Women want to be given special consideration for advancement to compensate for the discrimination they have suffered in the past.

Candid opinion:		
Want	Don't want	Neutral
Politically correct opinion:		
Want	Don't want	Neutral

2. Women want to be given exactly the same opportunities as men when it comes to competing occupationally.

Candid opinion:		
Want	Don't want	Neutral
Politically correct opinion:		
Want	Don't want	Neutral

3. Women want to have the best of both worlds—the rewards that come from competing in traditional male arenas and the special considerations that make many aspects of life less harsh for women than for men.

Candid opinion:		
Want	Don't want	Neutral
Politically correct opinion:		
Want	Don't want	Neutral

4. Men want women to stop pushing so hard—they have been in the workplace a relatively short time, and they can't expect to achieve overnight what it took men decades to accomplish.

Candid opinion:		
Want	Don't want	Neutral
Politically correct opinion:		
Want	Don't want	Neutral

5. Men want to work with women who are willing to share equally extra time and effort or blame when things go sour on the job, as well as praise when the task can be accomplished without a hitch.

Candid opinion:		
Want	Don't want	Neutral

Politically correct opinion:		
Want	Don't want	Neutral

6. Men want to compete with women for job assignments, promotions, travel opportunities, etc. without gender entering into the equation in any way.

Candid opinion:		
Want	Don't want	Neutral

Politically correct opinion:		
Want	Don't want	Neutral

EXERCISE 9
MALE SUPERIORITY

Method   MULTIPLE CHOICE

Problem   Men and women let stereotypes about which gender is superior at certain tasks complicate their workplace relationships. In this exercise participants register their beliefs about some common assumptions regarding the superiority of male workers. The results are tallied and discussed.

Objective   Demonstrate to the participants that equal opportunity laws and regulations have not eradicated misconceptions about the "natural" superiority of men in certain pursuits. Use the experience to create awareness of the limitations to stereotypical beliefs about male superiority, and to adjust both genders' perceptions to a more accurate view.

Procedure   ✓ Due to a great deal of publicity about sexual harassment, most people know the "politically correct" responses to questions about the capabilities of women and men in the modern workplace. When you begin the exercise, acknowledge this and then emphasize that participants' answers will be anonymous and that the usefulness of the training relies on their candid responses. Ask them to express their gut feelings rather than those they think are "right" and to avoid extreme responses that do not express their true beliefs.

                      ✓ Distribute the "Male Superiority" Quiz. (A sample is provided or you may create your own.) Ask members of the group to indicate their own gender and then mark each entry candidly by selecting the multiple choice item that indicates what they believe about male superiority.

                      ✓ Have the respondents fold their quizzes for privacy and ask two volunteers to collect the forms and tally the results. Have them tally the responses for men, women, and the total group on each question (i.e., how many men, women, and total group participants marked the various responses). Post the results before the group and discuss them.

Discussion Questions 1. Were you surprised at the answers of the opposite sex? your own gender? the group? Why or why not?

                      2. How do you account for the differences among the groups?

                      3. What messages do the results convey?

                      4. What are some possible implications for sexual harassment?

                      5. Why do you think men seem to be better at math while women excel in verbal skills? Is this the result of natural superiority or of different cultural experience and expectations based on long-held assumptions of the proper roles for women and men?

                      6. Are higher math or verbal test scores relevant to performing most jobs in the modern workplace? Why or why not?

WHAT'S THE POINT?

Many popular assumptions about male superiority are mythical and un-realistic and can reinforce irrational limitations on career opportunities for women. In fact, the differences between the genders are often not as significant as the differences between individuals. It is important to be objective about an associate's strengths and limitations before discriminating on the basis of imagined ones.

Materials

✓ Blackboard and chalk, or markers and board or pad to display results before the group

✓ Copies of the "Male Superiority" Quiz for individual members of the group

Time Required

Approximately 20 minutes

"MALE SUPERIORITY" QUIZ

Directions:

A. Check your gender, but *do not put your name* on this anonymous quiz.

☐ Male ☐ Female

B. Read each statement and circle the response that you think is factually correct.

1. Male laboratory animals are sometimes superior to female laboratory animals on certain measures. What does this reflect about the abilities of men and women?
   a. It is safe to assume that men are superior to women on similar measures.
   b. It is probable that the tests were conducted with a bias toward males and the results are incorrect.
   c. Test results from animal experiments bear only a limited relationship to men and women because human behavior is so much more complex than that of animals.
   d. Male superiority is confirmed as the overarching pattern in nature.
   e. Results of animal experiments have no value in explaining differences in the behavior of men and women.

2. Men have historically scored higher than women on standardized tests of mathematical skills, but the gap is gradually narrowing. What does this tell us about the attributes and abilities of women and men?
   a. Men are unquestionably superior to women in jobs that involve computation.
   b. The difference in scores is at least partly the result of different early life experiences of girls and boys in our culture.
   c. Young women should be encouraged to pursue occupations that make use of their usually superior verbal and nurturing skills.
   d. Girls who excel at math are less feminine than others.
   e. Tests are poor measures of mathematical ability.

3. As a group men are viewed as communicating more directly and authoritatively than women, who are more likely to conciliate and negotiate. How does the difference in style impact management effectiveness?
   a. Differences in management effectiveness between individual women or individual men are more significant than those between the two groups.
   b. Men are the more natural leaders because of an innate ability to communicate forcefully.
   c. Management styles are being deliberately changed to accommodate the feminine approach.
   d. Women will eventually learn to manage like men, and the difference in styles will mostly disappear.
   e. The ability to communicate has little to do with management effectiveness.

4. In humans, the male brain is larger, on average, than the female brain. How does this affect intellect and the ability to perform complex tasks?
   a. Male capacity for learning is significantly greater than that of women.
   b. If God intended woman to be the intellectual equal of man, he or she would have endowed her with a brain of comparable size.
   c. Women have to work harder to compensate for their smaller brains.
   d. Men's baldness can be partially attributed to their larger brain's demands on their cranial endocrine system.
   e. Size differences between the brains of women and men are essentially irrelevant to performance in the contemporary workplace.

5. The male trait of confrontation and the female trait of conciliation are …
   a. "Hard-wired" behavioral responses that are unlikely to change
   b. Largely cultural responses learned over eons of role specialization that will likely meld together the best of both approaches and narrow the differences as new generations grow up with less traditional role expectations
   c. Differences that explain male superiority in sports and business competition
   d. Unique to our culture and easily reversed by modern parenting
   e. A root cause for the failure of co-ed colleges and the resurgence of gender-specific colleges

---

Answers (mask or remove before copying): 1 = c, 2 = b, 3 = a, 4 = e, 5 = b. NOTE: Although these answers would be accepted by most current authorities, ambiguity continues to surround many questions regarding whether differences between the sexes have a significant effect on their abilities. Therefore, steer discussion toward the best current thinking, but make clear that knowledge on these topics is constantly evolving.

EXERCISE 10
REACTION DIFFERENCES

Method   MULTIPLE CHOICE

Problem   Men and women let stereotypes about how the opposite sex will react to various situations color their workplace relationships. In this exercise participants register their beliefs about some common gender stereotypes regarding reactions. The results are tallied and discussed.

Objective   Demonstrate to the participants that equal opportunity laws and regulations have not eradicated misconceptions about how their gender opposites will react in certain situations. Use the experience to create awareness of the limitations to stereotypical beliefs about reactions, and to adjust both genders' perceptions to a more accurate view.

Procedure   ✓ Due to a great deal of publicity about sexual harassment, most people know the "politically correct" responses to questions about the reactions of women and men in the modern workplace. When you begin the exercise, acknowledge this and then emphasize that participants' answers will be anonymous and that the usefulness of the training relies on their candid responses. Ask them to express their gut feelings rather than those they think are "right" and to avoid extreme responses that do not express their true beliefs.

✓ Distribute the "Reaction Differences" Quiz. (A sample is provided or you may create your own.) Ask members of the group to indicate their gender and then mark each entry candidly by selecting the multiple-choice item that indicates what they believe about how women and men can be expected to react.

✓ Have the respondents fold their quizzes for privacy and ask two volunteers to collect the forms and tally the results. Have them tally the responses for men, women, and the total group on each question (i.e., how many men, women, and total group participants marked the various responses). Post the results before the group and discuss them.

Discussion Questions
1. Were you surprised at the answers of the opposite sex? your own gender? the group? Why or why not?

2. How do you account for the differences among the groups?

3. What messages do the results convey?

4. What are some possible implications for sexual harassment?

5. Do you think the perceived differences in men's and women's reaction styles are valid for most members of each sex? If so, do they have a significant impact on their ability to do an effective job? manage people? How? Why?

WHAT'S THE POINT?

Much of the common wisdom about how men and women react is mythical and unrealistic and can reinforce irrational limitations on career opportunities for women. In fact, the differences between the genders are often not as significant as the differences between individuals. It is important to be objective about an associate's reaction potential rather than discriminate on the basis of imagined limitations.

Materials	✓ Blackboard and chalk, or markers and board or pad to display results before the group
	✓ Copies of the "Reaction Differences" Quiz for individual members of the group
Time Required	Approximately 20 minutes

REACTION DIFFERENCES" QUIZ

Directions:

A. Check your gender, but *do not put your name* on this anonymous quiz.

☐ Male ☐ Female

B. Read each statement and circle the response that you think is factually correct.

1. Faced with stern but constructive criticism by a superior before a working group of her peers, a woman is more likely than a man to …
   a. Counter with a spirited defense of her position
   b. Immediately accede to the presumed wishes of the superior
   c. Take the criticism as a personal rebuke and react emotionally, possibly reverting to tears
   d. View the criticism as constructive and respond accordingly
   e. Internalize her feelings, successfully hiding them from the group

2. Confused by driving instructions provided by a client company to locate their offices, a sales*man* is more likely than a sales*woman* to …
   a. Stop and ask directions
   b. Rely on his intuitive sense of direction
   c. Admit that he is lost and call for more specific directions
   d. Rely on street signs and printed instructions
   e. Ultimately locate the client's office

3. Asked for a public reaction to a colleague's conspicuously dumb idea, a woman is more apt than a man to …
   a. Criticize indirectly, and structure a face-saving situation for her associate
   b. Seize the opportunity to diminish the status of the competitor
   c. Fail to grasp the colleague's gaffe quickly enough to take advantage of it
   d. Describe the shortcomings of the idea succinctly
   e. Alter her position to oppose the discredited concept

4. In a business conversation, a woman is more apt than a man to …
   a. End her sentences with prepositions
   b. Be correct in her judgment
   c. Seize the initiative
   d. Dominate it
   e. Use body language and a conversational style seen as the language and style of a subordinate

5. A physician is more likely to …
   a. Show more concern for executive women than for men who lose work time due to treatment for an illness
   b. Diagnose chest pain as having an emotional cause in women and a circulatory one in men
   c. Prescribe drug dosages more accurately for women than for men
   d. Expect women patients to visit the doctor's office less often than men
   e. Revert instinctively to his or her knowledge of the anatomy and physiology of a woman rather than that of a man in a medical emergency

---

Answers (mask or remove before copying): 1 = c, 2 = b, 3 = a, 4 = e, 5 = b. NOTE: Although these answers would be accepted by most current authorities, ambiguity continues to surround many questions regarding whether differences between the sexes have a significant effect on their abilities. Therefore, steer discussion toward the best current thinking, but make clear that knowledge on these topics is constantly evolving.

EXERCISE 11

DIFFERENT DRUMMERS

Method   RATE THE ACCURACY

Problem   Sexual harassment problems can begin with the mismatched perceptions of a man and woman. In this exercise participants truthfully define their own opinions on statements about the mixed-gender working environment that are apt to be judged differently by women and men.

Objective   Demonstrate to the participants that men and women often have differing views on interactions between the sexes. Use the experience to create awareness of significant differences and to adjust both genders' perceptions to a more accurate norm.

Procedure

✓ Due to a great deal of publicity about sexual harassment, many people know the "politically correct" response to questions surrounding the issue. When you begin the exercise, acknowledge this and then emphasize that participants' answers will be anonymous and that the usefulness of the training relies on their candid responses. Ask them to express their gut feelings rather than those they think are "right" and to avoid extreme responses that do not express their true beliefs.

✓ Distribute the "Different Drummer" Survey Forms. (A sample page is provided or you may create your own.) Ask members of the group to indicate their gender and then rate each item candidly by circling a point on the scale. Also ask for a second rating that indicates what they *think* the politically correct (PC) answer would be. Clarify that the PC response might be the same as their gut feeling, and it may or may not be "right." The participants' objective is simply to state their gut feelings and then indicate what they perceive to be the socially acceptable response.

✓ Have the respondents fold their surveys for privacy and ask volunteers to collect and score the results. Have them calculate the average score for men, women, and the total group for each question (i.e., add up the individual scores and divide by the total number of surveys in that group for each question)—for candid and PC responses. Post the results before the group and discuss them.

Discussion Questions

1. Were you surprised that men and women responded differently? the same? Why or why not?

2. How do you account for the differences?

3. What do you think the fact that men and women answered differently has to say about the potential for misunderstandings that could lead to sexual harassment problems?

4. Are your candid and PC responses different? If so, why? Will that ever change? Why?

5. Are there ratings that you would change now that we've discussed them? Are there any that you are at least willing to rethink quietly on your own?

WHAT'S THE POINT?

Men and women at work are concerned about having their social interactions and career expectations reflect norms that won't place them on the fringes of acceptable standards in the new era of modern women workers. To do this successfully it is helpful to note where others, including gender opposites, stand on classic situations and issues they might encounter at work.

Materials

✓ Blackboard and chalk, or markers and board or pad to display results before the group

✓ Copies of the survey for individual members of the group

✓ A pocket calculator

Time Required

Approximately 25 minutes

"DIFFERENT DRUMMERS" SURVEY FORM

Directions:
A. Check your gender, but *do not put your name* on this anonymous survey.

☐ Male   ☐ Female

B. Read each statement and mark it twice: (1) circle the number on the scale that best represents your candid, personal opinion; and (2) circle the number that represents what you believe to be the "politically correct" response.

1. A woman who wears fashionably sexy (i.e., not extreme) clothes to work should not be surprised that she is drawing a different kind of attention from her male colleagues than her more conventionally dressed counterparts.

Candid opinion:

1   2   3   4   5   6   7   8   9   10

Accurate   Inaccurate

Politically correct opinion:

1   2   3   4   5   6   7   8   9   10

Accurate   Inaccurate

---

2. It is acceptable for a man who finds himself alone with a woman on an elevator to compliment her on her appearance, e.g., comment that she is wearing a pretty dress or that her new hairstyle is attractive.

Candid opinion:

1   2   3   4   5   6   7   8   9   10

Accurate   Inaccurate

Politically correct opinion:

1   2   3   4   5   6   7   8   9   10

Accurate   Inaccurate

---

3. It makes practical business sense to consider gender when handing out certain job assignments.

Candid opinion:

1   2   3   4   5   6   7   8   9   10

Accurate   Inaccurate

Politically correct opinion:

1   2   3   4   5   6   7   8   9   10

Accurate   Inaccurate

---

4. Women will soon (i.e., in the next few years) hold top executive positions in the same relative percentage as men do now.

Candid opinion:

1	2	3	4	5	6	7	8	9	10

Accurate   Inaccurate

Politically correct opinion:

1	2	3	4	5	6	7	8	9	10

Accurate   Inaccurate

EXERCISE 12

TYPICAL WOMAN/MAN

Method RATE THE ACCURACY

Problem Mismatched perceptions are often the beginning of sexual harassment problems between opposite-gender coworkers. In this exercise participants truthfully state their own opinions on statements about the mixed-gender working environment. The results will likely demonstrate that some of the gut feelings of today's modern workers of both sexes are not all that different from those that they intellectually know and agree are long out of date and inappropriate.

Objective Demonstrate to the participants that men and women often have different but deep-seated feelings about interactions between the sexes that are relevant to the harassment issue. Use the experience to create awareness of stereotypical thinking and to adjust both genders' perceptions to a more accurate norm.

Procedure
✓ Due to a great deal of publicity about sexual harassment, many people know the "politically correct" response to questions surrounding the issue. When you begin the exercise, acknowledge this and then emphasize that participants' answers will be anonymous and that the usefulness of the training relies on their candid responses. Ask them to express their gut feelings rather than those they think are "right" and to avoid extreme responses that do not express their true beliefs.

✓ Distribute "Typical Woman/Man" Survey Forms. (A sample page is provided or you may create your own.) Ask members of the group to indicate their gender and then rate each item candidly by circling a point on the scale—first from their own perspective, then from what they believe would be the perspective of their gender opposites. (A woman responds, and then indicates what she thinks a man would say on the same point and vice versa.)

✓ Have the respondents fold their surveys for privacy and ask volunteers to collect and score the results. Have them calculate the average score for men, women, and the total group for each question (i.e., add up the individual scores and divide by the total number of surveys in that group for each question)—for both responses. Post the results before the group and discuss them.

Discussion Questions
1. Were you surprised that men and women responded differently? the same? Why or why not?

2. How do you account for the differences?

3. What do you think the fact that men and women answered differently has to say about the potential for misunderstandings that could lead to sexual harassment problems?

4. Are the expected responses of gender opposites much different from personal responses? If so, why? Will that ever change? Why or why not?

5. Are there ratings that you would change now that we've discussed them? Are there any that you are at least willing to rethink quietly on your own?

WHAT'S THE POINT?

Sexual harassment issues among working women and men stem in part from their ingrained assumptions about what each gender group perceives about the beliefs, aspirations, character, and abilities of their opposites. A starting point for replacing the myths with realities is that participants candidly express thoughts leading to stereotypes about "typical" expectations or behavior for women and men. Just as important is what men *think* women believe and vice versa.

Materials

✓ Blackboard and chalk, or markers and board or pad to display results before the group

✓ Copies of the survey for individual members of the group

✓ A pocket calculator

Time Required

Approximately 25 minutes

"TYPICAL WOMAN/MAN" SURVEY FORM

Directions:

A. Check your gender, but *do not put your name* on this anonymous survey.

☐ Male   ☐ Female

B. Read each statement and mark it twice: (1) circle the number on the scale that best represents your candid, personal opinion; and (2) circle the number that represents what you believe would be your gender opposite's response.

1. A typical man would prefer the world as it was before women's liberation when men were "men" and women were "women."

My opinion:

1   2   3   4   5   6   7   8   9   10

Accurate   Inaccurate

My gender opposite would say:

1   2   3   4   5   6   7   8   9   10

Accurate   Inaccurate

---

2. A typical woman, in her heart of hearts, thinks she deserves to "have it all," e.g., be a successful professional with unlimited lifestyle freedom and advancement opportunities; the perfect mother of adorable children; and a romance-novel heroine fulfilling her romantic fantasies.

My opinion:

1   2   3   4   5   6   7   8   9   10

Accurate   Inaccurate

My gender opposite would say:

1   2   3   4   5   6   7   8   9   10

Accurate   Inaccurate

---

3. The typical man, in his heart of hearts, would like to have a successful career with unlimited advancement opportunities; a gorgeous, eternally youthful, and faithful wife who stays at home with perfect children; and the freedom to pursue romantic liaisons whenever he chooses.

My opinion:

1   2   3   4   5   6   7   8   9   10

Accurate   Inaccurate

My gender opposite would say:

1   2   3   4   5   6   7   8   9   10

Accurate   Inaccurate

---

4. A typical woman nurtures a fundamental belief that most men deal with women as sex objects first and as professional peers, intellectual counterparts, friends, etc. as a poor second.

My opinion:

1	2	3	4	5	6	7	8	9	10
Accurate								Inaccurate	

My gender opposite would say:

1	2	3	4	5	6	7	8	9	10
Accurate								Inaccurate	

EXERCISE 13

DOCTOR/PATIENT

Method SOLVE THE RIDDLE

Problem Men and women are conditioned to have preestablished expectations about gender roles in a variety of situations. Some of their automatic reactions are based on false gender role stereotypes that perpetuate unequal opportunity and can lead to sexual harassment.

Objective Demonstrate to the participants that expectations based on stereotypes pervade the thoughts of even the most enlightened men and women. By recognizing the point in a riddle that is apt to snare all but the most alert or those who have previously encountered such an example, participants experience a strong jolt of reality about subtle discrimination that an everyday intellectual discussion would not bring out nearly as powerfully.

Procedure

✓ Pass out copies of the "Doctor/Patient" Riddle Form to the participants. Riddles are most effective early in sexual harassment training sessions, before the group becomes predisposed to see them lurking in every situation. If your group jumps to the sexual harassment conclusion, use the occasion to discuss the points of the riddle, and contrast how their reactions might have differed in the training situation and real life (i.e., they may have been less prone to see the sexual harassment problem in real life).

✓ Ask them to work privately on solving the riddle and answering the questions that follow it. This experience will be diminished in value by allowing anyone to provide the answer before individuals ponder the puzzle on their own.

✓ After most group members indicate they have either solved the riddle or given up, interrupt them and begin discussing the solution and its ramification for relations between women and men at work.

Discussion Questions

1. Be totally honest. Was at least your initial thinking colored by stereotypes about the "normal" roles of men and women? Identify the stereotypes and discuss them.

2. Do you see any connection between the stereotypes brought out by the riddle and career limitations on women such as the glass ceiling? Discuss.

3. If you could predict the future, do you think this riddle would be a useful training device before a similar audience in 20 years? Why or why not? What changes currently taking place in the work force might alter the reactions of future audiences?

53

WHAT'S THE POINT?

We are so used to placing men and women in separate, gender-stratified roles in our society that we have a natural tendency to typecast people immediately according to their sex. These attitudes must change if women are to thrive in occupational roles previously held only by men and vice versa.

Materials

✓ "Doctor/Patient" Riddle Forms

Time Required

Approximately 25 minutes

"DOCTOR/PATIENT" RIDDLE FORM

Carefully read the following riddle, and privately explore your thoughts as you attempt to find the solution. Please do not discuss the riddle with others until the group addresses the solution. Answer the questions that follow.

"Doctor/Patient" Riddle

A man and his son are driving home following an evening together at a sports event. The highway is icy and in an ensuing head-on collision the man is killed instantly. His son is badly injured, and is taken by the rescue squad to the hospital. The head surgeon is consulted, looks at the young man, and reacts emotionally: "I can't perform this operation. That's my son!"

1. How can this be possible?
2. Explain the role stereotypes play in this situation. How might these relate to discrimination and sexual harassment issues?

Solution (mask or remove before copying): The surgeon is a woman, wife of the driver and mother of the prospective patient.

EXERCISE 14

CABINET SPOUSE

Method SOLVE THE RIDDLE

Problem Men and women are conditioned to have preestablished expectations about gender roles in a variety of situations. Some of their automatic reactions are based on false gender-role stereotypes that perpetuate unequal opportunity and can lead to sexual harassment.

Objective Demonstrate to the participants that expectations based on stereotypes pervade the thoughts of even the most enlightened men and women. By recognizing the point in a riddle that is apt to snare all but the most alert or those who have previously encountered such an example, participants experience a strong jolt of reality about subtle discrimination that an everyday intellectual discussion would not illustrate nearly as powerfully.

Procedure
✓ Pass out copies of the "Cabinet Spouse" Riddle Form to the participants. Riddles are most effective early in sexual harassment training sessions, before the group becomes predisposed to see them lurking in every situation. If your group jumps to the sexual harassment conclusion, use the occasion to discuss the points of the riddle, and contrast how their reactions might have differed in the training situation and real life (i.e., they may have been less prone to see the sexual harassment problem in real life).

✓ Ask them to work privately on solving the riddle and answering the questions that follow it. This experience will be diminished in value by allowing anyone to provide the answer before individuals ponder the puzzle on their own.

✓ After most group members indicate they have either solved the riddle or given up, interrupt them and begin discussing the solution and its ramification for relations between women and men at work.

Discussion Questions
1. Be totally honest. Was at least your initial thinking colored by stereotypes about the "normal" roles of men and women? Identify the stereotypes and discuss them.

2. Do you see any connection between the stereotypes brought out by the riddle and career limitations on women such as the glass ceiling problem? Discuss.

3. If you could predict the future, do you think this riddle would be a useful training device before a similar audience in 20 years? Why or why not? What changes currently taking place in the work force might alter the reactions of future audiences?

WHAT'S THE POINT?

We are so used to placing men and women in separate, gender-stratified roles in our society that we have a natural tendency to typecast people immediately according to their sex. These attitudes must change if women are to thrive in occupational roles previously held only by men and vice versa.

Materials   ✓ "Cabinet Spouse" Riddle Forms

Time Required   Approximately 25 minutes

"CABINET SPOUSE" RIDDLE FORM

Carefully read the following riddle and privately explore the thoughts you have in pursuing the solution. Please do not discuss it with others until the group addresses the solution. Answer the questions that follow.

"Cabinet Spouse" Riddle

The difficulties of being married to prominent political leaders were being discussed by a group of cabinet spouses in Washington. The conversation was just getting interesting when one of them checked the time and made a quick exit to keep an urgent personal medical appointment. The hostess, curious about the reason for the hasty departure, asked a woman, who was a good friend of the departing guest, what the problem was. She explained that there had been a last minute rescheduling of the other guest's follow-up visit for a massive coronary suffered about six months ago.

1. How could such a diagnosis be possible considering the circumstances and composition of the group?

2. Explain the role stereotypes play in this situation. How might these relate to discrimination and sexual harassment issues?

Solution (mask or remove before copying): The cabinet spouse who left for treatment was a man, *husband* of a *female* cabinet Secretary. Women also suffer heart attacks, but given the situation described, many people would picture a female cabinet spouse and puzzle over why she would be keeping a personal appointment about a massive coronary.

EXERCISE 15

50:50 SPLIT ON ATTRIBUTES

Method	SORT THE LISTS
Problem	Sexual harassment issues among working women and men are aggravated by their ingrained assumptions about the beliefs, aspirations, character, and abilities of their gender opposites. In this exercise participants execute a forced sorting of attributes into male and female lists to confront their likely predispositions to categorize colleagues based on subconscious gender stereotyping.
Objective	Demonstrate to the participants that men and women have preexisting expectations about the attributes that most appropriately describe members of each sex. Use the experience to create awareness of stereotypical thinking and to adjust both genders' perceptions to a more accurate norm.

Procedure

✓ Due to a great deal of publicity about sexual harassment, many people know the "politically correct" responses to questions surrounding the issue. When you begin the exercise, acknowledge this and then emphasize that participants' answers will be anonymous and that the usefulness of the training relies on their candid responses. Ask them to express their gut feelings rather than those they think are "right" and to avoid extreme responses that do not express their true beliefs.

✓ Distribute "50:50 Split on Attributes" Forms. (A sample is provided or you may create your own.) Ask members of the group to indicate their gender and then place the attributes in rank order under the male and female columns. Mention that both columns must contain the same number of attributes, and that the task may grow more difficult as they face forced choices toward the end.

✓ Have the respondents fold their surveys for privacy and ask volunteers to collect and score the results. Have them tally the responses for men, women, and the total group. Post the results before the group and discuss.

Discussion Questions

1. Were you surprised that men and women responded differently? the same? Why or why not?

2. How do you account for the differences?

3. Are there attribute placements you find easier to defend than others? Why?

4. Which attributes do you consider to be the most in transition and apt to change in our lifetimes?

5. What do you think the fact that men and women answered differently has to say about the potential for misunderstandings that could lead to sexual harassment problems?

6. Are there entries that you would change now that we've discussed them? Are there any that you are at least willing to rethink quietly on your own?

WHAT'S THE POINT?

Given a private situation and forced to assign attributes differently to male and female lists, men and women respond in certain patterns. This demonstrates that men and women see each other as having different kinds of strengths and weaknesses. Such attributes have career overtones, and the same thinking that comes into play during this sorting exercise can limit the potential of women at work.

Materials

✓ "50:50 Split on Attributes" Forms

✓ Chalkboard or pad on which to display the results

Time Required

Approximately 25 minutes

"50:50 SPLIT ON ATTRIBUTES" FORM

Directions:

A. Check your gender, but *do not put your name* on this anonymous form.

☐ Male   ☐ Female

B. Mentally inventory the list, and place each attribute under the male or female column. Don't choose based on what you think is the "right" answer; give your gut-level response.

C. You must end up with an even number of attributes under male and female.

Attributes

Assertive	Indecisive
Bitchy	Moody
Blunt	Picky
Clerical	Pushy
Delicate	Showing the years
Distinguished	Strong
Emotional	Temperamental
Executive	Trustworthy
Flexible	Well-preserved

Male	*Female*
1.	1.
2.	2.
3.	3.
4.	4.
5.	5.
6.	6.
7.	7.
8.	8.
9.	9.

EXERCISE 16

50:50 SPLIT ON ASPIRATIONS

Method SORT THE LISTS

Problem Sexual harassment issues among working women and men are aggravated by their ingrained assumptions about the beliefs, aspirations, character, and abilities of their gender opposites. In this exercise participants execute a forced sorting of aspirations into male and female lists to confront their likely predispositions to categorize colleagues based on subconscious gender stereotyping.

Objective Demonstrate to the participants that men and women have preexisting assumptions about the aspirations that most appropriately are assigned to members of each sex. Use the experience to create awareness of stereotypical thinking and to adjust both genders' perceptions to a more accurate norm.

Procedure
✓ Due to a great deal of publicity about sexual harassment, many people know the "politically correct" responses to questions surrounding the issue. When you begin the exercise, acknowledge this and then emphasize that participants' answers will be anonymous and that the usefulness of the training relies on the their candid responses. Ask them to express their gut feelings rather than those they think are "right" and to avoid extreme responses that do not express their true beliefs.

✓ Distribute "50:50 Split on Aspirations" Forms. (A sample is provided or you may create your own.) Ask members of the group to indicate their gender and then place the aspirations in rank order under the male and female columns. Emphasize that both columns must contain the same number of attributes, and that the task may grow more difficult as they face forced choices toward the end.

✓ Have the respondents fold their surveys for privacy and ask volunteers to collect and score the results. Have them tally the responses for men, women, and the total group. Post the results before the group and discuss.

Discussion Questions
1. Were you surprised that men and women responded differently? the same? Why or why not?

2. How do you account for the differences?

3. Are there assignments of aspirations that you find easier to defend than others? Why?

4. Which aspirations do you consider to be the most in transition and apt to change in our lifetimes?

5. What do you think the fact that men and women answered differently has to say about the potential for misunderstandings that could lead to sexual harassment problems?

6. Are there entries that you would change now that we've discussed them? Are there any that you are at least willing to rethink quietly on your own?

WHAT'S THE POINT?

Given anonymity and forced choices, men and women will assign aspirations differently to male and female lists, demonstrating that the sexes view each other as seeking different types of careers. Because aspirations partially determine career path, the stereotypical thinking that comes into play during this sorting exercise may hinder the potential of women to work in fields that have been traditionally viewed as more suitable for men.

Materials

✓ "50:50 Split on Aspirations" Forms

✓ Chalkboard or pad on which to display the results

Time Required

Approximately 25 minutes

"50:50 SPLIT ON ASPIRATIONS" FORM

Directions:
A. Check your gender, but *do not put your name* on this anonymous form.

☐ Male   ☐ Female

B. Mentally inventory the list, and place each aspiration under the male or female heading. Don't choose based on what you think is the "right" answer; give your gut-level response.
C. You must end up with an even number of aspirations under male and female.

Aspirations

Army General or Navy Admiral	Government pensioner
Astrophysicist	Homemaker
Bank executive	Librarian
CEO of a corporation	Middle manager
Chief nurse	Musical composer
College president	Musical conductor
Commercial pilot	Physician
Computer scientist	Plumber
Entrepreneur	Secretary of state
Executive secretary	Teacher

Male	*Female*
1.	1.
2.	2.
3.	3.
4.	4.
5.	5.
6.	6.
7.	7.
8.	8.
9.	9.
10.	10.

EXERCISE 17
NATURE/NURTURE QUIZ

Method TRUE/FALSE

Problem Many men harbor myths about their own "natural" superiority (nature) at certain things. Sometimes these notions contain a modicum of truth, but that bit of truth overrides broader considerations including the role cultural expectations and experiences (nurture) play in giving males favorable starting positions and in-place preparation to excel in particular occupations.

Objective Demonstrate to the participants that men and women have biased attitudes about the origins of their respective occupational strengths and weaknesses, which can influence how they view each others' potential. Use the experience to create awareness of stereotypical thinking and to adjust both genders' perceptions to a more accurate norm.

Procedure ✓ Due to a great deal of publicity about sexual harassment, many people know the "politically correct" responses to questions surrounding the issue. When you begin the exercise, acknowledge this and then emphasize that participants' answers will be anonymous and that the usefulness of the training relies on their candid responses. Ask them to express their gut feelings rather than those they think are "right" and to avoid extreme responses that do not express their true beliefs.

✓ Distribute "Nature/Nurture" Quiz. (A sample is provided or you may create your own.) Ask members of the group to indicate their gender, read each statement, and respond true or false.

✓ Have the respondents fold their quizzes for privacy and ask volunteers to collect and score the results. Have them tally the number of people who marked each statement true and false. Do this for the combined group and for women and men separately. Post the results before the group and discuss them.

Discussion Questions 1. Were you surprised that men and women responded differently? the same? Why or why not?

2. How do you account for the differences?

3. Are there statements you found easier to answer than others? Why?

4. What do you think the fact that men and women answered differently has to say about the potential for misunderstandings that could lead to sexual harassment problems?

5. Are there responses that you would change now that we've discussed them? Are there any that you are at least willing to rethink quietly on your own?

WHAT'S THE POINT?

Given anonymity, men and women will respond honestly to what they view as the basis for gender strengths and weaknesses. The results will demonstrate that men and women see each other as having different kinds of potential. Such beliefs have career overtones, and the stereotypical thinking that comes into play in judging the statements true and false may hinder the potential of women to work in fields that have been traditionally viewed as the males' domain.

Materials
✓ "Nature/Nurture" Quiz

✓ Chalkboard or pad on which to display the results

Time Required
Approximately 20 minutes

"NATURE/NURTURE" QUIZ

Directions:

A. Check your gender, but *do not put your name* on this anonymous form.

☐ Male ☐ Female

B. Read each question and circle either True (T) or False (F).

Nature (Because they were born that way)
vs.
Nurture (Because they grew up that way)

T F 1. Men are generally larger and stronger than women due to both nature and nurture.

T F 2. Women are more nurturing primarily because they are born to be mothers.

T F 3. Men are born leaders.

T F 4. Women solve problems in a more conciliatory way than men because such behavior enabled them to survive during the evolution of the species.

T F 5. Men's primitive drive to perpetuate the species is understandably stronger than modern social rules that demand self-control; thus sexual harassment is understandable and not apt to change with time.

T F 6. Under fire, women are more emotional than men; this is a result of body chemistry and will never change; women will never be rational managers.

Answers (mask or remove before copying): While there are no absolute answers to these questions and they are provided more to stimulate thought and discussion than to prove scientific facts, currently accepted expert opinion would answer: 1 = T Born bigger and stronger, emphasis on athletics and strength-enhancing play encourages further physical development. 2 = F Born to the nurturing role of mother, but that characteristic is strongly enhanced by cultural expectations, even for childless women. 3 = F Some native predisposition (physical strength, absence of maternal role, hormones) but heavily influenced by their cultural expectations. 4 = T Cultural role has been that of a subordinate, and learning conciliatory behavior was necessary to survive. 5 = F The drive is indisputably a factor, and while urges cannot be controlled, behavior can. 6 = F An element of truth in the hormonal influences, but generalizations are stereotypes. There is more variation in management style between individuals than between the sexes.

EXERCISE 18
CONVENTIONAL WISDOM QUIZ

Method	TRUE/FALSE
Problem	Many men and women harbor myths in the form of conventional wisdom about the influence of gender, which override their objectivity and slow the acceptance of women as men's peers in the modern workplace.
Objective	Demonstrate to the participants that men and women have biased attitudes about the role of gender at work, which can influence how they view each others' potential. Use the experience to create awareness of stereotypical thinking and to adjust both genders' perceptions to a more accurate norm.

Procedure

✓ Due to a great deal of publicity about sexual harassment, many people know the "politically correct" responses to questions surrounding the issue. When you begin the exercise, acknowledge this and then emphasize that participants' answers will be anonymous and that the usefulness of the training relies on their candid responses. Ask them to express their gut feelings rather than those they think are "right" and to avoid extreme responses that do not express their true beliefs.

✓ Distribute "Conventional Wisdom" Quiz. (A sample is provided or you may create your own.) Ask members of the group to indicate their gender, read each statement, and respond true or false.

✓ Have the respondents fold their quizzes for privacy and ask volunteers to collect and score the results. Have them tally the number of people who marked each statement true and false. Do this for the combined group and for women and men separately. Post the results before the group and discuss them.

Discussion Questions

1. Were you surprised that men and women responded differently? the same? Why or why not?

2. How do you account for the differences?

3. Are there statements you found easier to answer than others? Why?

4. What do you think the fact that men and women answered differently has to say about the potential for misunderstandings that could lead to sexual harassment problems?

5. Are there responses that you would change now that we've discussed them? Are there any that you are at least willing to rethink quietly on your own?

WHAT'S THE POINT?

Given anonymity, men and women will respond honestly to what they view as conventional wisdom about the role of gender in their work lives. The results will demonstrate that men and women see each other as having different kinds of potential. Such beliefs have career overtones, and the stereotypical thinking that comes into play in judging the statements about conventional wisdom true and false may hinder the potential of women to succeed in the modern workplace.

Materials

✓ "Nature/Nurture" Quiz

✓ Chalkboard or pad on which to display the results

Time Required
Directions:

Approximately 20 minutes

"CONVENTIONAL WISDOM" QUIZ

A. Check your gender, but *do not put your name* on this anonymous form.

☐ Male ☐ Female

B. Read each question and circle either True (T) or False (F).

T F 1. Women and men should behave differently in working situations than in conventional social settings.

T F 2. Each gender has a "sixth sense" that gives its members accurate insights about their gender opposites—there are things they just "know."

T F 3. Work is a logical place to find a gender-opposite who shares your social views, educational level, and values.

T F 4. It is more likely for a woman's than a man's sexual attractiveness to be an asset in professional advancement.

T F 5. Important scientific standards in fields such as medicine have been based on the female body because men have had such a fascination with it.

T F 6. Equal opportunity notwithstanding, women should still receive some special consideration when an assignment involves more than average risk to personal safety.

Answers (mask or remove before copying): While there are no absolute answers to these questions and they are provided more to stimulate thought and discussion than to espouse facts, currently accepted expert opinion would answer: 1 = T Many harassment situations originate with the inability to distinguish between appropriate work and social behaviors. 2 = F More often than not, "sixth sense" knowledge is based on stereotypes that fulfill what one wants to be true. 3 = T Jobs attract generally homogenous groups of workers. 4 = T Current popular fiction notwithstanding—for example, Michael Crichton's *Disclosure*—the predator, and the one most likely influenced by sexual attractiveness, remains the male. 5 = F The 70-kilogram man has become infamous as the standard upon which modern medicine was based. 6 = F True equal opportunity requires sharing the downside equally.

EXERCISE 19

NEWS FLASH

Method	SPONTANEOUS REACTION
Problem	Some men and women hold different ideals when it comes to the outcome of major issues separating them in their quest for occupational equity and fairness. Revealing the spontaneous feelings that underlie their more studied reasoning on the issues highlights another dimension of differences that must be understood if they are to be overcome.
Objective	Demonstrate to the participants that men and women coming from different perspectives often favor different outcomes in the workplace battle between the sexes. Misunderstandings about what they see as the goals of the opposite sex and how they go after those goals can adversely influence how they view each other as partners on the job. Use this experience to create awareness of significant differences in perspective and to adjust both genders' perceptions to a more accurate norm.

Procedure

✓ Due to a great deal of publicity about sexual harassment, many people know the "politically correct" responses to questions surrounding the issue. When you begin the exercise, acknowledge this and then emphasize that participants' answers will be anonymous and that the usefulness of the training relies on their candid responses. Ask them to express their gut feelings rather than those they think are "right" and to avoid extreme responses that do not express their true beliefs.

✓ Distribute "News Flash" Reaction Form. (A sample is provided or you may create your own.) Ask members of the group to indicate their gender, read each statement, and respond spontaneously with their first reaction to each item.

✓ Have the respondents fold their quizzes for privacy and ask volunteers to collect and score the results. Have them tally the number of people who marked each response for each statement. Do this for the combined group and for women and men separately. Post the results before the group and discuss them.

Discussion Questions

1. Were you surprised that men and women responded differently? the same? Why or why not?

2. How do you account for the differences?

3. Did you find some statements easier to answer than others? Why?

4. What do you think the fact that men and women answered differently has to say about the potential for misunderstandings that could lead to sexual harassment problems?

5. Are there responses that you would change now that we've discussed them? Are there any that you are at least willing to rethink quietly on your own?

WHAT'S THE POINT?

Reacting spontaneously, working people record different "best outcomes" for gender-related issues that they face in their work lives. These reactions show clearly that women and men sometimes have different goals in the gender-equity movement. These value differences have career overtones, and the same impulses that come into play when reacting to news flashes can limit the ability of women and men to work together without hidden agendas or carefully masked hostility toward their opposite-gender coworkers.

Materials

✓ "News Flash" Reaction Forms

✓ Chalkboard or pad on which to display the results

Time Required

Approximately 20 minutes

"NEWS FLASH" REACTION FORM

Directions:
A. Check your gender, but *do not put your name* on this anonymous form.

☐ Male   ☐ Female

B. Read each question and immediately make a single response—your initial reaction is wanted, so don't ponder the question. If you strongly associate another word with the statement, choose E (Other) and write it in.

1. Company "no fraternization" rule upheld by Supreme Court
   A. Right!
   B. Wrong!
   C. Positive Expletive!
   D. Negative Expletive!
   E. (Other/fill in the blank) _____

2. Woman's firing as CEO rescinded—PMS successfully used as defense
   A. Right!
   B. Wrong!
   C. Positive Expletive!
   D. Negative Expletive!
   E. (Other/fill in the blank) _____

3. Old Girls' Club replaces Old Boys' Club on Judiciary Committee
   A. Right!
   B. Wrong!
   C. Positive Expletive!
   D. Negative Expletive!
   E. (Other/fill in the blank) _____

4. New hormone supplement offers women male assertiveness trait while maintaining femininity
   A. Right!
   B. Wrong!
   C. Positive Expletive!
   D. Negative Expletive!
   E. (Other/fill in the blank) _____

5. New hormone supplement offers men female empathy trait while maintaining masculinity
   A. Right!
   B. Wrong!
   C. Positive Expletive!
   D. Negative Expletive!
   E. (Other/fill in the blank) _____

6. Women the same as men: All but childbearing differences vanish
   A. Right!
   B. Wrong!
   C. Positive Expletive!
   D. Negative Expletive!
   E. (Other/fill in the blank) _____

EXERCISE 20

OFFICE GOSSIP

Method   SPONTANEOUS REACTION

Problem   Some men and women hold different ideals when it comes to the outcome of major issues separating them in their quest for occupational equity and fairness. Revealing the spontaneous feelings that underlie their more studied reasoning on the issues highlights another dimension of differences that must be understood if they are to be overcome.

Objective   Demonstrate to the participants that men and women coming from different perspectives often favor different outcomes in the workplace battle between the sexes. Misunderstandings about what they see as the goals of the opposite sex and how they go after them can adversely influence how they view each other as partners on the job. Use this experience to create awareness of significant differences in perspective and to adjust both genders' perceptions to a more accurate norm.

Procedure   ✓ Due to a great deal of publicity about sexual harassment, many people know the "politically correct" responses to questions surrounding the issue. When you begin the exercise, acknowledge this and then emphasize that participants' answers will be anonymous and that the usefulness of the training relies on their candid responses. Ask them to express their gut feelings rather than those they think are "right" and to avoid extreme responses that do not express their true beliefs.

✓ Distribute "Office Gossip" Reaction Form. (A sample is provided or you may create your own.) Ask members of the group to indicate their gender, read each statement, and respond spontaneously with their first reaction to each item.

✓ Have the respondents fold their quizzes for privacy and ask volunteers to collect and score the results. Have them tally the number of people who marked each response for each statement. Do this for the combined group and for women and men separately. Post the results before the group and discuss them.

Discussion Questions
1. Were you surprised that men and women responded differently? the same? Why or why not?
2. How do you account for the differences?
3. Did you find some statements easier to answer than others? Why?
4. What do you think the fact that men and women answered differently has to say about the potential for misunderstandings that could lead to sexual harassment problems?

5. Are there responses that you would change now that we've discussed them? Are there any that you are at least willing to rethink quietly on your own?

WHAT'S THE POINT?

Reacting spontaneously, men and women record different judgments of gender-related issues that confront them informally in their work lives. These reactions show clearly that women and men sometimes have different goals in the gender-equity movement. These value differences have career overtones, and the same impulses that come into play when reacting to news flashes can limit the ability of women and men to work together without hidden agendas or carefully masked hostility toward their opposite-gender coworkers.

Materials

✓ "Office Gossip" Reaction Forms

✓ Chalkboard or pad on which to display the results

Time Required

Approximately 20 minutes

"OFFICE GOSSIP" REACTION FORM

Directions:

A. Check your gender, but *do not put your name* on this anonymous form.

☐ Male ☐ Female

B. Read each question and immediately make a single response—your initial reaction is wanted, so don't ponder the question. If you strongly associate another word with the statement, choose E (Other) and write it in.

1. The classified ad ended: "EEO/AA Employer," but someone on the selection committee told me the boss's hidden agenda is to hire a white male with the same background as his own—but no one is willing to call him on it.
   A. Right!
   B. Wrong!
   C. Positive Expletive!
   D. Negative Expletive!
   E. (Other/fill in the blank) _____

2. Julie McAver will be heading the study group, and everyone knows that gives her a lock on promotion to division chief. No one denies Jack Wilson has both more experience and more relevant experience in the area. It's a painless way for senior management to appease the affirmative action gods, and sometimes men just have to pay the price for the wrongs of the past.
   A. Right!
   B. Wrong!
   C. Positive Expletive!
   D. Negative Expletive!
   E. (Other/fill in the blank) _____

3. George, the boss, and Sam, one of his product managers, spend a lot of time together—old service buddies. It's fun to see such a great friendship! Versus: John, the boss, and Sandy, one of his product managers, spend a lot of time together—bet she's sleeping her way to the top!
   A. Right!
   B. Wrong!
   C. Positive Expletive!
   D. Negative Expletive!
   E. (Other/fill in the blank) _____

4. Katherine's husband left an important product development meeting this morning to pick up their daughter at school—she was very sick. He had to do it; Katherine was on the Coast closing a big deal for her division. Why do women like that have kids in the first place?
   A. Right!
   B. Wrong!
   C. Positive Expletive!
   D. Negative Expletive!
   E. (Other/fill in the blank) _____

5. Rob is a royal pain this morning; bright guys like him seem to run in cycles. Versus: Jennifer is hell on wheels today; guess what time of the month it is?
   A. Right!
   B. Wrong!
   C. Positive Expletive!
   D. Negative Expletive!
   E. (Other/fill in the blank) _____

6. They've settled out of court with Marge on her sexual harassment suit—$250,000 over five years and a promotion to vice president. Hell, *I'd* sleep with the guy for that!
   A. Right!
   B. Wrong!
   C. Positive Expletive!
   D. Negative Expletive!
   E. (Other/fill in the blank) _____

Section 2

ILLUSTRATING THE KINDS OF SEXUAL HARASSMENT

Rationale   The overarching thought behind the exercises of Section 2 is: As the issue became litigious and the subject of regulation, sexual harassment offenses were sorted into categories that are key to understanding the boundaries of acceptable behavior.

Selection of Exercises   Use these thumbnail sketches of the exercises in Section 2 to choose those best suited to your purposes.

AGREE/DISAGREE

21. *How Can I Offend Thee? Let Me Count the Ways*—Participants anonymously score statements identifying kinds of sexual harassment on an agree/disagree scale. Identifying themselves only as male or female raters, they mark each statement once with their candid opinion and once with the answer they believe is "politically correct." Trainers calculate averages, note extremes, and help participants sort the kinds of harassment in a guided discussion of *quid pro quo* and hostile environment sexual harassment.

DEMONSTRATION

22. *Interplanetary Harassment*—*Quid pro quo* and hostile environment harassment are demonstrated by teams of participants working in contexts of Planets A and B where the object of coercion is something other than sex as we define it. Guided discussion draws the parallels between the culturally neutral vulnerabilities of the inhabitants of Planets A and B, and sex in the contemporary workplace, and concludes that abusive use of power is at the root of the sexual harassment issue.

MAKE THE CASE

23. *All He Wanted Was a Date?*—One group is tasked with making the case for sexual harassment charges in a hypothetical workplace situation, and the other must defend against the charges in the same situation. Participants experience both sides of the case either directly or vicariously and learn the importance of perception, intent, and other fine points in judging a shades-of-gray sexual harassment case. Trainer-guided discussion reveals the variety of motivations at play in these situations.

MATCH THE ITEMS

24. *Identify the Harassment*—Participants are given a series of situations and are asked to match them to a type of sexual harassment. The re-

sults are tallied and trainers help participants examine their thinking and appreciate each others' positions in guided discussion.

MULTIPLE CHOICE

25. *Is It Either? Is It Neither? Or Is It Both?*—Participants judge the validity of a number of kinds of potential sexual harassment situations by selecting multiple-choice answers. Trainers tabulate and compare the results, then aid participants in examining the strengths and weaknesses of their choices during a guided discussion.

RATE THE ACCURACY

26. *Do I Have to Put Up with This?*—Individuals are asked to score several statements about sexual harassment anonymously on an accurate/inaccurate scale. Identifying themselves only as male or female raters, they mark the list once with their candid opinion and once with the answer they believe is "politically correct." Trainers calculate averages, note extremes, and help participants separate myth from reality in a guided discussion of their differences.

SOLVE THE RIDDLE

27. *Failed Attorney*—Participants are asked to solve a riddle in which traditional thinking about reasons for success and failure clouds their judgment and hinders their ability to find the solution. Trainers guide the discussion to reveal stereotypical views and their relevance to attitudes at work.

SORT THE LISTS

28. *50:50 Split on Kinds of Harassment*—Participants are asked to make forced choices among kinds of harassment—half must be listed under *quid pro quo* and half under hostile environment. The results are tallied and then examined during a guided discussion.

TRUE/FALSE

29. *Classifying Harassment*—Participants take a true/false quiz based on how incidents of workplace harassment are best classified under law. The results are tallied and the responses are examined during a guided discussion.

SPONTANEOUS REACTION

30. *It's Your Call*—Participants are presented with a workplace event that has sexual harassment overtones and are asked to respond with an immediate reaction as to what kind of harassment occurred, if any. The results are tallied for men, women, and the total group and the responses are examined during a guided discussion.

Optional Cross-References—The following chapter of *Working Together: The New Rules and Realities for Managing Men and Women at Work* (Baridon and Eyler, McGraw-Hill, 1994) is recommended if you need additional information to understand the issues and support your discussions:

Chapter 3, "Laws, Regulations, and Gender in the Workforce"

EXERCISE 21

HOW CAN I OFFEND THEE? LET ME COUNT THE WAYS

Method	AGREE/DISAGREE
Problem	Men and women are not always clear about the differences between actions that are simply obnoxious and those that cross the line into sexual harassment territory. In this exercise participants indicate their opinions on whether or not certain situations fall under the two categories of sexual harassment (*quid pro quo* and hostile environment). The results are then tallied and discussed.
Objective	Demonstrate to the participants that equal opportunity laws and regulations provide guidance on identifying workplace behavior that can be defined as sexual harassment. Use the opinion survey to help individuals decide whether the actions described fit into classes of legally prohibited behavior and judge where the line is crossed that might involve them in sexual harassment.
Procedure	✓ Men and women may hold different views about whether certain actions fit the categories of sexual harassment. To contrast their disparate views and increase mutual understanding, respondents are asked to indicate their gender before completing the anonymous questionnaire. Due to much publicity about this issue, many people of both genders know the "politically correct" answer but hold different personal views. To get both viewpoints, the survey asks participants to differentiate between what they honestly feel and what they believe to be the "right" response. Stress the anonymity aspect of the exercise and urge participants to respond candidly.
	✓ Distribute the rating scales. (A sample is provided or you may create your own.) Ask members of the group to indicate their gender and then rate each assumption candidly by circling a number on the scale. Also ask for a second rating that indicates what they *think* the politically correct answer (PC) would be. Clarify that the PC response does not have to be different from the one expressing their gut feeling. The two might be the same and they may or may not be "right." The objective is simply to react instinctively and then indicate what is perceived to be the socially acceptable response.
	✓ Have the respondents fold their surveys for privacy and ask volunteers to collect and score the results. Have them calculate the average score for men, women, and the total group on each question (i.e., add up the individual scores and divide by the total number of surveys in that group for each question)—for candid and PC responses. Post the results before the group and discuss them. Note that the objective of the exercise is to examine views and develop sensitivity, not to reach definitive conclusions to the hypothetical questions.

1. Were you surprised at the answers of the opposite sex? your own gender? the group? Why or why not?

2. How do you account for the differences among the groups?

3. What messages do the results convey?

4. What are some possible implications for sexual harassment?

5. Are there differences between the candid and politically correct responses? Do you think they might be narrowed in the future? If so, why? How?

WHAT'S THE POINT?

The law has placed offending behavior into two categories, *quid pro quo* and environmental sexual harassment. While this is a necessary and generally effective device for identifying harassment problems at work, men and women need an appreciation of the character and limitations of such schemes. They also need to understand that actions do not always fit neatly into distinct predetermined categories. By working with the categories participants learn more than how to sort behavior into two groups. They discover that some behavior overlaps the two categories, and they become aware of the pitfalls of using sex as a weapon to intimidate a coworker.

Materials

✓ Blackboard and chalk, or markers and board or pad to display results before the group

✓ Copies of the survey for individual members of the group

✓ A pocket calculator

Time Required

Approximately 30 minutes

"HOW CAN I OFFEND THEE?" SURVEY FORM

Directions:

A. Check your gender, but *do not put your name* on this anonymous survey.

☐ Male   ☐ Female

B. Read each statement and mark it twice: (1) circle the number on the scale that best represents your candid, personal opinion; and (2) circle the number that represents what you believe to be the "politically correct" response.

Definitions:

✓ Quid pro quo *sexual harassment*—making sexual favors a condition of employment or the basis for favorable or unfavorable employment decisions.

✓ *Hostile environment sexual harassment*—sexual conduct that unreasonably interferes with an individual's work performance or creates an intimidating, hostile, or offensive working environment.

1. A supervisor who demands in no uncertain terms that an attractive subordinate is to accompany him or her on extended business trips, even though there is no compelling business reason, commits *quid pro quo* sexual harassment.

Candid opinion:									
1	2	3	4	5	6	7	8	9	10
Agree								Disagree	

Politically correct opinion:									
1	2	3	4	5	6	7	8	9	10
Agree								Disagree	

2. The office manager likes staff social events that have an obvious sexual component, e.g., magicians who perform sexually suggestive tricks, comedians who tell sex-based jokes, etc. Some people go along and get ahead, others don't and fall into disfavor. The latter group has a case for hostile environment sexual harassment.

Candid opinion:									
1	2	3	4	5	6	7	8	9	10
Agree								Disagree	

Politically correct opinion:									
1	2	3	4	5	6	7	8	9	10
Agree								Disagree	

3. An instructor in a company management trainee course asks a student for an after-hours date, and the student refuses. The cycle is repeated twice more with the same results. At the end of the course, the student receives an evaluation much lower than had been anticipated. A case could be made for both *quid pro quo* and hostile environment sexual harassment complaints.

Candid opinion:

1   2   3   4   5   6   7   8   9   10

Agree   Disagree

Politically correct opinion:

1   2   3   4   5   6   7   8   9   10

Agree   Disagree

EXERCISE 22
INTERPLANETARY HARASSMENT

Method	DEMONSTRATION
Problem	Sexual harassment is an exercise in power expressed by forcing someone to grant or tolerate intimacy they otherwise would not. It might involve exchanging privileges for intimacy, *quid pro quo* harassment; or it might consist of forcing others to tolerate objectionable conditions in the workplace, hostile environment sexual harassment. Demonstrating harassment in an alien-world context helps participants understand the inappropriate application of power without experiencing the discomfort that many people feel when dealing with sexual issues in our culture. Trainers lead a discussion of the group's observations, pointing out parallels between alien and more familiar abuses of power that constitute sexual harassment.
Objective	Demonstrate to the participants that the sexual component of harassment is just the specific vulnerability exploited in the abuses of power we know as *quid pro quo* and hostile environment sexual harassment. Use the experience to open the participants' thinking to the possibility that the principles demonstrated on the fictional planets might be generalized to situations in which sex is used as the ultimate power tool in their own workplaces.
Procedure	✓ Select two teams from the group of participants—about six members each is ideal, but the number is not critical. Include members of both sexes. Designate them the Planet A and Planet B groups. ✓ Separate the teams so they are unable to listen to what their counterparts are planning. Ask the audience not to influence the outcome by commenting or providing guidance. ✓ Give each team the Workplace Environment Kit for its planet. ✓ Give the audience a sheet that informs the observers about what the teams are doing. ✓ After team members finish conferring, ask each team to demonstrate (through a brief skit or a spokesperson—their option) how team members would use their power to coerce the workers on their respective planets—first *quid pro quo,* and then hostile environment. If the spokesperson option is chosen, a male and female trainer may want to act out the skit described to give life to the exercise. ✓ When both teams finish, ask each to explain its approach. ✓ If it has not become obvious, clarify that each team has demonstrated the two kinds of sexual harassment as inappropriate expressions of power that didn't involve sexual favors as we define them. The objects of coercion on Planets A and B are different from each other and each is different from sexual harassment on earth, but the inappropriate use of power is the same—with or without sex.

1. How does each team use its power to exploit those they view as weak or subordinate?

2. How is their behavior the same? different?

3. What parallels do you see between these power plays and sexual harassment in the contemporary workplace?

4. If sex didn't exist, would another basis for expressing control and superiority be found?

5. Which is the most damaging—*quid pro quo* or hostile environment harassment? Why?

6. Can you give examples of the kinds of actions that are more commonly associated with *quid pro quo* harassment? hostile environment harassment?

WHAT'S THE POINT?

In our culture, sex is the ultimate gesture of intimacy between two people, and it is the vulnerability of choice exploited by sexual harassers. Sexual harassment is difficult to graphically demonstrate because of the emotions that accompany the intimacy of sexual relationships between human beings. In our demonstration examples, this kind of intimacy involved sharing the contents of "the mind's eye" and "the window to the brain"—gestures usually reserved for significant others. This exercise unmasks sexual harassment for what it is—the exertion of power by one gender over another—unemotionally by substituting culture-neutral icons for sex as the vulnerability exploited by abusers. Participants who might not comfortably engage in a training experience using sexual terminology are more apt to involve themselves in a less threatening demonstration of culturally neutral vulnerabilities.

Materials

✓ Break-out areas in which the Planet A and B groups can meet (corners of the room will do, just so they can get away to confer with some degree of confidentiality)

✓ Planet A and Planet B Workplace Environment Kits

✓ Audience Information Sheet

✓ Chalkboard or large pad to note major points in discussion

Time Required

Approximately 25 minutes

PLANET A WORKPLACE ENVIRONMENT KIT

Situation

The workplace on Planet A is in turmoil. Workers have difficulty pursuing their careers in peace because the ruling group sometimes departs from the behavioral norms of the society and coerces some individuals into sharing, and, in some instances, tolerating objectionable public emphasis on, a very private part of their lives. More specifically, the ruling group links favorable working conditions to a worker's willingness to permit gazing upon a green crystal diode deep within the right eye. What is seen there is "the mind's eye," which exposes the individual's hopes, dreams, fears, etc. to anyone who is permitted to look within. Therefore, this is an intimate experience normally reserved for significant others.

TASK 1. Demonstrate how this might occur on a *quid pro quo* basis.

TASK 2. Demonstrate how this might occur on a hostile environment basis.

Definitions:

✓ Quid pro quo *sexual harassment*—making sexual favors a condition of employment or the basis for favorable or unfavorable employment decisions.

✓ *Hostile environment sexual harassment*—conduct that unreasonably interferes with an individual's work performance or creates an intimidating, hostile, or offensive working environment.

PLANET B WORKPLACE ENVIRONMENT KIT

Situation

The workplace on Planet B is in turmoil. Workers have difficulty pursuing their careers in peace because the ruling group sometimes departs from the behavioral norms of the society and coerces some individuals into sharing, and, in some instances, tolerating objectionable public emphasis on, a very private part of their lives. More specifically, the ruling group links favorable working conditions to a worker's willingness to permit pressing the button found on each individual's forehead. This opens "the window to the brain" which exposes the individual's hopes, dreams, fears, etc. to anyone who is permitted to look within. Therefore, this is an intimate experience normally reserved for significant others.

TASK 1. Demonstrate how this might occur on a *quid pro quo* basis.

TASK 2. Demonstrate how this might occur on a hostile environment basis.

Definitions:

✓ Quid pro quo *sexual harassment*—making sexual favors a condition of employment or the basis for favorable or unfavorable employment decisions.

✓ *Hostile environment sexual harassment*—conduct that unreasonably interferes with an individual's work performance or creates an intimidating, hostile, or offensive working environment.

AUDIENCE INFORMATION SHEET

Situation

The workplaces on Planets A and B are in turmoil. Workers have difficulty pursuing their careers in peace because the ruling group sometimes departs from the behavioral norms of the society and coerces some individuals into sharing, and, in some instances, tolerating objectionable public emphasis on, a very private part of their lives. More specifically, the ruling group links favorable working conditions to a worker's willingness to permit gazing upon, in the case of Planet A, a green crystal diode deep within the right eye that opens "the mind's eye," and for Planet B, touching a button located on the forehead that is "the window to the brain"—intimate experiences normally reserved for significant others on both planets.

TASK 1. Demonstrate how this might occur on a *quid pro quo* basis.

TASK 2. Demonstrate how this might occur on a hostile environment basis.

Definitions:

✓ Quid pro quo *sexual harassment*—making sexual favors a condition of employment or the basis for favorable or unfavorable employment decisions.

✓ *Hostile environment sexual harassment*—conduct that unreasonably interferes with an individual's work performance or creates an intimidating, hostile, or offensive working environment.

EXERCISE 23

ALL HE WANTED WAS A DATE?

Method   MAKE THE CASE

Problem   Sexual harassment claims are not always clear—there are often two perspectives. A good trial lawyer steps back from the emotional aspects of the client's case and, using logic and reason, puts on the best defense possible. In this exercise participants are asked to defend sexual harassment positions with which they might adamantly disagree, illustrating the qualities of *quid pro quo* and hostile environment harassment in the process.

Objective   Provide participants with the occasion to understand sexual harassment issues from points of view that differ from their own. Have them think as advocates for a position possibly alien to their own. Use the experience to increase sensitivity on both sides of a shades-of-gray case of sexual harassment and to demonstrate how one's actions might be misinterpreted or how one might misinterpret behavior that initially seems like sexual harassment but may be shown by objective analysis to be something entirely different.

Procedure   ✓ Select two teams of about six each, consisting of both men and women.

                  ✓ Pass out Scenarios 1 and 2 to the teams and the audience.

                  ✓ Instruct the teams to read and discuss their scenarios and to come up with their strongest defense for their assigned position—whether they agree with it or not.

                  ✓ Ask each team to have a spokesperson describe its scenario and summarize its defense for the position. Other team members are encouraged to contribute to the defense. (If necessary to get the discussion started, you may suggest a line of defense.)

                  ✓ Ask one team to challenge the other's position. (If necessary to move the discussion forward, you may suggest some challenges.)

                  ✓ Briefly note key words and phrases on a pad or blackboard—this helps people go back and elaborate on earlier points.

                  ✓ Encourage the exchange of challenge and defense until you feel the relevant points have been made.

                  ✓ Solicit a vote from the entire audience, which serves as the jury. The question for the jury is: Does this case constitute either *quid pro quo* or hostile environment sexual harassment or both?

                  ✓ Note that the objective is to uncover points of view that participants might not have considered. The case is deliberately ambiguous, open-ended, and subject to various interpretations and judgments (just like real life situations). Acknowledge this so you don't leave the group frustrated that a "correct" judgment was not reached.

Discussion Questions

1. Do you see legitimate arguments for each of the positions in this case? If so, what are they?

2. Could there be some underlying traditional thinking at work that kept Joyce from getting the assignments she wanted? What might that be?

3. Do you think that Joyce could have made some assumptions about Tom that were unfair? If so, what might they be?

4. Do you think Joyce handled her complaint correctly? How might a less formal approach have helped solve the problem (if there was one)?

5. Do you think those advocating either position intend to discriminate deliberately against the loser of the position based on gender? Why or why not?

6. Do you believe that the people advocating the position different from yours sincerely feel the way they do? Or do you assume that their behavior is simply meant to offend you? Why?

WHAT'S THE POINT?

Aside from blatant cases where it's your career vs. sexual acquiescence and/or tolerance of conditions you abhor, sexual harassment of both varieties (*quid pro quo* and hostile environment) often involve a considerable amount of interpretation and judgment. Having to make that judgment enlightens participants and helps them separate harassment from the lesser offenses of boorishness and tastelessness that, while obnoxious, do not cross the sexual harassment line.

Materials

✓ Blackboard and chalk, or markers and board or pad to display notes before the group

✓ Copies of the scenarios for the teams and audience

Time Required

Approximately 35 minutes

"ALL HE WANTED WAS A DATE?" SCENARIO 1

Directions:

Discuss the scenario as a team. Understand that *your role as a team is to defend the position of the accused who denies harassing his colleague—whether you agree with him or not.* Think about what arguments a person advocating his innocence would use even if you would disagree. You will have a chance later to say why you consider the position you articulate in this situation to be wrong, if that is how you feel. The team will choose a spokesperson, but everyone is encouraged to contribute to the discussion.

Situation

✓ Tom and Joyce work in the same division. He is at level 3 in a hierarchy where 4 represents the top; she is at level 2. Neither is presently married, and a reasonable person would judge them a plausible couple. Tom's opinions and recommendations, at least informally, will help Joyce get the assignments she needs to move to level 3. He has been pursuing Joyce socially for some time, and, because she knows he is a key factor in her advancement, she is in a quandary. Should she just keep from discouraging or encouraging him, or should she come clean and tell him she's simply not interested? Joyce believes that the latter choice puts her at risk for not getting the crucial assignments. Months pass; she takes an indecisive stance, not accepting Tom's repeated social initiatives, but not clearly saying they are unwanted. Finding fewer and fewer of the desired assignments coming her way, Joyce concludes it is because she has been unresponsive to Tom's personal advances and lodges a sexual harassment complaint with human resources.

✓ Make the case that Tom did not commit *quid pro quo* sexual harassment.

✓ Make the case that Tom did not commit hostile environment sexual harassment.

Definitions:

✓ Quid pro quo *sexual harassment*—making sexual favors a condition of employment or the basis for favorable or unfavorable employment decisions.

✓ *Hostile environment sexual harassment*—sexual conduct that unreasonably interferes with an individual's work performance or creates an intimidating, hostile, or offensive working environment.

"ALL HE WANTED WAS A DATE?" SCENARIO 2

Directions:

Discuss the scenario as a team. Understand that *your role as a team is to support the position of the woman alleging sexual harassment, whether you agree with her or not.* Think about what arguments people would use to defend such a position even if you find it objectionable. You will have a chance later to say why you consider the position you articulate in this situation is wrong, if that is how you feel. The team will choose a spokesperson, but everyone is encouraged to contribute to the discussion.

Situation

✓ Tom and Joyce work in the same division. He is at level 3 in a hierarchy where 4 represents the top; she is at level 2. Neither is presently married, and a reasonable person would judge them a plausible couple. Tom's opinions and recommendations, at least informally, will help Joyce get the assignments she needs to move to level 3. He has been pursuing Joyce socially for some time, and, because she knows he is a key factor in her advancement, she is in a quandary. Should she just keep from discouraging or encouraging him, or should she come clean and tell him she's simply not interested? Joyce believes that the latter choice puts her at risk for not getting the crucial assignments. Months pass; she takes an indecisive stance, not accepting Tom's repeated social initiatives, but not clearly saying they are unwanted. Finding fewer and fewer of the desired assignments coming her way, Joyce concludes it is because she has been unresponsive to Tom's personal advances and lodges a sexual harassment complaint with human resources.

✓ Make the case that Tom committed *quid pro quo* sexual harassment.

✓ Make the case that Tom committed hostile environment sexual harassment.

Definitions:

✓ Quid pro quo *sexual harassment*—making sexual favors a condition of employment or the basis for favorable or unfavorable employment decisions.

✓ *Hostile environment sexual harassment*—sexual conduct that unreasonably interferes with an individual's work performance or creates an intimidating, hostile, or offensive working environment.

EXERCISE 24

IDENTIFY THE HARASSMENT

Method

MATCH THE ITEMS

Problem

It is useful to be able to distinguish between the two legally defined types of sexual harassment, *quid pro quo* and hostile environment. In this exercise participants indicate their opinions on whether or not the situations posed constitute one or the other kind of sexual harassment. The results are then tallied and discussed.

Objective

Demonstrate to the participants that sexual harassment stems from one of two basic forms of workplace intimidation or a combination thereof. Use the experience to create awareness of differences in perception regarding alleged sexual harassment behavior and help participants avoid the pitfalls—either by going too far and committing it or by not acting decisively soon enough to curtail it.

Procedure

✓ Men and women may hold different views about whether certain actions fit the categories of sexual harassment. To contrast their disparate views and increase mutual understanding, respondents are asked to indicate their gender before completing the anonymous questionnaire. Due to much publicity about this issue, many people of both genders know the "politically correct" answer but hold different personal views. To get both viewpoints, the survey asks participants to differentiate between what they honestly feel and what they believe to be the "right" response. Stress the anonymity aspect of the exercise and urge participants to respond candidly.

✓ Distribute the "Identify The Harassment" Matching Form. (A sample is provided or you may create your own.) Ask members of the group to indicate their gender and then mark each entry candidly by circling the selection they feel indicates the best answer. Also ask for a second matching that indicates what they *think* the politically correct (PC) answer would be. Clarify that the PC response does not have to be different from the one expressing their gut feeling. The two might be the same and they may or may not be "right." The objective is simply to react instinctively and then indicate what is perceived to be the socially acceptable response.

✓ Have the respondents fold their matching forms for privacy and ask volunteers to collect the forms and tally the results. Have them tally the responses for men, women, and the total group on each item (i.e., how many men, women, and total group participants marked the item *Quid Pro Quo,* Hostile Environment, Both, Neither)—for candid and PC responses. Post the results before the group and discuss them.

Discussion Questions

1. Were you surprised at the answers of the opposite sex? your own gender? the group? Why or why not?

2. How do you account for differences among the groups if there are any?

3. What messages do the results convey?

4. What are some possible implications for sexual harassment?

5. Are there differences between the candid and politically correct responses? If so, what are the differences? Why do you think they exist?

WHAT'S THE POINT?

Judgment and the ability to separate sexual harassment from less significant offending, but not illegal, behavior are important skills for both potential harassers and victims. A key item in fostering those skills in either situation is knowing at least the broad criteria that define *quid pro quo* and hostile environment sexual harassment. This exercise allows participants to apply their judgment, test it against that of other individuals and the group, and have it refined with the help of the trainers.

Materials

✓ Blackboard and chalk, or markers and board or pad to display results before the group

✓ Copies of the matching form for individual members of the group

Time Required

Approximately 20 minutes

"IDENTIFY THE HARASSMENT" MATCHING FORM

Directions:

A. Check your gender, but *do not put your name* on this anonymous survey.

☐ Male   ☐ Female

B. Read each statement and mark it twice: (1) circle the selection on the form that best matches your candid, personal opinion of what kind of harassment, if any, has taken place; and (2) circle the selection that matches what you believe to be the "politically correct" response.

Definitions:

✓ Quid pro quo *sexual harassment*—making sexual favors a condition of employment or the basis for favorable or unfavorable employment decisions.

✓ *Hostile environment sexual harassment*—sexual conduct that unreasonably interferes with an individual's work performance or creates an intimidating, hostile, or offensive working environment.

1. A hiring official in a private interview tells the job candidate he can guarantee her the position if she'll spend the coming weekend with him at the shore.

	Candid opinion:		
Quid Pro Quo	Hostile Environment	Both	Neither
	Politically correct opinion:		
Quid Pro Quo	Hostile Environment	Both	Neither

2. As he returns from a meeting one day, a young male subordinate finds in his desk drawer a pack of condoms; another day he finds a neatly wrapped pair of men's bikini shorts. Similar incidents continue intermittently for months. Each time a smiling middle-aged woman who evaluates his job performance observes him with a knowing smile from behind the curtained window of her nearby office.

	Candid opinion:		
Quid Pro Quo	Hostile Environment	Both	Neither
	Politically correct opinion:		
Quid Pro Quo	Hostile Environment	Both	Neither

3. A worker grows attached to a colleague with whom he has been teamed for more than a year. When work assignments change and she is assigned to a project team with another coworker, he appears to be slightly jealous and shows some reluctance in accepting the new arrangement.

	Candid opinion:		
Quid Pro Quo	Hostile Environment	Both	Neither
	Politically correct opinion:		
Quid Pro Quo	Hostile Environment	Both	Neither

4. Amanda takes a new job in what turns out to be a party office. After a short time in the company she learns that those who get ahead are active in an extended office group where couples form and sexually suggestive situations are common. She is approached to participate, says no, and is told her career could suffer.

	Candid opinion:		
Quid Pro Quo	Hostile Environment	Both	Neither

	Politically correct opinion:		
Quid Pro Quo	Hostile Environment	Both	Neither

Comments (cover or remove before copying for use in the exercise): Each situation contains sketchy information, and answers might be different with the introduction of additional information. The examples are intended to stimulate discussion and uncover relevant points, not establish indelible criteria or provide indisputable rulings of guilt or innocence. In general, an informed person would respond: 1. *Quid Pro Quo,* 2. Hostile Environment, 3. Neither, and 4. Both

EXERCISE 25

IS IT EITHER? IS IT NEITHER? OR IS IT BOTH?

Method   MULTIPLE CHOICE

Problem   Naturally occurring attractions between gender opposites may complicate their workplace relationships. Sometimes actions, usually those of the
male, cross professional boundaries and result in *quid pro quo* or hostile environment sexual harassment, or a combination of the two. In this exercise
participants are asked to judge whether or not sexual harassment is a factor in a number of common workplace situations. The results are tallied
and discussed.

Objective   Demonstrate to the participants that sexual harassment is one of many
possibilities on the continuum of human behavior. Because some actions
do not fit neatly into the discrete boundaries used in statutory definitions
such as *quid pro quo* and hostile environment harassment, men and
women need to develop the ability to distinguish between behavior that
is objectionable, even grossly so, and that which is illegal harassment.

Procedure   ✓ Due to a great deal of publicity about sexual harassment, most people
know the "politically correct" responses to questions about sexual harassment in the modern workplace. When you begin the exercise, acknowledge this and then emphasize that participants' answers will be
anonymous and that the usefulness of the training relies on their candid responses. Ask them to express their gut feelings rather than those
they think are "right" and to avoid extreme responses that do not express their true beliefs.

✓ Distribute the "Is It Either? Is It Neither? Or Is It Both?" Quiz. (A sample is provided or you may create your own.) Ask members of the
group to indicate their gender and then mark each entry candidly by
selecting the multiple-choice item that indicates what they believe
about sexual harassment.

✓ Have the respondents fold their quizzes for privacy and ask volunteers
to collect the forms and tally the results. Have them tally the responses
for men, women, and the total group on each question (i.e., how many
men, women, and total group participants marked the various responses). Post the results before the group and discuss them.

Discussion Questions 1. Were you surprised at the answers of the opposite sex? your own gender? the group? Why or why not?

2. How do you account for the differences among the groups?

3. What messages do the results convey?

4. What are some possible implications for sexual harassment?

98

5. Do you think gender stereotyping affected how you answered any of the questions? How your opposite-sex peers answered them? How? Why?

6. Do you think it is more important to understand the difference between *quid pro quo* and hostile environment harassment or between either type of harassment and simply offensive or obnoxious behavior? Why?

WHAT'S THE POINT?

Making the distinction between boorish, crude, inappropriate behavior and actions that constitute illegal sexual harassment is a necessary step in effectively dealing with the issue. In fact, the differences between *quid pro quo* and hostile environment are less important than those between harassment and just plain gender-based rudeness. The ability to define the behavior objectively and evaluate its threat will enable you to calibrate your reaction appropriately for either genuine harassment or equally inexcusable, but not illegal, offensive bad manners.

Materials

✓ Blackboard and chalk, or markers and board or pad to display results before the group

✓ Copies of the "Is It Either? Is It Neither? Or Is It Both?" Quiz for individual members of the group

Time Required

Approximately 20 minutes

"IS IT EITHER? IS IT NEITHER? OR IS IT BOTH?" QUIZ

Directions:
A. Check your gender, but *do not put your name* on this anonymous quiz.

☐ Male ☐ Female

B. Read each statement and circle the response that you think is factually correct.

Definitions:

✓ Quid pro quo *sexual harassment*—making sexual favors a condition of employment or the basis for favorable or unfavorable employment decisions.

✓ *Hostile environment sexual harassment*—conduct that unreasonably interferes with an individual's work performance or creates an intimidating, hostile, or offensive working environment.

1. Men find a kind of inspiration in the female form and the thoughts they associate with it. How does this cultural-biological reality play in the sexual harassment issues of the modern workplace?
   a. It is a legitimate excuse for most of the things men do that offend women.
   b. It is something that women should learn to live with—it's natural.
   c. It is most likely to manifest itself in *quid pro quo* sexual harassment (demanding sexual favors in return for favorable treatment).
   d. It is most likely to manifest itself in hostile environment sexual harassment (displaying pinups and the like in the workplace).
   e. All of the above.

2. Mentoring is a highly regarded method of developing new generations of leadership in businesses. What relationship does this favorable practice have to the kinds of sexual harassment?
   a. Because men now hold most senior positions, they are most apt to become mentors to up-and-coming leaders.
   b. Increasing numbers of women are among the ranks of the rising leadership generation; therefore, younger women are likely to be mentored by older men.
   c. Men in the mentoring role are expressing concern about being vulnerable to *quid pro quo* sexual harassment charges.
   d. Hostile environment sexual harassment is less relevant in mentoring.
   e. All of the above.

3. Tom is an old-fashioned macho-male manager who curses up a storm, tells off-color stories regularly, and makes no secret of his biases against women when he thinks he is among friends (both male and female). He also has hired and retained several top-flight female managers within his division. How does his style fit into the sexual harassment definitions?
   a. He's relatively harmless, though somewhat offensive, and will probably pass into retirement uncharged and unchanged.
   b. He's poisoning the workplace environment and is guilty of hostile environment sexual harassment.
   c. He almost certainly has a subordinate locked into a *quid pro quo* sexual harassment relationship.
   d. He's an accident waiting to happen, and all signs point to sexual harassment charges in the future.
   e. He's the kind of guy you've just got to admire in a lot of ways.

4. The big boss loves fine art. Among his choices for the executive suite are prints of reclining nude women painted by the masters. His secretary is stuck with them whether she likes them or not, and she puts up with a barrage of teasing, mostly from male coworkers, about being surrounded by naked women. What are her chances of a successful hostile environment sexual harassment filing?

a. Not good; classic art is not judged the same as magazine centerfolds.
b. Not bad; there should be an equal number of classic male nudes or none at all.
c. She would more likely succeed if she directs her case toward the men who make the comments than toward the boss who chose the art.
d. Excellent; no woman should have to look at such things *and* be teased about them.
e. Both a and c.

5. A busy male executive asked his female administrative assistant if she would stop by a lingerie shop and select a Valentine's Day gift for his significant other—and get something for herself for doing the favor. How would you classify this request in the context of *quid pro quo* and hostile environment sexual harassment?
a. *Quid pro quo* of course. Suggesting that she buy herself lingerie on his charge account was the first stop on the road to asking for another, more "personal" favor.
b. Bad judgment on the boss's part in the modern work environment, but at this level it hardly qualifies as either kind of sexual harassment.
c. Very thoughtful. We should all have such generous bosses!
d. If he makes this kind of request regularly, then comments that he'd like to see her model what she chose for herself, implying that if she agrees, she's bound to move up the corporate ladder, and so forth, he could find himself defending against both kinds of sexual harassment.
e. Both b and d

Answers (mask or remove before copying): 1 = d, 2 = e, 3 = a, 4 = e, 5 = e. NOTE: While these answers would be accepted by most current authorities, ambiguity continues to surround many questions regarding sexual harassment. Therefore, steer discussion toward the best current thinking, but make clear that knowledge on the topics is constantly evolving.

EXERCISE 26

DO I HAVE TO PUT UP WITH THIS?

Method	RATE THE ACCURACY
Problem	Sexual harassment problems occur for two basic reasons: (1) the genders have somewhat different opinions on appropriate workplace behavior; and (2) they make incorrect assumptions about what their gender counterparts think is appropriate workplace behavior. In this exercise participants truthfully express their own opinions on statements about harassment in the working environment. Such situations are frequently judged differently by women and men.
Objective	Demonstrate to the participants that men and women often have differing views on how the sexes should interact at work. Use the experience to create awareness of how their mismatched perceptions can lead to the two kinds of sexual harassment and to prepare both genders for avoiding them.

Procedure

✓ Due to a great deal of publicity about sexual harassment, most people know the "politically correct" responses to questions about the roles of women and men in the modern workplace. When you begin the exercise, acknowledge this and then emphasize that participants' answers will be anonymous and that the usefulness of the training relies on their candid responses. Ask them to express their gut feelings rather than those they think are "right" and to avoid extreme responses that do not express their true beliefs.

✓ Distribute the rating scales. (A sample is provided or you may create your own.) Ask members of the group to indicate their gender and then rate each assumption candidly by circling a number on the scale. Also ask for a second rating that indicates what they *think* the politically correct (PC) answer would be. Clarify that the PC response does not have to be different from the one expressing their gut feeling. The two might be the same and they may or may not be "right." The objective is simply to react instinctively and then indicate what is perceived to be the socially acceptable response.

✓ Have the respondents fold their surveys for privacy and ask volunteers to collect and score the results. Have them calculate the average score for men, women, and the total group for each question (i.e., add up the individual scores and divide by the total number of surveys in that group for each question)—for candid and PC responses. Post the results before the group and discuss them.

Discussion Questions

1. Were you surprised that men and women responded differently? the same? Why or why not?

2. How do you account for the differences?

3. What do you think the fact that men and women answered differently has to say about the potential for misunderstandings that could lead to sexual harassment problems?

4. Are your candid and PC responses different? If so, why? Will that ever change? Why?

5. Are there ratings that you would change now that we've discussed them? Are there any that you are at least willing to rethink quietly on your own?

WHAT'S THE POINT?

Men and women at work are concerned about finding themselves involved in a sexual harassment case without knowing how they got there. To avoid such a situation, workers need to know how others, including gender opposites, judge classic sexual harassment situations and issues they might encounter on the job.

Materials

✓ Blackboard and chalk, or markers and board or pad to display results before the group

✓ Copies of the survey for individual members of the group

✓ A pocket calculator

Time Required

Approximately 25 minutes

"DO I HAVE TO PUT UP WITH THIS?" SURVEY FORM

Directions:

A. Check your gender, but *do not put your name* on this anonymous survey.

☐ Male   ☐ Female

B. Read each statement and mark it twice: (1) circle the number on the scale that best represents your candid, personal opinion; and (2) circle the number that represents what you believe to be the "politically correct" response.

Definitions:

✓ Quid pro quo *sexual harassment*—making sexual favors a condition of employment or the basis for favorable or unfavorable employment decisions.

✓ *Hostile environment sexual harassment*—conduct that unreasonably interferes with an individual's work performance or creates an intimidating, hostile, or offensive working environment.

1. *Quid pro quo* sexual harassment isn't difficult to identify, someone is either demanding sex for job favors or they're not.

Candid opinion:

1	2	3	4	5	6	7	8	9	10

Accurate   Inaccurate

Politically correct opinion:

1	2	3	4	5	6	7	8	9	10

Accurate   Inaccurate

---

2. Hostile environment sexual harassment is a lot like the old adage, "Your individual right to express hostility ends where my nose begins." In other words, you behave as you choose, even play sexual games, until your behavior infringes on someone else's sensibilities.

Candid opinion:

1	2	3	4	5	6	7	8	9	10

Accurate   Inaccurate

Politically correct opinion:

1	2	3	4	5	6	7	8	9	10

Accurate   Inaccurate

---

3. If the tone of an office doesn't suit some people, when most are unwilling to make waves over some employees' use of reasonably discreet sexual favors to buy better treatment, those disagreeing should find a setting more to their liking instead of imposing their standards on others.

Candid opinion:

1	2	3	4	5	6	7	8	9	10

Accurate   Inaccurate

Politically correct opinion:

1	2	3	4	5	6	7	8	9	10

Accurate   Inaccurate

4. *Quid pro quo* and hostile environment sexual harassment are two sides of the same coin—power plays by people who use a perceived weakness to control others. One form of harassment is no worse than the other.

Candid opinion:

1	2	3	4	5	6	7	8	9	10

Accurate   Inaccurate

Politically correct opinion:

1	2	3	4	5	6	7	8	9	10

Accurate   Inaccurate

EXERCISE 27

FAILED ATTORNEY

Method   SOLVE THE RIDDLE

Problem   Men and women sometimes fail at jobs when there is every reason to believe they should succeed. These failures may have nothing to do with their qualifications or ability to make normal social adjustments to the work group. *Quid pro quo* and hostile environment sexual harassment are possible reasons that people, who have every expectation of success, fail instead.

Objective   Demonstrate to the participants that *quid pro quo* and hostile environment sexual harassment may have such an adverse impact on otherwise successful job candidates that they simply cannot do their jobs effectively. Making the point in a riddle presents sexual harassment in a context in which it operates in the background and not as a highly visible factor in workplace problem solving. If asked why the employee failed, many participants will probably list traditional reasons, such as personality conflicts, lacking the "right stuff" to work under pressure, unwillingness to put in long hours, etc.—with sexual harassment as an afterthought if it makes the list at all.

Procedure   ✓ Pass out copies of the "Failed Attorney" Riddle Form to the participants. Riddles are most effective early in sexual harassment training sessions, before the group becomes predisposed to see gender bias lurking in every situation. If your group jumps to the sexual harassment conclusion, use the occasion to discuss the points of the riddle, and contrast how their reactions might have differed in the training situation and real life (i.e., they may have been less prone to see the sexual harassment problem in real life).

                      ✓ Ask them to work privately on solving the riddle and answering the questions that follow it. This experience will be diminished in value by allowing anyone to provide the answer before individuals ponder the puzzle on their own.

                      ✓ After most group members indicate they have either solved the riddle or given up, interrupt them and begin discussing the solution and its ramification for relations between women and men at work.

Discussion Questions   1. What first occurred to you as possible reasons for the attorney's failure at a job that seemed a perfect match in terms of qualifications and past experience? Did you consider sexual harassment as a possible reason or even a contributing factor?

                      2. What gender did you ascribe to the attorney when you first read the riddle? Did this have any bearing on what you thought might be the reasons for failure? If so, why?

3. If you could predict the future, do you think this riddle would be a useful training device before a similar audience in 20 years? Why or why not? What changes currently taking place in the work force might alter the likely reactions of future audiences?

WHAT'S THE POINT?

We are accustomed to judging employees' failure to adapt to the job environment on the basis of superficial personality problems and the like. It is important to be alert to deeper conflicts and manipulation of personal vulnerabilities that occur because of prohibited behavior such as *quid pro quo* or hostile environment sexual harassment. This is especially true when the actions come from those normally expected to help rather than harm the workers they manage.

Materials	✓ "Failed Attorney" Riddle Forms
Time Required	Approximately 25 minutes

"FAILED ATTORNEY" RIDDLE FORM

Carefully read the following riddle, and privately explore your thoughts as you attempt to find the solution. Please do not discuss the riddle with others until the group addresses the solution. Answer the questions that follow.

"Failed Attorney" Riddle

An attorney accepts what seems to be a dream position in a large corporation. Within months the person dreads coming to work, receives negative job ratings, and noticeably fails to become part of the office team. Employment ends at the expiration of the probation period. When friends not intimately familiar with life at the firm see the vacancy advertised, compare their friend's qualifications to the letter, but notice that the ad now stresses ability to adapt to the "office culture," they marvel at how a colleague who had always fit in before was unsuccessful in what seemed to be a tailor-made situation.

1. How can this be possible?

2. Explain the role *quid pro quo* and/or hostile environment sexual harassment may have played in such a situation.

Solution (mask or remove before copying): The attorney encountered an office situation where she had to go along with, if not actively participate in, sexual banter and where liaisons with superiors were a necessary part of the job. A termination that resulted from not participating would constitute *quid pro quo* sexual harassment; being driven out by the intolerable atmosphere would constitute hostile environment sexual harassment. In this case, both forms of sexual harassment were present.

EXERCISE 28

50:50 SPLIT ON KINDS OF HARASSMENT

Method	SORT THE LISTS
Problem	Solving sexual harassment problems requires "knowing it when you see it." In this exercise participants develop their recognition skills by sorting a series of descriptive statements into the two categories of harassment.
Objective	Demonstrate to the participants that sexual harassment has identifiable characteristics that can be sorted into two basic categories of offenses, *quid pro quo* and hostile environment harassment. Use the experience to create awareness of potentially chargeable behavior under the law and clarify behavior boundaries for men and women who work together.

Procedure

✓ Due to a great deal of publicity about sexual harassment, most people know the "politically correct" responses to questions about the roles of women and men in the modern workplace. When you begin the exercise, acknowledge this and then emphasize that participants' answers will be anonymous and that the usefulness of the training relies on their candid responses. Ask them to express their gut feelings rather than those they think are "right" and to avoid extreme responses that do not express their true beliefs.

✓ Distribute "50:50 Split on Kinds of Harassment" Forms. (A sample is provided or you may or create your own.) Ask members of the group to place the descriptive statements under the *quid pro quo* and hostile environment columns. (VARIATION: To liven up the process, instead of having participants simply read the descriptive statements, have trainers or volunteers from the group read or act them out.) Mention that both columns must contain the same number of statements, and that the task may grow more difficult as forced choices must be made toward the end.

✓ Have the respondents fold their surveys for privacy and ask volunteers to collect and score the results. Have them tally the responses. Post the results before the group and discuss.

Discussion Questions

1. Did you have difficulty placing any of the statements under just one discrete category? Why? How did you arrive at your decision on where it fit best?

2. Do you think men and women tend to classify the statements differently? If so, why?

3. Are there situations you find less offensive than others? some that don't bother you at all? Why?

4. Which situations do you consider to be the most in transition and apt to change in our lifetimes?

5. What do you think the fact that men and women answered differently has to say about the potential for misunderstandings that could lead to sexual harassment problems?

6. Are there entries that you would change now that we've discussed them? Are there any that you are at least willing to rethink quietly on your own?

WHAT'S THE POINT?

It is possible and desirable to recognize descriptive statements about workplace situations as links to *quid pro quo* and hostile environment sexual harassment. This demonstrates to the participants that: (1) offending and harassing behavior can be identified and separated from harmless, but maybe obnoxious, workplace banter, and (2) harassment can be generally classified into the categories used by the courts in adjudicating sexual harassment cases. Again, keep in mind that in many situations, both kinds of harassment are going on simultaneously, and that the purpose of the exercise is to target offensive behavior, whatever category it fits.

Materials

✓ "50:50 Split on Kinds of Sexual Harassment" Forms

✓ Chalkboard or pad on which to display the results

Time Required

Approximately 25 minutes

"50:50 SPLIT ON KINDS OF SEXUAL HARASSMENT" FORM

Directions:

A. Mentally inventory the list, and place each descriptive statement under the *quid pro quo* or hostile environment column. If you see shades of both in a single statement, place it where you think it fits best and be prepared to explain your decision.

B. You must end up with the same number of statements in both columns.

Definitions:

✓ Quid pro quo *sexual harassment*—making sexual favors a condition of employment or the basis for favorable or unfavorable employment decisions.

✓ *Hostile environment sexual harassment*—conduct that unreasonably interferes with an individual's work performance or creates an intimidating, hostile, or offensive working environment.

Descriptive Statements

A. I can assure you a management position here at XYZ Corporation if you treat me right when we travel together.

B. The guys just seem to work better with naked women taped to the walls. Sorry you find it offensive; what can I say?

C. Look, every woman who ever held your position in the company did office parties like a trooper. You don't have to do anything "wrong" if that's how you feel, but come to the parties, smile, and look like you're having a good time.

D. My friend Al does the hiring over there. If you sleep with him you've got the job, I can promise you that.

E. I work my buns off for the guy and tread water in the same old job. She shows him a good time and gets a big promotion. I have a big problem with that.

F. I need someone to help me set things up in the new sales territory. It could be a real step up the ladder for you with very little effort on your part—just be extra "friendly" with me when we're out there working next month.

G. What's the matter, can't take a joke? You've seen body parts before! The ones on that piece of paper are no different than what you see in the mirror every day. Everyone else got a charge out of the expression on your face when you opened that drawer! You *never* seem to get used to it!

H. Mr. Wilson, I've told him every way I know how that I do not want to go out with him. I don't even want to be his friend. We work well together, and that's all it is and ever will be for me. He won't take no for an answer, and he's making my life at work miserable. Can't you do something?

I. I'm going to be announcing a reduction in force tomorrow, and I can see to it that your name won't be on that list if you'd show me the kind of gratitude that I'm sure you'd enjoy as much as I would. How about it?

J. It's not like he's propositioned me or anything, but I dread having to spend my days pushing his foot away from my leg under the table! This is really getting old and I shouldn't have to put up with it.

K. So you find my language a little sexist do you? Well, if you want to keep your job, get used to it! That's how I express myself, and I'm not about to change because you're so easily offended. Grow up!

L. So you thought I was *kidding* when I suggested that willingness to pool the old *per diem* and share a suite with a king size bed was my main criterion for selecting the new trade show associate. I've never been more serious in my life.

Quid Pro Quo	Hostile Environment
1.	1.
2.	2.
3.	3.
4.	4.
5.	5.
6.	6.

Answers (mask or remove before copying): A = QPQ, B = HE, C = HE, D = QPQ, E = HE, F = QPQ, G = HE, H = HE, I = QPQ, J = HE, K = QPQ, L = QPQ. While informed people would generally agree with these answers, some statements have aspects that could be interpreted differently, depending on the perspective of the person answering. The objective is to stimulate thinking and communicate basic guidelines rather than to provide definitive answers to legal questions.

EXERCISE 29

CLASSIFYING HARASSMENT

Method

TRUE/FALSE

Problem

At times the legal and regulatory classification of sexual harassment offenses into two discrete categories confuses workers and managers who, after dutifully learning the definitions, are presented with behavior that seems to fit neither category exactly, contains a little bit of both, or is grossly offensive but doesn't jibe with either definition. The value of sorting behavior into *quid pro quo* and hostile environment sexual harassment categories is in helping workers and managers recognize the elements that define harassing behavior. But even more crucial is realizing that the categories sometimes overlap and that both kinds of behavior must be dealt with at the same time.

Objective

Demonstrate to the participants that there is merit in recognizing sexual harassment in terms used by the regulatory statutes, but that recognizing objectionable behavior and distinguishing it from equally offensive, but not illegal actions, are even more important. Use the exercise to develop awareness of the classification scheme (*quid pro quo* vs. hostile environment sexual harassment) and the recognition factors, but broaden participants' thinking to embrace the full spectrum of possibilities, including combinations.

Procedure

✓ Due to a great deal of publicity about sexual harassment, many people know the "politically correct" response to questions surrounding the issue. When you begin the exercise, acknowledge this and then emphasize that participants' answers will be anonymous and that the usefulness of the training relies on their candid responses. Ask them to express their gut feelings rather than those they think are "right" and to avoid extreme responses that do not express their true beliefs.

✓ Distribute "Classifying Harassment" Quiz. (A sample is provided or you may create your own.) Ask members of the group to read each statement and respond true or false.

✓ Have the respondents fold their quizzes for privacy and ask volunteers to collect and score the results. Have them tally the number of people who marked each statement true and false. Post the results before the group and discuss them.

Discussion Questions

1. Did you think men and women respond differently to these situations? the same? Why or why not?

2. Do you think it is more important to understand the differences between *quid pro quo* and hostile environment harassment or to distinguish between harassment and offensive but not illegal behavior? Why?

3. Are there situations you found easier to classify than others? Why?

4. How do you think being able to identify and classify offensive behavior will impact potential misunderstandings that could lead to sexual harassment problems?

5. Could "knowing it when you see it" help prevent sexual harassment in the first place? How?

WHAT'S THE POINT?

In regulating the issue of sexual harassment, good faith efforts to categorize offenses by the courts and others produced dichotomies of terminology that are at once helpful in recognizing problem behavior and a hindrance in judging complex situations where the offending actions don't seem to fit neatly into either category. It is useful to sharpen participants' understanding of the differences between *quid pro quo* and environmental sexual harassment, and to emphasize that in many situations the two kinds of offenses are involved and overlap.

Materials	✓ "Classifying Harassment" Quiz
	✓ Chalkboard or pad on which to display the results
Time Required	Approximately 20 minutes

"CLASSIFYING HARASSMENT" QUIZ

Directions:
Read each statement and circle either True (T) or False (F).

Definitions:

✓ Quid pro quo *sexual harassment*—making sexual favors a condition of employment or the basis for favorable or unfavorable employment decisions.

✓ *Hostile environment sexual harassment*—conduct that unreasonably interferes with an individual's work performance or creates an intimidating, hostile, or offensive working environment.

T F 1. You do not find *quid pro quo* and hostile environment sexual harassment in the same incident.

T F 2. If making attendance mandatory at after-hours office functions were judged to be sexual harassment and the offender did not link the demands to better or worse treatment at work, the behavior would be classified as hostile environment harassment only.

T F 3. Some workers reluctantly give in to the sexual demands of their superiors in order to move up the career ladder more rapidly; others are unwilling, and although they are not directly punished or threatened, in order to avoid the atmosphere in the office, they spend as much time as possible in the field dealing directly with clients. This situation includes both *quid pro quo* and hostile environment harassment.

T F 4. Occasionally turning the office air blue with sexist profanity constitutes hostile environment sexual harassment.

T F 5. Two peers previously had a romantic relationship that one of them ended rather abruptly. One can make the other's life at work miserable by continuing to push for an unwanted relationship. This could constitute hostile environment sexual harassment.

T F 6. Hiring situations are more apt to involve *quid pro quo* than hostile environment sexual harassment.

Answers (mask or remove before copying): Although these questions are provided more to stimulate thought and discussion than to prove legal judgments, and other interpretations are possible, informed people would generally answer: 1 = F Both can be present in the same incident. 2 = T *Quid pro quo* requires the offer or threat of workplace consequences, good or bad. 3 = T Both forms of sexual harassment are present here. Participants exchange sex for favors (*quid pro quo*); nonparticipants aren't directly threatened but they may not have the same opportunities for advancement as those granting sexual favors. In addition, the environment may interfere with their work. 4 = F Occasional outbursts normally wouldn't be considered pervasive enough to constitute either kind of harassment even though the behavior is extremely offensive. 5 = T Hostile environment harassment would be the most likely claim in this situation as it involves making the workplace atmosphere unpleasant enough that one cannot effectively do the job required. If the offender were a superior and demanded that the relationship continue or the person would suffer negative job consequences, both kinds of harassment could be claimed. 6 = T A favor is asked; the encounter is probably too brief to generate a hostile environment case.

EXERCISE 30

IT'S YOUR CALL

Method   SPONTANEOUS REACTION

Problem   Sexual harassment issues are at the top of the sensitivity list in the modern workplace, and men and women sometimes react instinctively upon hearing of (or encountering) an incident. A spontaneous reaction that is based on emotion rather than an accurate evaluation (no matter how quick) of available facts will prevent workers and managers from protecting themselves and others from abuse. An informed reaction will also help people to avoid inflating a situation that may be obnoxious, but relatively harmless, into something that can't be resolved directly by those involved.

Objective   Demonstrate to the participants that when sexual harassment–related incidents elicit spontaneous reactions, such reactions are most apt to be effective when based on an accurate, dispassionate view of what actually occurred. Show that recognition of *quid pro quo* and hostile environment sexual harassment aids people in limiting personal vulnerability and may prevent them from trying to make a case of offensive behavior that does not fall within the legal definitions of harassment. Use the experience to heighten awareness of whether harassment has taken place and the kinds of incidents that can occur. Cite likely differences in male/female perceptions of such incidents, to more accurately calibrate both men's and women's reactions to them.

Procedure   ✓ Due to a great deal of publicity about sexual harassment, many people know the "politically correct" response to questions surrounding this issue. When you begin the exercise, acknowledge this and then emphasize that participants' answers will be anonymous and that the usefulness of the training relies on their candid responses. Ask them to express their gut feelings rather than those they think are "right" and to avoid extreme responses that do not express their true beliefs.

                ✓ Distribute "It's Your Call" Reaction Form. (A sample is provided or you may create your own.) Ask members of the group to indicate their gender, read each statement, and respond spontaneously with their first reaction to each item.

                ✓ Have the respondents fold their quizzes for privacy and ask volunteers to collect and score the results. Have them tally the number of people who marked each response for each statement. Do this for the combined group and for women and men separately. Post the results before the group and discuss them.

                ✓ Read illustrative item D elaborations to enliven the discussion. If the group is receptive, and volunteers come forward, act out some item D elaborations prior to discussing them.

Discussion Questions

1. Did the men and women view many of the situations differently? the same? Why or why not?

2. How do you account for the differences?

3. Were you surprised that some of the actions, which you might have thought were offensive, did not qualify as either *quid pro quo* or hostile environment harassment? Why?

4. What do you think the fact that men and women answered differently has to say about the potential for misunderstandings that could lead to sexual harassment problems?

5. Are there responses that you would change now that we've discussed them? Are there any that you are at least willing to rethink quietly on your own?

WHAT'S THE POINT?

Reacting spontaneously, men and women sometimes see different motivations, which they may immediately take to be factually correct, in potential sexual harassment incidents. The greater their awareness of what constitutes *quid pro quo* and hostile environment sexual harassment, the lower the likelihood they will either wrongly tolerate unacceptable illegal behavior or overreact to offensive actions that do not constitute harassment. Moving the genders nearer a common standard for acceptable behavior removes another obstacle to achieving equity in workplace opportunity.

Materials

✓ "It's Your Call" Reaction Forms

✓ Chalkboard or pad on which to display the results

Time Required

Approximately 20 minutes

"IT'S YOUR CALL" REACTION FORM

Directions:
A. Check your gender, but *do not put your name* on this anonymous form.

☐ Male   ☐ Female

B. Read each statement and immediately make a single response—your initial reaction is wanted, so don't ponder the question.

Definitions:

✓ Quid pro quo *sexual harassment*—making sexual favors a condition of employment or the basis for favorable or unfavorable employment decisions.

✓ *Hostile environment sexual harassment*—conduct that unreasonably interferes with an individual's work performance or creates an intimidating, hostile, or offensive working environment.

It's Your Call!

1. Boss privately compliments subordinate on how her stockings and high heels enhance the appearance of her legs as he follows her from the elevator into the office.
   A. *Quid Pro Quo*
   B. Hostile Environment
   C. Both
   D. Neither, but add _____
      and you've got a case of (circle 1)   A.   B.   C.

2. The division chief leaves a sealed envelope at the front desk for a colleague attending the same out-of-town business meeting. She opens it to find a key to his room, a hotel ballpoint pen, and her annual rating form.
   A. *Quid Pro Quo*
   B. Hostile Environment
   C. Both
   D. Neither, but add _____
      and you've got a case of (circle 1)   A.   B.   C.

3. Home-office VP distributes membership forms and events calendars for her ballroom dance group, and makes it known that she will view active participation by the single men very positively.
   A. *Quid Pro Quo*
   B. Hostile Environment
   C. Both
   D. Neither, but add _____
      and you've got a case of (circle 1)   A.   B.   C.

4. A woman pilot often finds pornographic solicitations from a male admirer among her charts in the flight planning room; most of the male pilots know about them and laugh at her embarrassment. She has taken to doing her flight planning in the airport lounge rather than put up with their teasing. The solution suggested when she complains to her supervisor is to acquiesce to the sexual demands of her tormentor and "get it over with."
   A. *Quid Pro Quo*
   B. Hostile Environment
   C. Both
   D. Neither, but add _____
      and you've got a case of (circle 1)   A.   B.   C.

5. A female graduate assistant to a college psychology professor is told by him that she must locate and transcribe quotes on human sexual behavior from popular men's magazines for a paper he is preparing to present at a professional meeting.
   A. *Quid Pro Quo*
   B. Hostile Environment
   C. Both
   D. Neither, but add _____
      and you've got a case of (circle 1)   A.   B.   C.

6. Job applicant being interviewed by a search committee at an airport hotel is asked to come to her prospective supervisor's room to complete the interpersonal skills phase of her interview.
   A. *Quid Pro Quo*
   B. Hostile Environment
   C. Both
   D. Neither, but add _____
      and you've got a case of (circle 1)   A.   B.   C.

Answers (cover or remove before copying): 1. D, if this is an isolated incident. 2. A, assuming a proposition is implied. 3. D, unless she really pushes the private relationship aspect. 4. C, *quid pro quo* since she's being asked to trade favors for peaceful work and hostile environment because her work environment is made unreasonably intimidating. 5. D, unless the task was linked to expected favors. 6. D, if the supervisor simply conducted this part of the interview one-on-one because he was the final decision maker, and this phase of the interview was the most important to him.

Advise the participants that careful judgment and consideration of nuance is required in judging instances of sexual harassment, and that knee-jerk answers are rarely possible. The answers given here are illustrative of informed reactions to the situations as they are stated, but if respondents used answer D to elaborate, add details, or change the situation even subtly, the answers change accordingly.

Section **3**

JUDGING WHEN WORKPLACE BEHAVIOR BECOMES SEXUAL HARASSMENT

Rationale

The overarching thought behind the exercises of Section 3 is: Although definitions are not carved in stone and evolve over time, continual testing in the courts is yielding the criteria against which offending behavior is judged. Workers need to be familiar with the emerging guidelines.

Selection of Exercises

Use these thumbnail sketches of the exercises in Section 3 to choose those best suited to your purposes.

AGREE/DISAGREE

31. *Accentuate the Positive?*—Participants anonymously score statements illustrating possible sexual harassment on an agree/disagree scale. Identifying themselves only as male or female raters, they mark each statement once with their candid opinion and once with what they believe is the "politically correct" answer. Trainers calculate averages, note extremes, and, in a guided discussion, help participants sort likely harassment from more benign behavior.

DEMONSTRATION

32. *Say It with Flowers*—Sexual harassment is demonstrated by teams of participants working in contexts of floral symbols where the object of coercion is something other than sex as we define it. Guided discussion draws the parallels between the culturally neutral vulnerabilities of the flowers and sex in the contemporary workplace, and concludes that abusive use of power is at the root of the sexual harassment issue.

MAKE THE CASE

33. *Counsel for the Defense*—One group is tasked with making the case for sexual harassment charges in a hypothetical workplace situation, and the other must defend against the charges in the same situation. Participants experience both sides of the case either directly or vicariously and learn the importance of perception, intent, and other fine points in judging a shades-of-gray sexual harassment case. Trainer-guided discussion reveals the variety of motivations at play in these situations.

121

MATCH THE ITEMS

34. *Call It as You See It*—Participants are given a series of situations and are asked to match them to possible levels of offensive behavior. The results are tallied and trainers use guided discussion to help participants examine their thinking and appreciate each others' positions.

MULTIPLE CHOICE

35. *What's a Guy (or Gal) To Do?*—Participants judge whether a number of situations rise to the level of sexual harassment by selecting multiple-choice answers. Trainers tabulate and compare the results, then aid participants in examining the strengths and weaknesses of their choices during a guided discussion.

RATE THE ACCURACY

36. *What Was That Supposed To Mean?*—Individuals are asked to score several scenarios about sexual harassment anonymously on an accurate/inaccurate perception scale. Identifying themselves only as male or female raters, they mark the list once with their candid opinion and once with the answer they believe is "politically correct." Trainers calculate averages, note extremes, and help participants hone their judgment in a guided discussion of their differences.

SOLVE THE RIDDLE

37. *That's Not Like Her*—Participants are asked to solve a riddle in which traditional thinking about a prospective employee's reasons for rejecting an assignment clouds their judgment and hinders their ability to find the solution. Trainers guide the discussion to reveal less obvious reasons and their relevance to attitudes at work.

SORT THE LISTS

38. *50:50 Split on "Is It Harassment?"*—Participants are asked to make forced choices on whether statements fall under "harassment" or "not harassment" headings; half must be listed under each. The results are tallied and examined during a guided discussion.

TRUE/FALSE

39. *This Is Sexual Harassment!*—Participants take a true/false quiz based on a series of affirmations that various workplace incidents are sexual harassment. The results are tallied and the responses are examined during a guided discussion.

SPONTANEOUS REACTION

40. *He's Right!/She's Right!*—Participants are presented with situations that have workplace sexual harassment overtones and are asked to respond with an immediate reaction as to who is right, the man or the woman. The results are tallied for men, women, and the total group and the responses are examined during a guided discussion.

Optional Cross-References—The following chapters of *Working Together: The New Rules and Realities for Managing Men and Women at Work* (Baridon and Eyler, McGraw-Hill, 1994) are recommended if you need additional information to understand the issues and support your discussions:

Chapter 3, "Laws, Regulations, and Gender in the Workforce"

Chapter 4, "Workplace Etiquette for Men and Women"

Chapter 5, "Managing Men and Women"

EXERCISE 31

ACCENTUATE THE POSITIVE?

Method	AGREE/DISAGREE
Problem	Men and women are not always clear about the differences between behavior that is simply naive or obnoxious and that which crosses the line to become sexual harassment. In this exercise participants are asked to indicate their opinions on whether or not certain situations involve sexual harassment.
Objective	Demonstrate to the participants that equal opportunity laws and regulations provide useful guidance on identifying workplace behavior that can be defined as sexual harassment. Use the opinion survey to help individuals sharpen their ability to judge whether the actions described constitute legally prohibited behavior or merely bad manners.

Procedure

✓ Men and women may hold different views about whether certain actions constitute sexual harassment. To contrast their disparate views and increase mutual understanding, respondents are asked to indicate their gender before completing the anonymous questionnaire. Due to much publicity about this issue, many people of both genders know the "politically correct" answer but hold different personal views. To get both viewpoints, the survey asks participants to differentiate between what they honestly feel and what they believe to be the "right" response. Stress the anonymity aspect of the exercise and urge participants to respond candidly.

✓ Distribute the rating scales. (A sample is provided or you may create your own.) Ask members of the group to indicate their gender and then rate each statement candidly by circling a number on the scale. Also ask for a second rating that indicates what they *think* the politically correct (PC) answer would be. Clarify that the PC response does not have to be different from the one expressing their gut feeling. The two might be the same and they may or may not be "right." The objective is simply to react instinctively and then indicate what is perceived to be the socially acceptable response.

✓ Have the respondents fold their surveys for privacy and ask volunteers to collect and score the results. Have them calculate the average score for men, women, and the total group on each question (i.e., add up the individual scores and divide by the total number of surveys in that group for each question)—for candid and PC responses. Post the results before the group and discuss them. Note that the objective of the exercise is to examine views and develop sensitivity, not to reach definitive conclusions to the hypothetical questions.

Discussion Questions

1. Were you surprised at the answers of the opposite sex? your own gender? the group? Why or why not?
2. How do you account for the differences among the groups?
3. What messages do the results convey?
4. What are some possible implications for sexual harassment?
5. Why do you think there are differences between the candid and politically correct responses? Do you think they might be narrowed in the future? If so, why? How?

WHAT'S THE POINT?

The law is gradually refining its definition of what kinds of behavior constitute sexual harassment. Knowing the boundaries is essential if we are to protect victims from harassment and keep offenders (villainous and otherwise) from generating unacceptable workplace environments filled with tension. Workers and managers need to understand that actions do not always fit neatly into predetermined discrete "it is"/"it is not" harassment categories. By applying their judgment on a continuous scale, participants learn to sort offending behavior more accurately. As the group results are discussed, some individuals may use the experience to adjust certain opinions nearer to the group norm and to commit to mutually acceptable boundaries.

Materials

✓ Blackboard and chalk, or markers and board or pad to display results before the group
✓ Copies of the survey for individual members of the group
✓ A pocket calculator

Time Required

Approximately 30 minutes

125

"ACCENTUATE THE POSITIVE?" SURVEY FORM

Directions:

A. Check your gender, but *do not put your name* on this anonymous survey.

☐ Male   ☐ Female

B. Read each statement and mark it twice: (1) circle the number on the scale that best represents your candid, personal opinion; and (2) circle the number that represents what you believe to be the "politically correct" response.

1. Juliet was infatuated with her supervisor and clearly encouraged a sexual liaison with him. When the relationship soured, she charged harassment but got nowhere because it was determined that she had welcomed the relationship. She was not sexually harassed.

Candid opinion:

1	2	3	4	5	6	7	8	9	10

Agree   Disagree

Politically correct opinion:

1	2	3	4	5	6	7	8	9	10

Agree   Disagree

---

2. Travis became involved in an affair with the woman who heads his division. Eventually she made so many demands on his time, both on and off the job, that he charged harassment. He won his case because it was determined that, while he voluntarily participated in the relationship, it was an unwelcome liaison he felt he must tolerate because he feared the loss of his job. He was sexually harassed.

Candid opinion:

1	2	3	4	5	6	7	8	9	10

Agree   Disagree

Politically correct opinion:

1	2	3	4	5	6	7	8	9	10

Agree   Disagree

---

3. Normally a single incident of sexually offensive behavior isn't enough to sustain charges. However, Jason was dismissed from a management training program after charges that he overtly fondled the breasts of an unwilling female associate. He said it was a joke and wouldn't happen again, but his offense was judged sufficiently severe and physical that once was enough. She was sexually harassed.

Candid opinion:

1	2	3	4	5	6	7	8	9	10
Agree								Disagree	

Politically correct opinion:

1	2	3	4	5	6	7	8	9	10
Agree								Disagree	

Legal principles (mask or remove before copying): The courts generally agree with all three positions represented. Situations 1 and 2 demonstrate the principle that it is the "welcomeness" of the behavior or relationship and not the voluntary acquiescence of the victim that plays the greater role in determining whether harassment occurred. Situation 3 illustrates that severe or overtly physical incidents are often exceptions to the normal expectation that a sustained pattern of behavior is necessary to constitute harassment. These illustrations are broad and general. Actual cases may have mitigating circumstances, and other outcomes are possible.

EXERCISE 32

SAY IT WITH FLOWERS

Method   DEMONSTRATION

Problem   Sexual harassment is an exercise in power expressed by forcing someone to grant or tolerate intimacy they otherwise would not. Demonstrating harassment in a context in which flowers are a code for sexy clothing or body parts helps participants understand inappropriate applications of power without experiencing the discomfort many people feel when dealing with sexuality more directly. Trainers lead a discussion of the group's observations, pointing out parallels between floral power brokering and more familiar abuses that constitute sexual harassment.

Objective   Demonstrate to the participants that the sexual component of harassment is no more than the specific vulnerability exploited in the abuses of power we know as sexual harassment. Use the experience to open the participants' thinking to the possibility that the principles demonstrated in the floral examples might be generalized to situations of their own in which sex is used as the ultimate power tool in their own workplaces.

Procedure

✓ Select two teams from the participants—about six members each is ideal, but the number is not critical. Include members of both sexes. Designate them Groups A and B.

✓ Separate the teams so they are unable to listen to what the other is planning. Ask the audience not to influence the outcome by commenting or providing guidance.

✓ Give each team the Floral Intimacy Kit for its group.

✓ Give the audience the Audience Floral Intimacy Kit that informs the observers about what the teams are doing.

✓ After team members finish conferring, ask each team to demonstrate (through a brief skit or a spokesperson—their option) how it would use flowers to exercise power in the workplace. First, Group A demonstrates how it might constitute harassment; next, Group B demonstrates how it might be more innocent. If the spokesperson option is chosen, a male and female trainer may want to act out the skit described to give the exercise life.

✓ When both teams finish, ask each to explain its approach.

✓ If it isn't apparent, draw parallels between the role of flowers in the example culture and sexy clothes and body parts in the real world.

✓ If it has not become obvious, clarify that each team has demonstrated the parameters of sexual harassment with inappropriate expressions of power that didn't involve sexual favors as we define them. The objects used to coerce potential harassment victims in each group's culture are

128

different (flowers in the imaginary society vs. sexual activity in ours), but the inappropriate use of power is the same—with or without sex.

Discussion Questions

1. Do you think harassers are looking primarily for free sex? If not, then what are they looking for?

2. How does each team use its power to exploit those they view as weak or subordinate?

3. How is their behavior the same? different?

4. What parallels do you see between these power plays and sexual harassment in the contemporary workplace?

5. If sex didn't exist, would another basis for expressing control and superiority be found?

6. Can you give examples of the kinds of actions that are more commonly associated with sexual harassment in the contemporary workplace?

WHAT'S THE POINT?

The "ultimate intimacy" is the vulnerability of choice used by on-the-job harassers to exert their power. In our demonstration example, this kind of intimacy involved interactions based on intimacy-significant flowers. In the real world, sex is the ultimate gesture of intimacy between two people, and it is the vulnerability of choice exploited by sexual harassers. Sexual harassment is difficult to demonstrate graphically because of the emotions that accompany the intimacy of sexual relationships between human beings. This exercise unmasks sexual harassment for what it is—the exertion of power by one gender over another—here represented unemotionally by substituting culture-neutral flowers for sex as the vulnerability exploited by abusers. Participants who might not comfortably engage in a training experience using sexual terminology are more apt to involve themselves in a less threatening demonstration of culturally neutral vulnerabilities.

Materials

✓ Break-out areas in which Groups A and B can meet (corners of the room will do, just so they can get away to confer with some degree of confidentiality)

✓ Floral Intimacy Kits for Groups A, B, and the audience

✓ Chalkboard or large pad to note major points in discussion

Time Required

Approximately 25 minutes

FLORAL INTIMACY KIT A

Situation

In this mythical culture, intimacy between the sexes is communicated in the symbolism of flowers. It is a rite of passage for young women to use flowers, either real or artificial, as part of their clothing and accessories. Each woman creates her own unique style with the choice of blooms and their form and placement on her person, but certain flowers carry the following universal connotations:

1. Daisies = friendship
2. Tulips = innocent pleasure
3. Lilies = emotional sharing
4. Roses = romantic interest
5. Orchids = passionate desire

It is absolutely proper and routine for all of the flowers to be worn freely and often. They are the spice of nonverbal communication between men and women of all ages and motivations in this culture. Flowers are objects of admiration but evoke their full meaning only when individual men and women signal mutual agreement that their message goes beyond their intrinsic beauty and enchanting fragrances.

Task for Group A

Demonstrate workplace scenarios in which male/female interactions involving flowers might cross the line and become sexual harassment—show what the exchanges and patterns of behavior might be like. Use these scenario starters:

1. "You've got some awesome tulips ¼ "
2. "Those roses sure smell delicious ¼ "
3. "Don't take this the wrong way, but those orchids ¼ "

FLORAL INTIMACY KIT B

Situation

In this mythical culture, intimacy between the sexes is communicated in the symbolism of flowers. It is a rite of passage for young women to use flowers, either real or artificial, as part of their clothing and accessories. Each woman creates her own unique style with the choice of blooms and their form and placement on her person, but certain flowers carry the following universal connotations:

1. Daisies = friendship
2. Tulips = innocent pleasure
3. Lilies = emotional sharing
4. Roses = romantic interest
5. Orchids = passionate desire

It is absolutely proper and routine for all of the flowers to be worn freely and often. They are the spice of nonverbal communication between men and women of all ages and motivations in this culture. Flowers are objects of admiration but evoke their full meaning only when individual men and women signal mutual agreement that their message goes beyond their intrinsic beauty and enchanting fragrances.

Task for Group B

Demonstrate workplace scenarios in which male/female interactions involving flowers might approach but remain safely below the level of sexual harassment—show what the exchanges and patterns of behavior might be like. Use these scenario starters:

1. "Your lilies are fantastic ¼"
2. "Nice roses ¼"
3. "I like what you've done with your orchids ¼"

AUDIENCE FLORAL INTIMACY KIT

Situation

In this mythical culture, intimacy between the sexes is communicated in the symbolism of flowers. It is a rite of passage for young women to use flowers, either real or artificial, as part of their clothing and accessories. Each woman creates her own unique style with the choice of blooms and their form and placement on her person, but certain flowers carry the following universal connotations:

1. Daisies = friendship
2. Tulips = innocent pleasure
3. Lilies = emotional sharing
4. Roses = romantic interest
5. Orchids = passionate desire

It is absolutely proper and routine for all of the flowers to be worn freely and often. They are the spice of nonverbal communication between men and women of all ages and motivations in this culture. Flowers are objects of admiration but evoke their full meaning only when individual men and women signal mutual agreement that their message goes beyond their intrinsic beauty and enchanting fragrances.

Task for Group A

Demonstrate workplace scenarios in which male/female interactions involving flowers might cross the line and become sexual harassment—show what the exchanges and patterns of behavior might be like. Use these scenario starters:

1. "You've got some awesome tulips ¼"

2. "Those roses sure smell delicious ¼"

3. "Don't take this the wrong way, but those orchids ¼"

Task for Group B

Demonstrate workplace scenarios in which male/female interactions involving flowers might approach but remain safely below the level of sexual harassment—show what the exchanges and patterns of behavior might be like. Use these scenario starters:

1. "Your lilies are fantastic ¼"

2. "Nice roses ¼"

3. "I like what you've done with your orchids ¼"

EXERCISE 33

COUNSEL FOR THE DEFENSE

Method   MAKE THE CASE

Problem   Many people view sexual harassment from narrow perspectives that result in hasty judgments and exclude other opinions and plausible resolutions to problems. A good trial lawyer steps back from the emotional aspects of the client's case and puts on the best possible defense. In this exercise participants do the same for sexual harassment positions with which they might adamantly disagree.

Objective   Provide participants with the occasion to consider sexual harassment points of view that differ from their own. Have them change positions and think as advocates for an alien position. Use the experience to soften the resentment toward different, but not threatening, perspectives and, in the process, facilitate the growth of more mutually acceptable behavior.

Procedure   ✓ Select two teams of about six each, consisting of men and women.

✓ Pass out Scenarios 1 and 2 to the teams and audience.

✓ Instruct the teams to read and discuss their scenarios and to come up with their strongest defense for their assigned position—whether they agree with it or not.

✓ Ask each team to have a spokesperson describe its scenario and summarize its defense for the position. Other team members are encouraged to contribute to the defense. (You may suggest a line of defense if necessary to get the discussion started.)

✓ Ask one team to challenge the other's position. (You may suggest some challenges if necessary to move the discussion forward.)

✓ Briefly note key words and phrases on a pad or blackboard—this helps people go back and elaborate on earlier points.

✓ Encourage the exchange of challenge and defense until you feel the relevant points have been made.

✓ Solicit a vote from the entire audience, which serves as the jury. The question for the jury is: Does the behavior in this case involve sexual harassment?

✓ Note that the objective is to uncover points of view that participants might not have considered. The case is deliberately ambiguous, open-ended, and subject to various interpretations and judgments (just like real life situations). Acknowledge this so you don't leave the group frustrated that a "correct" judgment was not reached.

Discussion Questions   1. Is Jake's casual touching wrong ? If so, how? What would indicate his having gone too far?

133

2. Do you see legitimate arguments for each of the positions in this case? If so, what are they? What are the issues and considerations?

3. Where would you place each position on a chronology of socially progressive thinking? Caveman? American frontier? Roaring 20s? World War II? 50s? 60s? 90s? etc.?

4. Is either position out of vogue with mainstream thinking in the 90s? If so, did you realize this prior to this training exercise? Does it matter to you? Do you see any practical reasons to reconsider any of your assumptions?

WHAT'S THE POINT?

It is often revealing to be forced to advocate something you don't necessarily believe. Doing so conscientiously can give you perspectives on the opposing view that you had not considered before. Understanding (if not accepting) a position you oppose can help you deal more effectively with those who espouse it.

Materials
✓ Blackboard and chalk, or markers and board or pad to display notes before the group
✓ Copies of the scenarios for the teams

Time Required
Approximately 35 minutes

"COUNSEL FOR THE DEFENSE" SCENARIO 1

Directions:

Understand that *your role as a team is to defend the position of the man whether you agree with it or not*. Think about the arguments wrong-thinking people would use to advocate such a position, even if you would not. You will have a chance to say why you consider the position you articulate in this game is wrong. The team should select a spokesperson, but everyone is encouraged to contribute to the discussion.

Situation

✓ Jake is a backslapping kind of a guy who has spent his whole life communicating with words and touch. He won't make a pass or do anything overt, but he will freely put his hand on a woman's shoulder while standing and talking with her about something on her computer screen, or in the small of her back as he follows her through a door. In fact, whenever a woman is near him, he always seems to be touching her, although he never gropes or fondles. One of the women has taken offense at these practices and has brought a case of sexual harassment.

✓ Make the case that Jake is not engaged in sexual harassment.

"COUNSEL FOR THE DEFENSE" SCENARIO 2

Directions:

Discuss the scenario as a team. Understand that *your role as a team is to support the position of the woman alleging sexual harassment, whether you agree with it or not.* Think about the arguments people would use to defend such a position even if you find it objectionable. You will have a chance later to say why you consider the position you articulate in this situation is wrong, if that is how you feel. The team should select a spokesperson, but everyone is encouraged to contribute to the discussion.

Situation

✓ Jake is a backslapping kind of a guy who has spent his whole life communicating with words and touch. He won't make a pass or do anything overt, but he will freely put his hand on a woman's shoulder while standing and talking with her about something on her computer screen, or in the small of her back as he follows her through a door. In fact, whenever a woman is near him, he always seems to be touching her, although he never gropes or fondles. One of the women has taken offense at these practices and has brought a case of sexual harassment.

✓ Make the case that Jake's behavior constitutes sexual harassment.

EXERCISE 34

CALL IT AS YOU SEE IT

Method   MATCH THE ITEMS

Problem   It is useful to be able to distinguish between sexual harassment, border-line behavior that invites caution, and merely obnoxious behavior that, unpleasant as it is, does not fit within the definitions of illegal harassment. In this exercise participants indicate their opinions on which of these options best describes the situations posed. The results are then tallied and discussed.

Objective   Demonstrate to the participants that sexual-harassment-related behavior exists on a continuum, but that actions crossing the line into sexual harassment territory have identifiable characteristics. Use the experience to create awareness of differences in perception regarding alleged sexual harassment behavior and help participants avoid the pitfalls—either by going too far and committing it or by not acting decisively soon enough to curtail it.

Procedure   ✓ Men and women may hold different views about where certain actions cross the lines and become sexual harassment. To contrast their disparate views and increase mutual understanding, respondents are asked to indicate their gender before completing the anonymous questionnaire. Due to much publicity about this issue, many people of both genders know the "politically correct" answer but hold different personal views. To get both viewpoints, the survey asks participants to differentiate between what they honestly feel and what they believe to be the "right" response. Stress the anonymity of the exercise and urge participants to respond candidly.

✓ Distribute the "Call It As You See It" Matching Form. (A sample is provided or you may create your own.) Ask members of the group to indicate their gender and then mark each entry candidly by circling the selection they feel indicates the best answer. Also ask for a second matching that indicates what they think the politically correct (PC) answer would be. Clarify that the PC response does not have to be different from the one expressing their gut feeling. The two might be the same and they may or may not be "right." The objective is simply to react instinctively and then indicate what is perceived to be the socially acceptable response.

✓ Have the respondents fold their matching forms for privacy and ask volunteers to collect the forms and tally the results. Have them tally the responses for men, women, and the total group on each item (i.e., how many men, women, and total group participants marked the item Not Harassment, Borderline Behavior, or Harassment)—for candid and PC responses. Post the results before the group and discuss them.

137

Discussion Questions	1.	Were you surprised at the answers of the opposite sex? your own gender? the group? Why or why not?
	2.	How do you account for differences among the groups if there are any?
	3.	What messages do the results convey?
	4.	What are some possible implications for sexual harassment?
	5.	Are there differences between the candid and politically correct responses? Do you think those differences might be narrowed in the future? If so, why? How?

WHAT'S THE POINT?

Judgment and the ability to separate sexual harassment from less significant offensive, but not illegal, behavior are important skills for both potential harassers and victims. A key item of personal knowledge in fostering those skills in either situation is recognizing when actions make the transition from being simply boorish or grossly inappropriate to sexual harassment. This exercise allows participants to apply their judgment, test it against that of other individuals and the group, and have it refined with the help of the trainers.

Materials

✓ Blackboard and chalk, or markers and board or pad to display results before the group

✓ Copies of the matching form for individual members of the group

Time Required

Approximately 20 minutes

"CALL IT AS YOU SEE IT" MATCHING FORM

Directions:

A. Check your gender, but *do not put your name* on this anonymous survey.

☐ Male   ☐ Female

B. Read each statement and mark it twice: (1) circle the selection on the form that best matches your candid, personal opinion of what has taken place; and (2) circle the selection that matches what you believe to be the "politically correct" response.

1. Colleagues who have traveled together and talked in jest about a potential sexual relationship consider a private holiday trip together. He makes it clear that he likes her a lot and enjoys her company more than most people's, but that the trip wouldn't be an attractive option without sex.

	Candid opinion:	
Not Harassment	Borderline Behavior	Harassment
	Politically correct opinion:	
Not Harassment	Borderline Behavior	Harassment

2. At a group meeting around a conference table, a woman discreetly passes a note under the table to a male associate whose views she opposes. Even after he retrieves the note, her hand remains, distracting him to the point of reducing his composure and lessening his effectiveness.

	Candid opinion:	
Not Harassment	Borderline Behavior	Harassment
	Politically correct opinion:	
Not Harassment	Borderline Behavior	Harassment

3. A consultant who does business with a company several times a year never misses an opportunity to press a personal relationship with the accounts manager assigned to his contracts. She has rejected his every initiative, but he keeps pushing. When he is in town, she makes a point of being out of the office simply to avoid him.

	Candid opinion:	
Not Harassment	Borderline Behavior	Harassment
	Politically correct opinion:	
Not Harassment	Borderline Behavior	Harassment

4. A team of four cash management bankers are on a week-long swing across the South calling on major clients. The man heading the team insists that the group (another man and two women) have a "relaxed" meeting in the hotel's hot tub each evening to discuss the day's business. One of the women makes it plain that she is decidedly uncomfortable with the setting.

| | Candid opinion: | |
| Not Harassment | Borderline Behavior | Harassment |

| | Politically correct opinion: | |
| Not Harassment | Borderline Behavior | Harassment |

Comments (mask or remove before copying): Each situation contains sketchy information, and answers might be different with the introduction of additional information. The examples are intended to stimulate discussion and uncover relevant points, not establish indelible criteria or provide indisputable rulings of guilt or innocence. In general, an informed person would respond: 1. Not Harassment, 2. Harassment, 3. Borderline Behavior, 4. Borderline Behavior.

EXERCISE 35

WHAT'S A GUY (OR GAL) TO DO?

Method   MULTIPLE CHOICE

Problem   Naturally occurring attractions between gender opposites may complicate their workplace relationships. Sometimes actions, usually those of the
male, cross professional boundaries and result in sexual harassment. In
this exercise participants are asked to judge whether or not sexual harassment is a factor in a number of common workplace situations. The results
are tallied and discussed.

Objective   Demonstrate to the participants that sexual harassment is one of many
possibilities on the continuum of human behavior. Because some actions
do not fit neatly into the discrete boundaries used in statutory definitions
of sexual harassment, men and women need to develop the ability to distinguish between behavior that is objectionable, even grossly so, but not
illegal and that which is illegal harassment.

Procedure   ✓ Due to a great deal of publicity about sexual harassment, most people
know the "politically correct" responses to questions about sexual harassment in the modern workplace. When you begin the exercise, acknowledge this and then emphasize that participants' answers will be
anonymous and that the usefulness of the training relies on their candid responses. Ask them to express their gut feelings rather than those
they think are "right" and to avoid extreme responses that do not express their true beliefs.

✓ Distribute the "What's a Guy (or Gal) to Do?" Quiz. (A sample is provided or you may create your own.) Ask members of the group to indicate their gender and then mark each entry candidly by selecting the
multiple-choice item that indicates what they believe about sexual harassment.

✓ Have the respondents fold their quizzes for privacy and ask volunteers
to collect the forms and tally the results. Have them tally the responses
for men, women, and the total group on each question (i.e., how many
men, women, and total group participants marked the various responses). Post the results before the group and discuss them.

Discussion Questions 1. Were you surprised at the answers of the opposite sex? your own gender? the group? Why or why not?

2. How do you account for the differences among the groups?

3. What messages do the results convey?

4. What are some possible implications for sexual harassment?

5. Do you think gender stereotyping affected how you answered any of the
questions? how your opposite-sex peers answered them? How? Why?

6. Do you think it is important to understand the difference between sexual harassment and simply offensive or obnoxious behavior? Why?

WHAT'S THE POINT?

Making the distinction between boorish and crude, but not illegal, inappropriate behavior, and actions that constitute illegal sexual harassment is a necessary step in effectively dealing with the issue. The difference between harassment and just plain gender-based rudeness is an important understanding to have in the workplace. The ability to objectively define the behavior and evaluate its threat will enable you to calibrate your reaction appropriately for either genuine harassment or equally inexcusable, but not illegal, offensive bad manners.

Materials

✓ Blackboard and chalk, or markers and board or pad to display results before the group

✓ Copies of the "What's a Guy (or Gal) to Do?" Quiz for individual members of the group

Time Required

Approximately 20 minutes

"WHAT'S A GUY (OR GAL) TO DO?" QUIZ

Directions:

A. Check your gender, but *do not put your name* on this anonymous quiz.

☐ Male   ☐ Female

B. Read each statement and circle the response that you think is factually correct.

1. If you are interested in a personal relationship with a colleague but are not sure if the feeling is returned, use the following suggestions both to find out and to avoid behavior that might raise questions of sexual harassment.
   a. Show you care by being a little possessive.
   b. Show that your interest is genuine by suggesting a personal relationship repeatedly in the face of apparent rejection.
   c. Set up occasions when the two of you can be alone together.
   d. Subtly reward acquiescence and either ignore or punish rejection.
   e. None of the above.

2. If you think you are on the receiving end of sexual harassment, the best way to sort it out and deal with it is ¼
   a. Ignore the offending behavior and it will probably go away, leaving both your reputation and career unscathed.
   b. Rationally evaluate whether you are being asked to trade favors for career considerations and whether the work environment is adversely affecting your ability to pursue your professional goals. If you think harassment is an issue, make your displeasure with it indisputably clear.
   c. Consider sex a small price to pay for furthering your career.
   d. Accept one date and persuade your harasser to stop tormenting you.
   e. Do whatever you must to protect your paycheck, but keep good records and sue later.

3. You are in a lunch-time job interview at a hotel with an out-of-town company representative. You're being sexually harassed when the interviewer ¼
   a. Asks if he might call and invite you to dinner the next time he's in town.
   b. Inquires about what your husband would think if you had to travel with male colleagues.
   c. Promises you the job if you accompany him to his room "to get better acquainted" after lunch.
   d. Tells an off-color joke to test your reaction to what he thinks you'll encounter with clients if you accept the position.
   e. All of the above.

4. A woman who enjoys tasteful business clothes that complement her attractive body legitimately begins to consider sexual harassment charges when a male colleague ¼
   a. Comments on how well she wears a particular dress.
   b. Suggests she could make a lot more money in another line of work and says he'd be her first customer.
   c. Says that her dressing well is a positive factor in her job rating.
   d. Instructs her to wear a sexy dress when they travel to meet foreign clients on the coast next week, and says that if she'll do whatever it takes to get the contract, she'll receive a substantial bonus.
   e. All of the above.

5. Touching is likely to be judged as sexually harassing behavior in which of the following situations ¼
   a. A man places his hand in the small of a woman's back to guide her through a doorway in front of him.

b. As a woman helps a man solve a computer malfunction, she leans too close to his hand which brushes her breast while he carefully keeps the mouse in hand moving "purposefully."

c. A man walks by and pats a temporary worker on the rear as she bends over to lift a bundle of mail.

d. A man meets a woman colleague's flight and greets her with an unexpected hug.

e. All of the above

Answers (mask or remove before copying): 1 = e, 2 = b, 3 = c, 4 = d, 5 = c. NOTE: Although these answers would be accepted by most current authorities, remind the group that refinements can be added to many situations that might alter the judgment of whether harassment occurred.

EXERCISE 36

WHAT WAS THAT SUPPOSED TO MEAN?

Method

RATE THE ACCURACY

Problem

Sexual harassment problems occur for two basic reasons: (1) the genders have somewhat different opinions on appropriate workplace behavior; and (2) they make incorrect assumptions about what their gender counterparts think is appropriate workplace behavior. In this exercise participants truthfully express their own opinions on statements about harassment in the working environment. Such situations are frequently judged differently by women and men.

Objective

Demonstrate to the participants that men and women often have differing views on how the sexes should interact at work. Use the experience to create awareness of how their mismatched perceptions can lead to sexual harassment and to prepare both genders for avoiding it.

Procedure

✓ Due to a great deal of publicity about sexual harassment, most people know the "politically correct" responses to questions about the roles of women and men in the modern workplace. When you begin the exercise, acknowledge this and then emphasize that participants' answers will be anonymous and that the usefulness of the training relies on their candid responses. Ask them to express their gut feelings rather than those they think are "right" and to avoid extreme responses that do not express their true beliefs.

✓ Distribute the rating scales. (A sample is provided or you may create your own.) Ask members of the group to indicate their gender and then rate each assumption candidly by circling a number on the scale. Also ask for a second rating that indicates what they *think* the politically correct (PC) answer would be. Clarify that the PC response does not have to be different from the one expressing their gut feeling. The two might be the same and they may or may not be "right." The objective is simply to react instinctively and then indicate what is perceived to be the socially acceptable response.

✓ Have the respondents fold their surveys for privacy and ask volunteers to collect and score the results. Have them calculate the average score for men, women, and the total group for each question (i.e., add up the individual scores and divide by the total number of surveys in that group for each question)—for candid and PC responses. Post the results before the group and discuss them.

Discussion Questions

1. Were you surprised that men and women responded differently? the same? Why or why not?

2. How do you account for the differences?

3. What do you think the fact that men and women answered differently has to say about the potential for misunderstandings that could lead to sexual harassment problems?

4. Are your candid and PC responses different? If so, why? Will that ever change? Why?

5. Are there ratings that you would change now that we've discussed them? Are there any that you are at least willing to rethink quietly on your own?

WHAT'S THE POINT?

Men and women at work are concerned about finding themselves involved in a sexual harassment case without knowing how they got there. To avoid such a situation, workers need to know how others, including gender opposites, judge classic sexual harassment situations and issues they might encounter on the job.

Materials

✓ Blackboard and chalk, or markers and board or pad to display results before the group

✓ Copies of the survey for individual members of the group

✓ A pocket calculator

Time Required

Approximately 25 minutes

"WHAT WAS THAT SUPPOSED TO MEAN?" SURVEY FORM

Directions:

A. Check your gender, but *do not put your name* on this anonymous survey.

☐ Male ☐ Female

B. In the context of workplace sexual harassment, read each scenario and judge the accuracy of perception twice: (1) circle the number on the scale that best represents your candid, personal opinion; and (2) circle the number that represents what you believe to be the "politically correct" response.

1. She took his arm after the office party and radiated warmth and affection on the way back to work. The next week she stopped by his office and suggested they have a long lunch; they did dinner instead. At her request, he agreed to show her his new apartment, and when he made his move, she consented to having sex. When he wanted to leave it at that and not develop an exclusive "relationship," she brought sexual harassment charges. He thought she had signaled a willingness to have sex with him—in fact encouraged him—and was dumbfounded when she alleged he'd taken advantage of her. How would you judge his perception?

Candid opinion:

1   2   3   4   5   6   7   8   9   10

Accurate   Inaccurate

Politically correct opinion:

1   2   3   4   5   6   7   8   9   10

Accurate   Inaccurate

---

2. They had known each other professionally for years. Although they worked for different firms, they were in the same business and often were teamed by their companies on jobs for mutual clients. Since they enjoyed a platonic private friendship as well, they decided to pool their resources and buy a house—one that was big enough that each could have separate quarters, but would give each of them the benefit of a beautiful home in an exclusive neighborhood that neither could have afforded alone. Her employer took umbrage, and indicated that the two of them could no longer act as a business team given their "lifestyle." His employer had no such concerns. They maintained that their living arrangements were private, did not affect their business objectivity, and that they were being sexually harassed by her employer's linking their personal living arrangement to employment opportunities with clients. How would you judge their perception?

Candid opinion:

1   2   3   4   5   6   7   8   9   10

Accurate   Inaccurate

Politically correct opinion:

1   2   3   4   5   6   7   8   9   10

Accurate   Inaccurate

---

3. He gave her a ride to the train station when she was doing business at his location, and she took him to a cozy, hole-in-the-wall restaurant for lunch the last time he was in her town. Both occasions were spontaneous and more enjoyable than either expected. The next year he returned to her locale on other business not involving her company, invited her to dinner at his hotel, and hinted unmistakably that he would like her to spend the night. She ignored his hints, and when he got home, his boss was outraged that he had propositioned a client (even though he was on other business)—she had made a formal complaint. His view was that they "had something going" last year, and he was just following through like any guy would. How would you rate his perception?

Candid opinion:

1	2	3	4	5	6	7	8	9	10

Accurate   Inaccurate

Politically correct opinion:

1	2	3	4	5	6	7	8	9	10

Accurate   Inaccurate

---

4. They traveled together on business often and sometimes shared two-bedroom suites in order to afford better living quarters while on the road. She trusted him implicitly and never doubted her safety with him—there'd never been more than ritual propositions he'd never pushed, and she was convinced that their mild sexual banter was harmless. When he opened the door of her room and slipped into her bed one night after they had said goodnight, she was mortified, felt totally betrayed, and indignantly rejected his initiative. She adamantly refused to travel with him ever again. Had she wanted to press the point, she reasoned, there were more than enough grounds for a successful sexual harassment filing. How would you judge her perception of the situation?

Candid opinion:

1	2	3	4	5	6	7	8	9	10

Accurate   Inaccurate

Politically correct opinion:

1	2	3	4	5	6	7	8	9	10

Accurate   Inaccurate

EXERCISE 37

"THAT'S NOT LIKE HER"

Method

SOLVE THE RIDDLE

Problem

Men and women sometimes forgo career opportunities when logic says they should accept them and forge ahead in their careers. These missed opportunities may have nothing to do with their qualifications or ability to meet the job's challenges. Sexual harassment is a possible reason that people who have a chance at what others see as the brass ring refuse to reach out and grasp it.

Objective

Demonstrate to the participants that sexual harassment may have such an adverse impact on otherwise successful job aspirants that they simply cannot seize what appears to be an opportunity tailor-made for them. Making the point in a riddle presents sexual harassment in a context in which it operates in the background and not as a highly visible factor in workplace problem solving. If asked why the employee failed to take a career step that would seem to be a golden opportunity, many participants will probably list traditional reasons, such as personality conflicts, lacking the "right stuff" to work under pressure, unwillingness to put in long hours, etc.—with sexual harassment as an afterthought if it makes the list at all.

Procedure

✓ Pass out copies of the "That's Not Like Her" Riddle Form to the participants. Riddles are most effective early in sexual harassment training sessions, before the group becomes predisposed to see gender bias lurking in every situation. If your group jumps to the sexual harassment conclusion, use the occasion to discuss the points of the riddle, and contrast how their reactions might have differed in the training situation and real life (i.e., whether they would have been less prone to see the sexual harassment problem in real life).

✓ Ask them to work privately on solving the riddle and answering the questions that follow it. This experience will be diminished in value by allowing anyone to provide the answer before individuals ponder the puzzle on their own.

✓ After most group members indicate they have either solved the riddle or given up, interrupt them and begin discussing the solution and its ramifications for relations between women and men at work.

Discussion Questions

1. What first occurred to you as possible reasons for this woman's refusal of a job opportunity that she had been working toward all of her professional career and was the envy of most of her peers? Did you think of prior sexual harassment as a potential reason for her refusal?

149

2. Do you think her course of action (inaction?) was correct? Why? If not, what do you think she should have done?

3. If you could predict the future, do you think this riddle would be a useful training device before a similar audience in 20 years? Why or why not? What changes currently taking place in the work force might alter the reactions of future audiences?

WHAT'S THE POINT?

We are accustomed to judging employees' failure to accept new career opportunities on the basis of superficial personality problems and the like. It is important to be alert to deeper conflicts and manipulation of personal vulnerabilities that occur because of prohibited behavior such as sexual harassment. This is especially true when the actions come from those normally expected to help rather than harm the workers they manage.

Materials	✓ "That's Not Like Her" Riddle Forms
Time Required	Approximately 25 minutes

"THAT'S NOT LIKE HER" RIDDLE FORM

Carefully read the following riddle, and privately explore your thoughts as you attempt to find the solution. Please do not discuss the riddle with others until the group addresses the solution. Answer the questions that follow.

"That's Not Like Her" Riddle

It was several months into the new administration in Washington, and new ambassadors were being posted throughout the world. A mid-career foreign service officer concluding a routine Washington assignment at the State Department and ready for her next posting receives seemingly wonderful news. She's been selected for a top job at the embassy in a major European capital. She has never shirked personal hardships to move forward in her chosen career and she has just been offered the job of her dreams— all the more so because the ambassador was her graduate school mentor years ago. To everyone's surprise, she announces: "I am honored by the confidence shown in me by the proposed assignment. However, at this time I must decline and complete the important study to which I have devoted the past 17 months."

1. How can this be possible?
2. Why would she pass on an opportunity for which she has worked and sacrificed during her entire professional career?

Solution (mask or remove before copying): The foreign service officer was sexually harassed during her graduate school years by the man who would now be her boss in the new job—her mentor the ambassador. She is unwilling to subject herself again to what she feels would likely be several more years of the same objectionable behavior, the job of her dreams notwithstanding.

EXERCISE 38

50:50 SPLIT ON "IS IT HARASSMENT?"

Method   SORT THE LISTS

Problem   Solving sexual harassment problems requires "knowing it when you see it." In this exercise participants develop their recognition skills by sorting a series of descriptive statements into the two categories, Harassment and Not Harassment.

Objective   Demonstrate to the participants that sexual harassment has identifiable characteristics that can be separated from rude but less harmful behavior. Use the experience to create awareness of potentially chargeable behavior under the law and clarify behavior boundaries for men and women who work together.

Procedure   ✓ Due to a great deal of publicity about sexual harassment, most people know the "politically correct" responses to questions about the roles of women and men in the modern workplace. When you begin the exercise, acknowledge this and then emphasize that participants' answers will be anonymous and that the usefulness of the training relies on their candid responses. Ask them to express their gut feelings rather than those they think are "right" and to avoid extreme responses that do not express their true beliefs.

✓ Distribute 50:50 Split on "Is It Harassment?" Forms. (A sample is provided or you may create your own.) Ask members of the group to place the descriptive statements under the Harassment and Not Harassment columns. (VARIATION: To liven up the process, instead of having participants simply read the descriptive statements, have trainers or volunteers from the group read or act them out.) Mention that both columns must contain the same number of statements, and that the task may grow more difficult as forced choices must be made toward the end.

✓ Have the respondents fold their surveys for privacy and ask volunteers to collect and score the results. Have them tally the responses. Post the results before the group and discuss.

Discussion Questions   1. Did you have difficulty deciding whether any of the behavior described was harassment? Why? What criteria did you use in making your decisions?

2. Do you think men and women tend to classify the statements differently? If so, why?

3. Are there situations you find less offensive than others? Some that don't bother you at all? Why?

4. Which situations do you consider to be the most in transition and apt to change in our lifetimes?

5. What do you think the fact that men and women answered differently has to say about the potential for misunderstandings that could lead to sexual harassment problems?

6. Are there entries that you would change now that we've discussed them? Are there any that you are at least willing to rethink quietly on your own?

WHAT'S THE POINT?

It is possible and desirable to recognize descriptive statements about workplace situations as either sexual harassment or more benign behavior. This demonstrates to the participants that offending and harassing behavior can be identified and separated from harmless, but maybe obnoxious, actions on the basis of guidelines used by the courts in adjudicating sexual harassment cases.

Materials

✓ 50:50 Split on "Is It Harassment?" Forms

✓ Chalkboard or pad on which to display the results

Time Required

Approximately 25 minutes

"50:50 SPLIT ON 'IS IT HARASSMENT?'" FORM

Directions:

A. Mentally inventory the list, and place each descriptive statement under the "Harassment" or "Not Harassment" column. If you see shades of both in a single statement, place it where you think it fits best and be prepared to explain your decision.

B. You must end up with the same number of statements in both columns.

Descriptive Statements

A. You are one fine-looking woman—if I were 20 years younger I'd probably make a pest of myself.

B. You are much too pretty to be stuffing envelopes in a back room where no one can see you, and you shouldn't have to live in that run-down apartment either. I'll book a room at the Marriott tomorrow—we can have a very private lunch and talk about how I can make your job and living conditions a lot more enjoyable.

C. You just don't seem to understand, I really want to get to know you better outside the office. Let's talk about it over dinner sometime, and maybe I can convince you at least to give it a chance.

D. I need your help on the presentation to the XYZ people in L.A. next week, and it'll mean a few nights away from home. Why don't you make the travel arrangements?

E. Instead of hopping on a plane with the rest of the lemmings Friday, let's spend a few nights getting to know each other better at a hot tub country inn in Big Sur country. It could bode well for your future in my department.

F. Just because things didn't work out personally for the two of us doesn't mean you have to make life miserable for every guy who takes me out to lunch. It's not fair. You're saying I can't work in peace and have a personal life that doesn't include you as long as you're the one pulling the strings in this company.

G. I was so embarrassed. To thank me for wowing his board with my presentation, he sent these beautiful roses to the office! Last month it was candy. I have no personal interest whatsoever in this man, and even though he means well, he's disrupting my life!

H. There's this guy in accounting who's a real piece of work. Every time we're alone—in the elevator or something—he nonverbally "admires" my body! Sounds a little crazy, but you'd have to be there. He never says anything out of line; he doesn't stand too close or do anything else offensive. But it's ogling to the 10th power! It's nice to be appreciated, but this kind of "compliment" I don't need!

I. The old man wants me to go out with his son. No, I mean he *really* wants to fix me up with him. As I understand it, I don't have much choice if I want to keep working here.

J. At first I felt flattered. What guy would complain about having an attractive woman boss who likes his body? Well, I'm not flattered anymore. The fun's gone and I want her to knock it off. But she's made it clear without saying a word that if I don't handle this right, I can start looking for another job.

K. O.K., maybe I deserved a little talking to about coming in late and leaving early, but to say I think I can get away with anything because I have a "well-stacked" body that's "easy on the eyes" was out of line. He's never said anything like that before. How would you take it?

L. He's a good looking kid, so I thought suggesting he try modeling was good advice. He was really enthusiastic about it at first, but now he won't go near that studio. It seems the photographers over there want to do more than just take his picture in high fashion clothes.

Harassment	Not Harassment
1.	1.
2.	2.
3.	3.
4.	4.
5.	5.
6.	6.

Answers (mask or remove before copying): A = NH, B = H, C = NH, D = NH, E = H, F = H, G = NH, H = NH, I = H, J = H, K = NH, L = H. Although informed people would generally agree with these answers, some statements have aspects that could be interpreted differently, depending on the perspective of the person answering. The objective is to stimulate thinking and communicate basic guidelines rather than to provide definitive answers to legal questions.

EXERCISE 39

THIS IS SEXUAL HARASSMENT!

Method   TRUE/FALSE

Problem   Distinguishing between behavior that legally constitutes sexual harassment and that which is crude, but may not be actionable under law, sometimes confuses modern workers and managers. Being able to identify behavior as sexual harassment or offensive, but not illegal, is a tool that will help workers and managers avoid unconsciously harassing others and having to deal with illegal behavior if it happens to them.

Objective   Demonstrate to the participants that "knowing it when they see it" will assist them in promoting reasonable operating boundaries between men and women at work. Use the exercise to develop awareness of the recognition factors, and to broaden participants' thinking to embrace the full spectrum of possibilities, including successfully determining what constitutes a reasonable response in various circumstances.

Procedure   ✓ Due to a great deal of publicity about sexual harassment, many people know the "politically correct" response to questions surrounding the issue. When you begin the exercise, acknowledge this and then emphasize that participants' answers will be anonymous and that the usefulness of the training relies on their candid responses. Ask them to express their gut feelings rather than those they think are "right" and to avoid extreme responses that do not express their true beliefs.

                      ✓ Distribute "This Is Sexual Harassment!" Quiz. (A sample is provided or you may create your own.) Ask members of the group to read each statement and respond true or false.

                      ✓ Have the respondents fold their quizzes for privacy and ask volunteers to collect and score the results. Have them tally the number of people who marked each statement true and false. Post the results before the group and discuss them.

Discussion Questions 1. Did men and women judge the situations differently? the same? Why or why not?

                      2. Do you think men and women tend to view particular types of behavior in a certain way simply because they have different gender experiences throughout their lives?

                      3. Are there situations you found easier to classify than others? Why?

                      4. How do you think being able to identify and classify offensive behavior will impact the potential for misunderstandings that could lead to sexual harassment problems?

                      5. Could "knowing it when you see it" help prevent sexual harassment in the first place? How?

WHAT'S THE POINT?

It is desirable to raise awareness of what constitutes sexual harassment on the job, but there is a practical necessity to distinguish between valid complaints and merely offensive behavior. Both deserve attention, but the laws must focus on serious violations, not just crudeness or bad manners. The sorting process begins on the workplace floor, where employees and managers trained to know the difference between simply objectionable, but not illegal, behavior and legally prohibited harassment can successfully resolve many problems without outside intervention.

Materials

✓ "This Is Sexual Harassment!" Quiz

✓ Chalkboard or pad on which to display the results

Time Required

Approximately 20 minutes

"THIS IS SEXUAL HARASSMENT!" QUIZ

Directions:
Read each statement and circle either True or False.

T F 1. Sexual harassment is occurring if, in a workplace relationship, favorable or unfavorable employment conditions are exchanged for sexual favors.

T F 2. Although she was disgusted by even the thought, she consented to the affair with her supervisor because she feared the loss of her job. This situation constitutes sexual harassment.

T F 3. He loved to tell 1950s-vintage jokes larded with sexism to his inner-circle staff that included several women. Subjecting these women to such jokes constitutes sexual harassment.

T F 4. Her efficiency ratings showed a downward trend from the moment she showed revulsion at the prospect of participating in the entrenched pattern of sexual liaisons among the office staff. This situation is one of sexual harassment.

T F 5. She was once romantically involved with a ranking member of the job search committee at the company where she now seeks employment. Failing to get the job, she sued on sexual harassment grounds. She will almost certainly win this suit.

T F 6. He continued to press for a personal relationship with a woman who worked for him even though she made it clear she wasn't interested. He was engaging in sexual harassment.

Answers (mask or remove before copying): Although these questions are provided more to stimulate thought and discussion than to establish legal judgments and other interpretations are possible, informed people would generally answer: 1 = T When sex is linked to workplace treatment, harassment occurs. 2 = T Voluntary participation is secondary to willingness. 3 = F Probably not serious and pervasive enough to create a hostile environment; would most likely qualify as simply crude behavior. 4 = T Her career prospects were hurt because she didn't acquiesce to the sexual demands of the office culture. 5 = F Establishing harassment would require proof that sexual favors had been linked to getting the present position. 6 = F Unless he persisted to the point of hampering her ability to do her job in peace or linked job treatment to his demands, he behaved badly, but did not engage in sexual harassment.

EXERCISE 40

HE'S RIGHT!/SHE'S RIGHT!

Method   SPONTANEOUS REACTION

Problem   Sexual harassment issues are at the top of the sensitivity list in the modern workplace, and men and women sometimes react instinctively upon hearing of (or encountering) an incident. A spontaneous reaction that is based on emotion rather than an accurate evaluation (no matter how quick) of available facts will prevent workers and managers from protecting themselves and others from abuse. An informed reaction will also help people to avoid inflating a situation that may be obnoxious, but relatively harmless, into something that cannot be resolved directly by those involved.

Objective   Demonstrate to the participants that when sexual-harassment-related incidents elicit spontaneous reactions, such reactions are most apt to be effective when based on an accurate, dispassionate view of what actually occurred. Show that accurate recognition of sexual harassment aids people in limiting personal vulnerability and may prevent them from trying to make a case of offensive behavior that does not fall within the legal definitions of harassment. Use the experience to heighten awareness of whether harassment has taken place and the kinds of incidents that can occur. Cite likely differences in male/female perceptions of them, to adjust both men's and women's reactions to them.

Procedure   ✓ Due to a great deal of publicity about sexual harassment, many people know the "politically correct" response to questions surrounding the issue. When you begin the exercise, acknowledge this and then emphasize that participants' answers will be anonymous and that the usefulness of the training relies on their candid responses. Ask them to express their gut feelings rather than those they think are "right" and to avoid extreme responses that do not express their true beliefs.

✓ Distribute "He's Right!/She's Right!" Reaction Forms. (A sample is provided or you may create your own.) Ask members of the group to indicate their gender, read each statement, respond spontaneously with their first reaction to each item, and be prepared to defend their responses.

✓ Have the respondents fold their quizzes for privacy and ask volunteers to collect and score the results. Have them tally the number of people who marked each response for each statement. Do this for the combined group and for women and men separately. Post the results before the group and discuss them.

Discussion Questions   1. Did the men and women view many of the situations differently? the same? Why or why not?

159

2. How do you account for the differences?

3. Were you surprised that some of the actions, which you might have thought were grossly offensive, did not qualify as harassment? Why?

4. What do you think the fact that men and women answered differently has to say about the potential for misunderstandings that could lead to sexual harassment problems?

5. Are there responses that you would change now that we've discussed them? Are there any that you are at least willing to rethink quietly on your own?

WHAT'S THE POINT?

Reacting spontaneously, men and women sometimes see different motivations, which they may immediately take to be factually correct, in potential sexual harassment incidents. The greater their awareness of what constitutes legally defined sexual harassment, the lower is the likelihood they will either wrongly tolerate unacceptable illegal behavior or overreact to offensive actions that fall short of harassment. Moving the genders nearer a common standard for acceptable behavior removes another obstacle to achieving equity in workplace opportunity.

Materials

✓ "He's Right!/She's Right!" Reaction Forms

✓ Chalkboard or pad on which to display the results

Time Required

"HE'S RIGHT!/SHE'S RIGHT!" REACTION FORM

Approximately 20 minutes

Directions:

A. Check your gender, but *do not put your name* on this anonymous form.

☐ Male ☐ Female

B. Read each statement and immediately make a single response—your initial reaction is wanted, so don't ponder the question.

He's Right!/She's Right! Reaction

1. She found the prospect of extending their next business trip together into a minivacation tantalizing enough to discuss it with their usual mildly flirtatious banter. He thought her reaction encouraging enough to make reservations that included sharing a room. When he told her what he'd done, she considered accusing him of sexual harassment—she was just kidding around as usual, and he should have known that she didn't intend to "deliver"!

    A. He's Right!   **B.** She's Right!

2. She recruited him, guided him through the executive job interview process, coached him on salary negotiations, and now stood ready to collect a substantial fee from the company hiring him. He got the kind of job he had always wanted and was grateful for her help. The entire process had been an intense, do-or-die effort for both of them, which ended on the highest note on the scale—he got the job and she got an enormous placement fee. He thought the energy they'd shared so intensely would logically translate to the ultimate expression of sharing—sex—and would be a welcome way to celebrate. She didn't agree, was grossly offended by his assumption, and threatened to pull the plug on the deal by charging him with harassment.

    A. He's Right!   **B.** She's Right!

3. He wanted the assignment, and his female supervisor could definitely make it happen. When she showed more than professional interest in him, he reciprocated by spending long periods in her office feeding her substantial ego. Salary increases and an inflated job description followed. The careers and salaries of others in the office remained static while he advanced rapidly. His retort was, "That's how the game's played. It's not as if I slept with her." A woman who claimed he traded favors for preferred treatment disagreed and filed hostile environment sexual harassment charges.

    A. He's Right!   **B.** She's Right!

4. As the only woman on the hospital's surgical team, she felt scrub-room teasing that included speculation about her bra size and sexual prowess was out of place in the professional setting. When she objected, the chief of surgery explained that she had come a long way, was easing the path for women who would follow in her professional footsteps, and should accept the "compliments" as a modest price to pay for the privilege of being one of "them." "After all," he explained patiently, "the operating theater is a man's world, and that's the way we talk. Think of yourself like a lone man in a group of women gossiping about the soaps and talking about shopping."

    A. He's Right!   **B.** She's Right!

5. He says sex is here to stay and that men and women, whether they're working together or meeting in a smoke-filled bar after the five o'clock whistle blows, have to expect to deal with the chemistry that's bound to arise between them. She agrees that attractions are inevitable, but insists that "follow-through" behavior is not. Therefore, she maintains that "biology" is not a valid excuse for actions in the workplace that more appropriately belong in a social setting.

A. He's Right!   **B.** She's Right!

6. He said she wore that dress knowing she'd get rather graphic compliments from some of the guys. She said she didn't mind some teasing, but enough was enough, and that they'd better knock it off or she'd haul them up on harassment charges. He made no secret of his opinion that "She asked for it!"

A. He's Right!   **B.** She's Right!

Answers (mask or remove before copying): 1 = B—She used poor judgment in encouraging his fantasies, but he made an assumption that simply wasn't warranted by their past relationship. 2 = B—Emotional highs between the sexes in business can feel extremely intimate, but the sexual aggressor should confirm mutual intent before assuming more than business. 3 = A—Unless sex was traded for the favors (he said it wasn't), this sounds more like office politics and poor judgment on the part of the boss than harassment. 4 = B—A woman is legally protected from having to tolerate sustained, pervasive, and objectionable personal references about her anatomy if they are a condition of employment or poison her work environment. 5 = B.—He is right about sexual chemistry being here to stay, but her argument is controlling—different codes exist for pursuing sexual interests at work and in social situations. 6 = B —"She asked for it" is not a valid defense in the modern workplace, her poor judgment notwithstanding.

APPLYING THE REASONABLE PERSON STANDARD TO SEXUAL HARASSMENT

Rationale

The overarching thought behind the exercises of Section 4 is: Case law has yielded the reasonable person standard for determining whether or not objectionable behavior is sexual harassment—the actions must be severe, threatening, or pervasive enough to adversely affect the work environment *in the judgment of a reasonable person.*

Selection of Exercises

Use these thumbnail sketches of the exercises in Section 4 to choose those best suited to your purposes.

AGREE/DISAGREE

41. *That Sounds Reasonable Enough*—Based on what they think is reasonable, participants anonymously score statements illustrating possible sexual harassment on an agree/disagree scale. Identifying themselves only as male or female raters, they mark each statement once with their candid opinions and once with the answer they believe is "politically correct." In a guided discussion, trainers calculate averages, note extremes, and help participants sort likely harassment from more benign behavior.

DEMONSTRATION

42. *Reasonable Numbers*—Sexual harassment is demonstrated by teams of participants working in contexts of numerical symbols, where the object of coercion is something other than sex as we define it. Guided discussion draws the parallels between the culturally neutral vulnerabilities of the erotic numbers and sex in the contemporary workplace, and concludes that abusive use of power is at the root of the sexual harassment issue.

MAKE THE CASE

43. *It Depends on Your Perspective*—One group is tasked with making a case, based on the reasonable person standard, for sexual harassment charges in a hypothetical workplace situation; the other group must defend against the charges in the same situation. Participants experience both sides of the case either directly or vicariously and learn the importance of commonsense reason in judging a shades-of-gray sexual harassment case. Trainer-guided discussion reveals the variety of motivations at play in these situations.

MATCH THE ITEMS

44. *How Reasonable Is It To…?*—Participants are given a series of situations and are asked to match them to judgments of reasonableness to decide whether or not they involve sexual harassment. The results are tallied and trainers help participants examine their thinking and appreciate each others' positions in guided discussion.

MULTIPLE CHOICE

45. *Making the Reasonable Choice*—Participants judge whether a number of situations can reasonably be classified as sexual harassment by selecting multiple-choice answers. Trainers tabulate and compare the results, then aid participants in examining the strengths and weaknesses of their choices during a guided discussion.

RATE THE ACCURACY

46. *It's Only Reasonable*—Individuals are asked to score several scenarios about sexual harassment anonymously on an accurate/inaccurate perception scale. Identifying themselves only as male or female raters, they mark the list once with their candid opinions and once with the answer they believe is "politically correct." Trainers calculate averages, note extremes, and help participants hone their judgment in a guided discussion of their differences on what is reasonable.

SOLVE THE RIDDLE

47. *The Reasonable Judge*—Participants are asked to solve a riddle in which the labels applied to the charges discussed were emotionally laden enough to make it appear that an employee's complaints sustained her charges of harassment. Trainers guide the discussion to reveal how reasonable judgments established over time become standards to which individual cases are ultimately compared, with sometimes surprising results.

SORT THE LISTS

48. *50:50 Split on "Is It Reasonable?"*—Participants are asked to make forced choices on whether incidents constitute reasonable or unreasonable charges of sexual harassment; half must be listed under each heading. The results are tallied and examined during a guided discussion.

TRUE/FALSE

49. *This Is Reasonable!*—Participants take a true/false quiz that requires them to judge whether a reasonable person would classify various workplace incidents as sexual harassment. The results are tallied and the responses are examined during a guided discussion.

SPONTANEOUS REACTION

50. *He's Unreasonable!/She's Unreasonable!*—Participants are presented with situations that have workplace sexual harassment overtones and are asked to respond with an immediate reaction based on common sense as to who is being unreasonable, the man or the woman. The results are tallied for men, women, and the total group, and the responses are examined during a guided discussion.

Optional Cross-References—The following chapters of *Working Together: The New Rules and Realities for Managing Men and Women at Work* (Baridon and Eyler, McGraw-Hill, 1994) are recommended if you need additional information to understand the issues and support your discussions:

Chapter 3, "Laws, Regulations, and Gender in the Workforce"

Chapter 4, "Workplace Etiquette for Men and Women"

Chapter 5, "Managing Men and Women"

EXERCISE 41

THAT SOUNDS REASONABLE ENOUGH

Method	AGREE/DISAGREE
Problem	Men and women are not always clear about the differences between behavior that is simply naive or obnoxious and that which crosses the line to become sexual harassment. In this exercise participants are asked to decide whether or not a reasonable person would judge certain things to be sexual harassment.
Objective	Demonstrate to the participants that reasoned, rather than emotional, judgment should guide their evaluation of whether or not workplace behavior can be defined as sexual harassment. Use the opinion survey to help individuals sharpen their reasoning ability to judge whether the actions described constitute legally prohibited behavior or something less.
Procedure	✓ Reasonable men and women may hold different views about whether certain actions constitute sexual harassment. To contrast their disparate views and increase mutual understanding, respondents are asked to indicate their gender before completing the anonymous questionnaire. Due to much publicity about sexual harassment issues, many people of both genders know the "politically correct" answer but hold different personal views. To get both viewpoints, the survey asks participants to differentiate between what they honestly feel and what they believe to be the "right" response. Stress the anonymity aspect of the exercise and urge participants to respond candidly.
	✓ Distribute the rating scales. (A sample is provided or you may create your own.) Ask members of the group to indicate their gender and then rate each statement candidly by circling a number on the scale. Also ask for a second rating that indicates what they *think* the politically correct (PC) answer would be. Clarify that the PC response does not have to be different from the one expressing their gut feeling. The two might be the same and they may or may not be "right." The objective is simply to react instinctively and then indicate what is perceived to be the socially acceptable response.
	✓ Have the respondents fold their surveys for privacy and ask volunteers to collect and score the results. Have them calculate the average score for men, women, and the total group on each question (i.e., add up the individual scores and divide by the total number of surveys in that group for each question)—for candid and PC responses. Post the results before the group and discuss them. Note that the objective of the exercise is examining views and developing sensitivity, not reaching definitive conclusions to the hypothetical questions.

1. Were you surprised at the answers of the opposite sex? your own gender? the group? Why or why not?

2. Do you think that the reasonable person standard is applied the same way by men and women? Why or why not?

3. What messages do the results of this exercise convey?

4. What are some possible implications for sexual harassment?

5. Why do you think there are differences between the candid and politically correct responses? Do you think they might be narrowed in the future? If so, why? How?

WHAT'S THE POINT?

The law is gradually refining its definition of what kinds of behavior constitute sexual harassment. Knowing the boundaries is essential if we are to protect victims from harassment and keep offenders (villainous and otherwise) from generating unacceptable workplace environments filled with tension. Workers and managers need to understand that actions do not always fit neatly into predetermined discrete "it is/it is not" harassment categories. By applying a standard based on what most would consider reasonable, participants learn to sort offending behavior more accurately. As the group results are discussed, some individuals may use the experience to adjust certain opinions nearer to the group norm, and to commit to mutually acceptable boundaries.

Materials

✓ Blackboard and chalk, or markers and board or pad to display results before the group

✓ Copies of the survey for individual members of the group

✓ A pocket calculator

Time Required

Approximately 30 minutes

"THAT SOUNDS REASONABLE ENOUGH" SURVEY FORM

Directions:

A. Check your gender, but *do not put your name* on this anonymous survey.

☐ Male ☐ Female

B. Read each statement and mark it twice: (1) circle the number on the scale that best represents your candid, personal opinion; and (2) circle the number that represents what you believe to be the "politically correct" response.

1. Centerfolds and calendars adorned with scantily clad women have hung in the shop for generations. Lori made the choice to become an automotive service technician and put herself in an environment where most of her peers are guys. She finds the "decorations" sexist, objectionable, and demeaning, but it's hardly reasonable for her to complain. After all, she voluntarily moved into a working environment full of red-blooded males and should accept it as it is!

					Candid opinion:					
1	2	3	4	5	6	7	8	9	10	
Agree								Disagree		

				Politically correct opinion:						
1	2	3	4	5	6	7	8	9	10	
Agree								Disagree		

2. The guys invited Connie and Ann along for an evening in the bar district of the local border town after a day of business meetings in San Diego. Although no one approached them directly, as the night wore on, Connie and Ann expressed offense at what they viewed as the crude exploitation of women in another culture. They made it clear to their male colleagues that the evening was an awful experience they'd not repeat, but a reasonable person would not back their complaints if they claimed sexual harassment.

					Candid opinion:					
1	2	3	4	5	6	7	8	9	10	
Agree								Disagree		

				Politically correct opinion:						
1	2	3	4	5	6	7	8	9	10	
Agree								Disagree		

3. Jeff encountered Elaine, a casual acquaintance from the office, at a busy coffee bar and well-known singles hangout. They spent the evening in animated conversation that both appeared to enjoy. When, at the office several days later, Jeff tried to pick up where they had left off he was puzzled by Elaine's formality and businesslike tone. When he asked if there was a problem, she explained that she distinguishes between social and professional behavior and doesn't mix the two. She didn't mean to be unpleasant, but if he pushed the personal side at work she'd consider it unwelcome and maybe worse. It's reasonable for a woman to expect a man to separate "business and pleasure."

Candid opinion:

1	2	3	4	5	6	7	8	9	10

Agree   Disagree

Politically correct opinion:

1	2	3	4	5	6	7	8	9	10

Agree   Disagree

Answers (cover or remove before copying): The courts generally agree with the last two positions and reject the first. In Situation 1, women entering a previously male domain are not expected to tolerate offensive behavior or environment merely because it's always been that way. Situation 2 is a voluntary social situation in which neither woman was threatened; they were simply offended by their observations. Situation 3 represents the choice to behave as one likes, and the good judgment to set separate standards for social and professional relationships. These illustrations are broad and general. Actual cases may have mitigating circumstances, and other outcomes are possible.

EXERCISE 42
REASONABLE NUMBERS

Method DEMONSTRATION

Problem Sexual harassment is an exercise in power expressed by forcing someone to grant or tolerate intimacy they otherwise would not. Demonstrating behavior that common sense would define as harassment in a context in which Roman numerals are code for sexy pictures or comments helps participants understand inappropriate applications of power without experiencing the discomfort many people feel when dealing with sexuality more directly. Trainers lead a discussion of the group's observations, pointing out parallels between numerical power brokering and more familiar abuses that constitute sexual harassment.

Objective Demonstrate to the participants that the sexual component of harassment is simply the specific vulnerability exploited in the abuses of power we know as sexual harassment. Use the experience to open the participants' thinking to the possibility that the principles demonstrated in the numbers examples might be generalized to situations in their own experience in which sex is used as the ultimate power tool where they work.

Procedure
- ✓ Select two teams from the participants—about six members each is ideal, but the number is not critical. Include members of both sexes. Designate them Groups A and B.
- ✓ Separate the teams so they are unable to listen to what the other is planning. Ask the audience not to influence the outcome by commenting or providing guidance.
- ✓ Give each team the Reasonable Numbers Kit for its group.
- ✓ Give the audience the Reasonable Numbers Kit that informs the observers about what the teams are doing.
- ✓ After team members finish conferring, ask each team to demonstrate (through a brief skit or a spokesperson—their option) how they would use Roman numerals to exercise power in the workplace. First, Group A demonstrates how such use might constitute harassment; next, Group B demonstrates how the numbers might be more innocent. If the spokesperson option is chosen, a male and female trainer may want to act out the skit described to give the exercise life.
- ✓ When both teams finish, ask each to explain its approach.
- ✓ If it isn't apparent, draw parallels between the role of Roman numeral symbols in the example culture and sexy pictures and comments in the real world.
- ✓ If it has not become obvious, clarify that each team has demonstrated sexual harassment with inappropriate expressions of power that didn't

involve sexual favors as we define them. The objects used to coerce potential harassment victims in each group's cultures are different (Roman numerals in the imaginary society vs. sexual activity in ours), but reasonable people will recognize the inappropriate use of power—with or without sex.

Discussion Questions

1. Do you think harassers are looking primarily for free sex? If not, then what are they looking for?

2. How does each team use its power to exploit those they view as weak or subordinate?

3. How is their behavior the same? different?

4. What parallels do you see between these power plays and sexual harassment in the contemporary workplace?

5. If sex didn't exist, would another basis for expressing control and superiority be found?

6. Can you give examples of the kinds of actions that most people would reasonably associate with sexual harassment in the contemporary workplace?

WHAT'S THE POINT?

The "ultimate intimacy" is the vulnerability of choice used by on-the-job harassers to exert their power. In our demonstration example, this kind of intimacy involved interactions based on intimacy-significant Roman numerals. In the real world, sex is the intimacy exploited by sexual harassers. Sexual harassment is difficult to demonstrate graphically because of the emotions that accompany sexual relationships between human beings. This exercise unmasks sexual harassment unemotionally by substituting culture-neutral numbers for sex. Participants who might not comfortably engage in a training experience using sexual terminology are more apt to involve themselves in a less threatening demonstration of culturally neutral vulnerabilities.

Materials

✓ Break-out areas in which Groups A and B can meet (corners of the room will do, just so they can get away to confer with some degree of confidentiality)

✓ Reasonable Numbers Kits for Groups A, B, and the audience

✓ Chalkboard or large pad to note major points in discussion

Time Required

Approximately 25 minutes

REASONABLE NUMBERS KIT A

Situation

In this mythical culture, intimacy between the sexes is communicated symbolically by Roman numerals. Patterns of the ancient numbers have erotic meanings long understood within the culture. Elaborate displays of the numerical combinations carry universal sexual connotations. Here are several examples:

VI = innocent "hearts and flowers" young love

VII = romance that may or may not include sex

XI = mature man-woman relationship, including courtship and marriage, with sex as an accepted component

XII = intense coupling dominated by bondage/deviant sexual practices

It is customary for the symbols to be displayed in a variety of media—print, video, clothing, decorations on fabrics, glassware, china, etc. Their possession and viewing under the right circumstances is a rite of passage for men and women rising to adulthood. Thereafter, the erotically symbolic numerals have a more discreet and private role in the personal sexuality of the society. While there is commercial exploitation of the symbols and extreme applications occupy an exotic place in fringe art and entertainment, tensions between men and women over the symbolism rarely occur outside the workplace.

Task for Group A

Demonstrate workplace or work-related scenarios in which male-female interactions involving erotically symbolic numbers cross the line and become sexual harassment in the eyes of a reasonable person—show what the exchanges and patterns of behavior might be like. Use these scenario starters and describe conditions that would make a reasonable person consider them to be sexual harassment:

1. VIIs and XIIs are the predominant paintings and sculptures in the company boardroom and hallways of the executive suites.

2. A few of the guys ask their female peers to join them as they huddle around the latest edition of a men's magazine admiring the XIs.

3. Some people bring candy or exotic coffees from other regions to share with office mates upon returning from business trips; Jack prefers to share XII items, especially with his opposite-sex coworkers.

REASONABLE NUMBERS KIT B

Situation

In this mythical culture, intimacy between the sexes is communicated symbolically by Roman numerals. Patterns of the ancient numbers have erotic meanings long understood within the culture. Elaborate displays of the numerical combinations carry universal sexual connotations. Here are several examples:

VI = innocent "hearts and flowers" young love

VII = romance that may or may not include sex

XI = mature man-woman relationship, including courtship and marriage, with sex as an accepted component

XII = intense coupling dominated by bondage/deviant sexual practices

It is customary for the symbols to be displayed in a variety of media—print, video, clothing, decorations on fabrics, glassware, china, etc. Their possession and viewing under the right circumstances is a rite of passage for men and women rising to adulthood. Thereafter, the erotically symbolic numerals have a more discreet and private role in the personal sexuality of the society. While there is commercial exploitation of the symbols and extreme applications occupy an exotic place in fringe art and entertainment, tensions between men and women over the symbolism rarely occur outside the workplace.

Task for Group B

Demonstrate workplace or work-related scenarios in which male-female interactions involving erotically symbolic numbers DO NOT cross the line and become sexual harassment in the eyes of a reasonable person—show what the exchanges and patterns of behavior might be like. Use these scenario starters and describe conditions that would make a reasonable person consider them not to be sexual harassment:

1. VIs and XIs are the predominant paintings and sculptures in the company boardroom and hallways of the executive suites.

2. A few of the guys ask their female peers to join them as they huddle around the latest edition of a men's magazine admiring the VIIs.

3. Some people bring candy or exotic coffees from other regions to share with office mates upon returning from business trips; Jack prefers to share VII items, especially with his opposite-sex coworkers.

AUDIENCE REASONABLE NUMBERS KIT

Situation

In this mythical culture, intimacy between the sexes is communicated symbolically by Roman numerals. Patterns of the ancient numbers have erotic meanings long understood within the culture. Elaborate displays of the numerical combinations carry universal sexual connotations. Here are several examples:

VI = innocent "hearts and flowers" young love

VII = romance that may or may not include sex

XI = mature man-woman relationship, including courtship and marriage, with sex as an accepted component

XII = intense coupling dominated by bondage/deviant sexual practices

It is customary for the symbols to be displayed in a variety of media—print, video, clothing, decorations on fabrics, glassware, china, etc. Their possession and viewing under the right circumstances is a rite of passage for men and women rising to adulthood. Thereafter, the erotically symbolic numerals have a more discreet and private role in the personal sexuality of the society. While there is commercial exploitation of the symbols and extreme applications occupy an exotic place in fringe art and entertainment, tensions between men and women over the symbolism rarely occur outside the workplace.

Task for Group A

Demonstrate workplace or work-related scenarios in which male-female interactions involving erotically symbolic numbers cross the line and become sexual harassment in the eyes of a reasonable person—show what the exchanges and patterns of behavior might be like. Use these scenario starters and describe conditions that would make a reasonable person consider them to be sexual harassment:

1. VIIs and XIIs are the predominant paintings and sculptures in the company boardroom and hallways of the executive suites.

2. A few of the guys ask their female peers to join them as they huddle around the latest edition of a men's magazine admiring the XIs.

3. Some people bring candy or exotic coffees from other regions to share with office mates upon returning from business trips; Jack prefers to share XII items, especially with his opposite-sex coworkers.

Task for Group B

Demonstrate workplace or work-related scenarios in which male-female interactions involving erotically symbolic numbers DO NOT cross the line and become sexual harassment in the eyes of a reasonable person—show what the exchanges and patterns of behavior might be like. Use these scenario starters and describe conditions that would make a reasonable person consider them not to be sexual harassment:

1. VIs and XIs are the predominant paintings and sculptures in the company boardroom and hallways of the executive suites.

2. A few of the guys ask their female peers to join them as they huddle around the latest edition of a men's magazine admiring the VII's.

3. Some people bring candy or exotic coffees from other regions to share with office mates upon returning from business trips; Jack prefers to share VII items, especially with his opposite-sex coworkers.

EXERCISE 43

IT DEPENDS ON YOUR PERSPECTIVE

Method   MAKE THE CASE

Problem   Many people view sexual harassment from emotional perspectives that result in hasty judgments and exclude other opinions and plausible resolutions to problems. A good trial lawyer steps back from the emotional aspects of the client's case and puts on the best possible defense, one that is based on a reasoned assessment of the facts of the case. In this exercise participants do the same—from the perspective of a reasonable person—for sexual harassment positions with which they might adamantly disagree.

Objective   Provide participants with the occasion to consider sexual harassment points of view that differ from their own. Have them change positions and think as advocates for an alien position—appreciating that one party's reasonable judgment may differ from another's. Use the experience to soften the resentment toward different, but not threatening, perspectives and in the process facilitate the growth of more mutually acceptable standards of reasonableness.

Procedure   ✓ Select two teams of about six each consisting of men and women.

✓ Pass out Scenarios 1 and 2 to the teams and audience.

✓ Instruct the teams to read and discuss their scenarios and to come up with their strongest defense for their assigned position—whether they agree with it or not.

✓ Ask each team to have a spokesperson describe its scenario and summarize its defense for the position. Other team members are encouraged to contribute to the defense. (You may suggest a line of defense if necessary to get the discussion started.)

✓ Ask one team to challenge the other's position. (You may suggest some challenges if necessary to move the discussion forward.)

✓ Briefly note key words and phrases on a pad or blackboard—this helps people go back and elaborate on earlier points.

✓ Encourage the exchange of challenge and defense until you feel the relevant points have been made.

✓ Solicit a vote from the entire audience which serves as the jury. The question for the jury is this: Based on common sense reasoning, does the behavior in this case involve sexual harassment?

✓ Note that the objective is to uncover points of view that participants might not have considered. The case is deliberately ambiguous, open-ended, and subject to various interpretations and judgments (just like real life situations). Acknowledge this so you don't leave the group frustrated that a "correct" judgment was not reached.

1. Is this manager wrong in expressing his personal preferences and opinions? If so, why? What are the issues and considerations? What might be some indicators that he has gone too far?

2. Do you see reasonable arguments for each of the positions in this case? If so, what are they?

3. Do you think that men and women coming from different emotional directions in a case like this can come to a commonsense reasonable judgment on what is right?

4. Where would you place each position on a chronology of socially progressive thinking? Caveman? American frontier? Roaring 20s? World War II? 50s? 60s? 90s? etc.?

5. Is either position out of vogue with mainstream thinking in the 90s? If so, did you realize this prior to this training exercise? Does it matter to you? Do you see any practical reasons to reconsider any of your assumptions?

WHAT'S THE POINT?

It is often revealing to be forced to advocate something you don't necessarily believe. Conscientiously doing so can give you perspectives on the opposing view that you had not considered before. Understanding (if not accepting) a position you oppose can help you deal more effectively with those who espouse it. This is an opportunity for participants to compare their judgment of a sexual harassment situation to the group's judgment—which may be closer to the social norm or reasonable person standard that would prevail in court.

Materials

✓ Blackboard and chalk, or markers and board or pad to display notes before the group

✓ Copies of the scenarios for the teams

Time Required

Approximately 35 minutes

"IT DEPENDS ON YOUR PERSPECTIVE" SCENARIO 1

Directions:

Understand that *your role as a team is to defend the charged party based on the reasonableness of his position whether you agree with it or not.* Think about the arguments that would be used to defend his view even if you do not agree with them. You will have a chance later to say why you consider the position you articulate in this situation is wrong, if that is how you feel. The team should choose a spokesperson, but everyone is encouraged to contribute to the discussion.

Situation

✓ He is a manager from the old school. As a matter of fact, his present position is a second career for this retired police officer, and most of the clients who deal with his business are males with a similar background. Although both male and female employees acknowledge that he is a fundamentally good person, they are often discomfited by his vocal expression of personal beliefs and preferences that are seen by some as racist and sexist. He made it clear that the new receptionist *would* be a woman selected largely on the basis of her attractiveness. A current part-time employee who was turned down for the job has filed sexual harassment charges telling all who will listen that only "pretty and willing" women get ahead in this company.

✓ Defend the boss from the perspective that reasonable people *would not* consider his workplace behavior problematic enough to make him guilty of sexual harassment.

"IT DEPENDS ON YOUR PERSPECTIVE" SCENARIO 2

Directions:

Discuss the scenario as a team. Understand that *your role as a team is to support the position of the woman alleging sexual harassment, whether you agree with it or not.* Think about the arguments people would use to defend her position even you find it objectionable. You will have a chance later to say why you consider the position you articulate in this situation is wrong, if that is how you feel. The team should choose a spokesperson, but everyone is encouraged to contribute to the discussion.

Situation

✓ He is a manager from the old school. As a matter of fact, his present position is a second career for this retired police officer, and most of the clients who deal with his business are males with a similar background. Although both male and female employees acknowledge that he is a fundamentally good person, they are often discomfited by his vocal expression of personal beliefs and preferences that are seen by some as racist and sexist. He made it clear that the new receptionist *would* be a woman selected largely on the basis of her attractiveness. A current part-time employee who was turned down for the job has filed sexual harassment charges telling all who will listen that only "pretty and willing" women get ahead in this company.

✓ Attack the manager's position from the perspective that reasonable people *would* consider his workplace behavior problematic enough to make him guilty of sexual harassment.

EXERCISE 44

HOW REASONABLE IS IT TO...?

Method

MATCH THE ITEMS

Problem

The application of commonsense reason, rather than subjective emotion, is essential in distinguishing among sexual harassment, borderline behavior that invites caution, and merely obnoxious behavior that, unpleasant as it is, does not fit within the definitions of illegal harassment. Making the necessary distinctions is essential for both the potential offenders and their victims. Training is needed to convey the standards of a reasonable person. In this exercise participants indicate commonsense opinions about which of these options best describes the situations posed. The results are then tallied and discussed.

Objective

Demonstrate to the participants that sexual-harassment-related behavior exists on a continuum, but that actions crossing the line into sexual harassment territory have qualities that make them identifiable when reasonable judgment is applied. Use the experience to create awareness of differences in perception regarding alleged sexual harassment behavior and help participants avoid the pitfalls—either by going too far and committing it or by not acting decisively soon enough to curtail it.

Procedure

✓ Reasonable men and women may hold different views about where certain actions cross the line and become sexual harassment. To contrast their disparate views and increase mutual understanding, respondents are asked to indicate their gender before completing the anonymous questionnaire. Due to much publicity about the this issue, many people of both genders know the "politically correct" answer but hold different personal views. To get both viewpoints, the survey asks participants to differentiate between what they honestly feel and what they believe to be the "right" response. Stress the anonymity aspect of the exercise and urge participants to respond candidly.

✓ Distribute the "How Reasonable Is It To..." Matching Form. (A sample is provided or you may create your own.) Ask members of the group to indicate their gender and then mark each entry candidly by circling the selection they feel indicates the best answer. Also ask for a second matching that indicates what they *think* the politically correct (PC) answer would be. Clarify that the PC response does not have to be different from the one expressing their gut feeling. The two might be the same and they may or may not be "right." The objective is simply to react instinctively and then indicate what is perceived to be the socially acceptable response.

✓ Have the respondents fold their matching forms for privacy and ask volunteers to collect the forms and tally the results. Have them tally the responses for men, women, and the total group on each item (i.e., how many men, women, and total group participants marked each item)—for candid and PC responses. Post the results before the group and discuss them.

<table>
<tr><td>Discussion Questions</td><td>

1. Were you surprised at the answers of the opposite sex? your own gender? the group? Why or why not?

2. Do you think that the reasonable person standard is applied the same way by men and women? Why or why not?

3. What are some possible implications for sexual harassment when reasonable men and women disagree on what actions constitute harassment?

4. What messages do the results of the exercise convey?

5. Are there differences between the candid and politically correct responses? Do you think those differences might be narrowed in the future? If so, why? How?
</td></tr>
</table>

WHAT'S THE POINT?

Judgment and the ability to separate sexual harassment from less significant offensive, but not illegal, behavior are important skills for both potential harassers and victims. A key item of personal knowledge in fostering those skills in either situation is using commonsense reason to help recognize when actions make the transition from simply boorish or grossly inappropriate to sexual harassment. This exercise allows participants to apply their reasoned judgment, test it against what other individuals and the group consider reasonable, and have it refined with the help of the trainers.

<table>
<tr><td>Materials</td><td>

✓ Blackboard and chalk, or markers and board or pad to display results before the group

✓ Copies of the matching form for individual members of the group
</td></tr>
<tr><td>Time Required</td><td>Approximately 20 minutes</td></tr>
</table>

"HOW REASONABLE IS IT TO...?" MATCHING FORM

Directions:

A. Check your gender, but *do not put your name* on this anonymous survey.

☐ Male ☐ Female

B. Read each statement and mark it twice: (1) circle the selection on the form that best matches your candid, personal opinion of the reasonableness shown in the situation; and (2) circle the selection that matches what you believe to be the "politically correct" response.

1. In the heat of working intensely together researching an important case, an attorney suggested to his paralegal that their mutual passion for the law might form the basis for an even more fiery relationship in the bedroom. She was tempted but decided against it, and his interest in her immediately cooled, both personally and professionally. How reasonable is it for her to view the loss of their productive working relationship as sexual harassment?

Candid opinion:		
Reasonable	Questionable	Unreasonable

Politically correct opinion:		
Reasonable	Questionable	Unreasonable

2. A woman civil engineering technician working in an isolated location with a survey crew had a reputation for routinely trading wits and sexual innuendoes with her male counterparts. A new man joined the crew who took the practice too far for her comfort. She complained to the crew chief about the hostile environment and said that she feared for her safety. How reasonable is it that she complain about being treated like "one of the boys" under these circumstances?

Candid opinion:		
Reasonable	Questionable	Unreasonable

Politically correct opinion:		
Reasonable	Questionable	Unreasonable

3. A nurse practitioner working in the urology section of an HMO routinely conducts physical examinations on male patients and finds nude men in the clinical setting unremarkable. To ease their embarrassment, she is relaxed, friendly, and generously tolerant of nervous jokes about her work. Darren was an exception who took her sense of humor as an opening for making unwelcome suggestions that a private sexual relationship between them might be "fun." She immediately refused, but he persisted for weeks, even to the point of leaving graphic messages on her voice mail. How reasonable is it to expect her to overlook such behavior as something that comes with the territory?

Candid opinion:		
Reasonable	Questionable	Unreasonable

Politically correct opinion:		
Reasonable	Questionable	Unreasonable

4. After weeks of observing Mariah admiringly at the health club, Andrew found himself behind her in the checkout line of the convenience store next door. When he blurted that her fitness program was obviously having positive results, she looked at him as if he were a monster and left without comment. When Andrew checked in at the club the next afternoon, he was stopped at the reception desk and informed that any further unwanted advances toward a female member would result in the termination of his membership. How reasonable was Mariah's reaction under the circumstances?

	Candid opinion:	
Reasonable	Questionable	Unreasonable

	Politically correct opinion:	
Reasonable	Questionable	Unreasonable

Answers (cover or remove before copying): Each situation contains sketchy information, and answers might be different with the introduction of additional information. The examples are intended to stimulate discussion and uncover relevant points, not establish indelible criteria or provide indisputable rulings of guilt or innocence. In general, an informed person would respond: 1. Unreasonable—unless he linked an affair to job treatment or conditions. 2. Reasonable—she has no obligation to accept the situation simply because that's the way it's always been. 3. Unreasonable—he has no right to assume her interest in personal intimacy simply because her work requires professional intimacy that includes viewing him nude. 4. Unreasonable—he made no physical or verbal advances—simply blurted out an awkward compliment.

EXERCISE 45

MAKING THE REASONABLE CHOICE

Method   MULTIPLE CHOICE

Problem   Naturally occurring attractions between gender opposites may compli-
                        cate their workplace relationships. Sometimes actions, usually those of the
                        male, cross professional boundaries and result in sexual harassment. In
                        this exercise participants are asked to judge reasonably whether or not
                        sexual harassment is a factor in a number of common workplace situa-
                        tions. The results are tallied and discussed.

Objective   Demonstrate to the participants that sexual harassment is one of many
                        outcomes on the continuum of human behavior. Because some actions
                        do not fit neatly into the discrete boundaries used in statutory defini-
                        tions of sexual harassment, men and women need to develop the ability
                        to use commonsense reasoning in distinguishing between behavior that
                        is objectionable, even grossly so, but not illegal, and that which is illegal
                        harassment.

Procedure   ✓ Due to a great deal of publicity about sexual harassment, most people
                        know the "politically correct" responses to questions about sexual ha-
                        rassment in the modern workplace. When you begin the exercise, ac-
                        knowledge this and then emphasize that participants' answers will be
                        anonymous and that the usefulness of the training relies on their can-
                        did responses. Ask them to express their gut feelings rather than those
                        they think are "right" and to avoid extreme responses that do not ex-
                        press their true beliefs.

                        ✓ Distribute the "Making the Reasonable Choice" Quiz. (A sample is pro-
                        vided or you may create your own.) Ask members of the group to in-
                        dicate their gender and then mark each entry candidly by selecting the
                        multiple choice item that indicates their belief about sexual harassment.

                        ✓ Have the respondents fold their quizzes for privacy and ask volunteers
                        to collect the forms and tally the results. Have them tally the responses
                        for men, women, and the total group on each question (i.e., how many
                        men, women, and total group participants marked the various re-
                        sponses). Post the results before the group and discuss them.

Discussion Questions 1. Were you surprised at the answers of the opposite sex? your own gen-
                        der? the group? Why or why not?

                        2. How do you account for the differences among the groups?

                        3. What messages do the results convey?

                        4. What are some possible implications for sexual harassment?

5. Do you think gender stereotyping rather than logic or reason affected how you answered any of the questions? how your opposite-sex peers answered them? How? Why?

6. Do you think most people use commonsense reason in judging the difference between sexual harassment and behavior that is simply offensive or obnoxious? If not, how do they make up their minds?

WHAT'S THE POINT?

Making the distinction between boorish and crude, but not illegal, inappropriate behavior, and actions that constitute illegal sexual harassment is a necessary step in effectively dealing with the issue. The difference between harassment and just plain gender-based rudeness is an important understanding to have in the workplace. The ability to judge how a reasonable person would categorize behavior—as sexually harassing or something less—is an essential skill for men and women in the contemporary workplace.

Materials

✓ Blackboard and chalk, or markers and board or pad to display results before the group

✓ Copies of the "Making the Reasonable Choice" Quiz for individual members of the group

Time Required

Approximately 20 minutes

"MAKING THE REASONABLE CHOICE" QUIZ

Directions:
A. Check your gender, but *do not put your name* on this anonymous quiz.

☐ Male   ☐ Female

B. Read each statement and circle the response that you think a reasonable person would choose.

1. Sonya wasn't actually looking for a relationship when she began working extended hours with Timothy, but after a number of dates and their first night together, she readily admitted the relationship was welcome.
   a. Timothy has violated Sonya's rights by sleeping with her.
   b. Sonya waives all sexual harassment rights by getting involved with Timothy.
   c. Either has grounds for a sexual harassment complaint against the other should the relationship sour.
   d. Sonya and Timothy are two consenting adults in a mutually welcome relationship—no signs of sexual harassment here.
   e. All of the above.

2. Jimmy had been through flight training with Nora eight years before they found themselves representing different defense contractors at a national sales meeting. Remembering her reputation as a "good-time girl" then, he refused to take no for an answer after a few drinks and forced a level of intimacy she didn't want. Nora filed sexual harassment charges.
   a. Jimmy deserves to walk on this one. After all, she was "that kind of woman" when they knew each other before.
   b. Nora, regardless of what she did in the past, has a right to expect no to be to clearly understood and respected.
   c. If Jimmy can resurrect a few people from flight class who will testify that Nora was free with her sexual favors then, her sexual harassment claims won't have a prayer now.
   d. Nora is only asking for further unwanted attention by highlighting her past.
   e. a and c

3. Certain members of the staff who had known each other for years regularly engaged in witty repartee that sometimes pushed the limits of polite conversation. After one such exchange, Kevin suggested privately that Janet come to his apartment after work so that he could disprove the aspersions she had cast upon his masculinity. Janet angrily recoiled at the suggestion and claimed he had sexually harassed her.
   a. While Janet had the right to refuse him and avoid such exchanges in the future, Kevin's suggestion could be viewed as "more of the same" and wouldn't constitute harassment in this case.
   b. A woman is more sensitive than a man. Therefore, Kevin shouldn't have jumped to conclusions about Janet's willingness and should have to defend against charges of harassment.
   c. Kevin should have known that Janet was kidding—they'd been doing it for years—and not forced the issue by propositioning her.
   d. Their supervisor is at fault for letting the situation get out of hand.
   e. All of the above.

4. Calvin and Marty had worked together for several months. She made it clear that his interest in her was not reciprocated, and his periodic invitations to join him for after-work social activities were beginning to wear on her. She finally threatened to file a formal complaint if he didn't leave her alone.
   a. Calvin has a right to express his interest in Marty.
   b. Marty has a right to discourage Calvin's interest.

c. If Calvin's attentions reach the point where they interfere with Marty's ability to work in peace, she has grounds for a sexual harassment complaint.

d. If Calvin stops short of interfering with Marty's working in peace, and just occasionally proffers unwanted invitations, he is not engaged in sexual harassment.

e. All of the above.

5. When they learned a woman would be joining the crew, the guys in the shop decided to surprise her by substituting a beefcake male centerfold for the girlie one inside her male predecessor's locker door.

a. She should consider this a fine welcome—these are sensitive fellows who understand that her tastes in erotica are different from theirs.

b. They are being presumptuous—she should be left to select her own beefcake.

c. The fact that the locker door has historically been a place to display sexy pictures doesn't justify placing a pinup inside and assuming that the new employee will wish to continue the practice.

d. Sexual harassment charges would never stick because the guys didn't hang around to watch her reaction.

e. All of the above

Answers (mask or remove before copying): 1 = d, 2 = b, 3 = a, 4 = e, 5 = c. NOTE: Although these answers would be accepted by most current authorities, remind the group that refinements can be added to many situations that might alter the judgment of whether harassment occurred.

EXERCISE 46

IT'S ONLY REASONABLE

Method   RATE THE ACCURACY

Problem   Sexual harassment problems occur for two basic reasons: (1) the genders have somewhat different opinions on appropriate workplace behavior; and (2) they make incorrect assumptions about what their gender counterparts think is appropriate workplace behavior. In this exercise participants are asked to use commonsense reason in judging statements about harassment in the working environment. Such situations are frequently judged differently by reasonable women and men.

Objective   Demonstrate to the participants that men and women often have differing views on how the sexes should interact at work. Use the experience to create awareness that using commonsense reasoning can minimize mismatched perceptions that can lead to sexual harassment and to prepare both genders to avoid it.

Procedure   ✓ Due to a great deal of publicity about sexual harassment, most people know the "politically correct" responses to questions about the roles of women and men in the modern workplace. When you begin the exercise, acknowledge this and then emphasize that participants' answers will be anonymous and that the usefulness of the training relies on their candid responses. Ask them to express their gut feelings rather than those they think are "right" and to avoid extreme responses that do not express their true beliefs.

                      ✓ Distribute the rating scales. (A sample is provided or you may create your own.) Ask members of the group to indicate their gender and then rate each assumption candidly by circling a number on the scale. Also ask for a second rating that indicates what they *think* the politically correct (PC) answer would be. Clarify that the PC response does not have to be different from the one expressing their gut feeling. The two might be the same and they may or may not be "right." The objective is simply to react instinctively and then indicate what is perceived to be the socially acceptable response.

                      ✓ Have the respondents fold their surveys for privacy and ask volunteers to collect and score the results. Have them calculate the average score for men, women, and the total group for each question (i.e., add up the individual scores and divide by the total number of surveys in that group for each question)—for candid and PC responses. Post the results before the group and discuss them.

Discussion Questions 1. Do you think men and women end up with the same answers when you ask them for an opinion based on commonsense reasoning in cases like these?

2. If not, how do you account for the differences?

3. What do you think the fact that men and women sometimes come to different conclusions has to say about the potential for misunderstandings that could lead to sexual harassment problems?

4. Are your candid and PC responses different? If so, why? Will that ever change? Why?

5. Are there ratings that you would change now that we've discussed them? Are there any that you are at least willing to rethink quietly on your own?

WHAT'S THE POINT?

Men and women at work are concerned about finding themselves involved in a sexual harassment case without knowing how they got there. To avoid such a situation, workers need to know what others, including gender opposites, consider reasonable workplace behavior. Judging classic sexual harassment situations and issues helps them prepare for situations they might encounter on the job.

Materials

✓ Blackboard and chalk, or markers and board or pad to display results before the group

✓ Copies of the survey for individual members of the group

✓ A pocket calculator

Time Required

Approximately 25 minutes

"IT'S ONLY REASONABLE" SURVEY FORM

Directions:
A. Check your gender, but *do not put your name* on this anonymous survey.

☐ Male   ☐ Female

B. In the context of workplace sexual harassment, read each scenario and judge the response of a reasonable person twice: (1) circle the number on the scale that best represents your candid, personal opinion of reasonableness; and (2) circle the number that represents what you believe to be the "politically correct" response.

1. Mark and Terri knew each other at the office. They also both lived in the same building and enjoyed early evening swims at their nearby apartment pool when most of their colleagues were sitting in the traffic of their evening commutes. Terri filed sexual harassment charges when her "friend" Mark became so possessive that she was unable to pursue other personal relationships in her private life because Mark made life miserable for her at work when he became aware of them. A reasonable person would back Terri on this one—Mark appears to be harassing her.

Candid opinion:									
1	2	3	4	5	6	7	8	9	10
Accurate								Inaccurate	

Politically correct opinion:									
1	2	3	4	5	6	7	8	9	10
Accurate								Inaccurate	

2. It was a daily event—a group of women from the division down the hall would have an extended lunch break in the workroom of another division where space had been designated for the purpose. They talked loudly and with little inhibition about soaps, movies, and sometimes their personal lives. In time the guys from the host organization who passed through the workroom in the course of their duties became familiar enough with the discussions to enter into them. At one point, opinions about a particular topic varied widely between the men and women, the discussion grew heated, and an angry woman on the losing end of the argument accused two of the men of sexual harassment. The guys were taken aback; they thought they were taking part in candid, unofficial, lunchtime personal discussions that were unrelated to job relationships. Besides, these women don't even work directly with the men in question. The men are right—this is not harassment.

Candid opinion:									
1	2	3	4	5	6	7	8	9	10
Accurate								Inaccurate	

Politically correct opinion:									
1	2	3	4	5	6	7	8	9	10
Accurate								Inaccurate	

3. It was common knowledge that the boss and his administrative assistant were having an affair. Other workers, men and women who reported to the executive in question, became involved in disputes with the administrative assistant; it became apparent to them that they were heading for the losing end of the office power play. They charged sexual harassment, claiming that the special relationship between boss and assistant unleveled the professional playing field to their detriment. A reasonable person would not condemn the couple simply because they had a personal relationship, but sympathies would shift to the other workers if the outcome was unfair working conditions resulting from the sexual liaison.

				Candid opinion:					
1	2	3	4	5	6	7	8	9	10
Accurate								Inaccurate	

				Politically correct opinion:					
1	2	3	4	5	6	7	8	9	10
Accurate								Inaccurate	

4. Marianne and Patrick had been coworkers and lovers for several years. But their combination personal and professional relationship was now fraying at the edges, stressed by uneven career growth—she was on the move, he was stalled. She moved out, and the harder she tried to pull away on the job, the more desperately he tightened the reins, making their shared professional lives increasingly contentious. Finally, Marianne announced that if Patrick persisted, she would pursue harassment charges against him. A reasonable person would find for Marianne only if Patrick were preventing her from doing her job in peace—"normal" spillover of a lovers' breakup wouldn't suffice to constitute harassment.

				Candid opinion:					
1	2	3	4	5	6	7	8	9	10
Accurate								Inaccurate	

				Politically correct opinion:					
1	2	3	4	5	6	7	8	9	10
Accurate								Inaccurate	

EXERCISE 47

THE REASONABLE JUDGE

Method   SOLVE THE RIDDLE

Problem   The mere mention of hot-button topics can trigger a rush judgment on sexual harassment charges—a judgment that might be wrong. The actual results of rude and inappropriate behavior may be less severe than the instinctive, emotional reaction to their occurrence. Although any inappropriate behavior of a sexual nature has no place at work, it is necessary to separate legal harassment from more petty conflicts between men and women that are better defined as management and human relations problems than as legal ones. Reasonably judging the difference between them is key to applying resources effectively in the fight against true sexual harassment.

Objective   Demonstrate to participants that the *appearance* of sexual harassment in a case does not mean that it has happened from a legal standpoint. The standards of reason must be applied carefully to judge the severity of the alleged behavior, its pervasiveness, and its ultimate impact on the charging party's ability to perform effectively in the work environment. This riddle presents a case with an apparent outcome that, scrutinized more closely, rises to a level of conflict that calls for corrective action but fails to sustain a charge of hostile environment sexual harassment. Participants need to realize that simply articulating the terminology of harassment in a case doesn't necessarily establish that it occurred.

Procedure   ✓ Pass out copies of the "The Reasonable Judge" Riddle Form to the participants. Riddles are most effective early in sexual harassment training sessions, before the group becomes predisposed to see harassment lurking in every situation. If your group jumps to the sexual harassment conclusion, use the occasion to discuss the points of the riddle, and contrast how their reaction might have differed in the training situation and real life (i.e., whether they would have been less prone to see the sexual harassment problem in real life).

                ✓ Ask them to work privately on solving the riddle and answering the questions that follow it. This experience will be diminished in value by allowing anyone to provide the answer before individuals ponder the puzzle on their own.

                ✓ After most group members indicate they have either solved the riddle or given up, interrupt them and begin discussing the solution and its ramification for relations between women and men at work.

Discussion Questions   1. Do you think Shannon was harassed? Why or why not?

                2. Do you think her course of action (inaction?) was correct? Why? If not, what do you think she should have done?

                3. Why do you think the jury was right? wrong?

4. Was the judge correct to reverse on appeal? Why or why not?

3. If you could predict the future, do you think this riddle would be a useful training device before a similar audience in 20 years? Why or why not?

WHAT'S THE POINT?

The terminology of sexual harassment has become familiar, and if certain words have been uttered and the facts establish that particular incidents have occurred, many people tend to assume that harassment did too. In fact, sexual harassment in the legal arena is limited to correcting reasonably severe situations in which the harassing behavior is pervasive and truly hinders the individual's ability to get the job done and pursue a career on a reasonably level playing field. Workers need to keep in mind that sexual harassment law was not created to correct bad manners, impolite competition, slights, affronts to the overly sensitive, and the like. Sustaining harassment charges requires passing the tests of reasonableness measured by the standards of cumulative case law.

Materials ✓ "The Reasonable Judge" Riddle Forms

Time Required Approximately 25 minutes

"THE REASONABLE JUDGE" RIDDLE FORM

Carefully read the following riddle and privately explore your thoughts as you attempt to find the solution. Please do not discuss the riddle with others until the group addresses the solution. Answer the questions that follow.

"The Reasonable Judge" Riddle
Shannon's sexual harassment case against Oliver Industries reached the jury stage after attempts to resolve it out of court failed. Testimony established that certain incidents had occurred: she had been called unflattering names; sexual objects had been displayed on the desks of several of her coworkers; pornography had been left on the lunchroom table in the place where she normally sat; anonymous phone calls had been placed in her voice mail; and some of her work files had disappeared on occasion. A sympathetic jury determined that she had been sexually harassed. But on appeal, the judge failed to sustain the jury's decision, and he was on firm legal ground.

1. How can this be possible?

2. Why might someone broadly familiar with the law, like a judge, rule differently than a jury of Shannon's peers in a case like this?

3. Discuss how the judge and jury may have legitimately differed on their interpretation of the topics covered in the testimony.

Solution (mask or remove before copying): The judge compared the actual incidents with case law and determined that, although the incidents had occurred, none was severe or pervasive enough to constitute hostile environment sexual harassment. Each was irritating, inappropriate, and in bad taste, but in the end, the incidents were more annoying than substantially detrimental to her ability to do her job. There had never been a question about *quid pro quo* harassment—Shannon was not asked for sexual favors—so everything hinged on comparing the incidents in her case to patterns amassed in previous cases in which reasonable people determined when inappropriate, obnoxious behavior rose to a level in which a significantly hostile work environment constituted legal sexual harassment. Shannon continued to work effectively despite the incidents, was promoted several times, and had made no moves to change jobs. The judge thought the jury reacted emotionally and that their decision was inconsistent with the standards for such cases.

EXERCISE 48

50:50 SPLIT ON "IS IT REASONABLE?"

Method	SORT THE LISTS
Problem	Solving sexual harassment problems requires a reasonable approach to "knowing it when you see it." In this exercise participants develop their recognition skills by sorting a series of descriptive statements into the two categories of reasonable and unreasonable judgments about whether or not certain behavior constitutes harassment.
Objective	Demonstrate to the participants that sexual harassment has identifiable characteristics that can be separated from rude but less harmful behavior by a reasonable person. Use the experience to create awareness of potentially chargeable behavior under the law and clarify reasonable behavior boundaries for men and women who work together.

Procedure

✓ Due to a great deal of publicity about sexual harassment, most people know the "politically correct" responses to questions about the roles of women and men in the modern workplace. When you begin the exercise, acknowledge this and then emphasize that participants' answers will be anonymous and that the usefulness of the training relies on their candid responses. Ask them to express their gut feelings rather than those they think are "right" and to avoid extreme responses that do not express their true beliefs.

✓ Distribute 50:50 Split On "Is It Reasonable?" Forms. (A sample is provided or you may create your own.) Ask members of the group to place the descriptive statements under the Reasonable and Unreasonable columns. Mention that both columns must contain the same number of statements, and that the task may grow more difficult as forced choices must be made toward the end. (VARIATION: To liven up the process, instead of having participants simply read the descriptive statements, have trainers or volunteers from the group read or act them out.)

✓ Have the respondents fold their surveys for privacy and ask volunteers to collect and score the results. Have them tally the responses. Post the results before the group and discuss.

Discussion Questions

1. Did you have difficulty deciding whether any of the behavior described could reasonably be defined as harassment? Why? What criteria did you use in making your decisions?

2. Do you think men and women tend to classify the statements differently? If so, do they view reasonable behavior differently? Why?

3. Are there situations you find less offensive than others? some that don't bother you at all? Why? Do your gender opposites have a different opinion? Why?

4. Which situations do you consider to be the most in transition and apt to change in our lifetimes?

5. What do you think the fact that men and women answered differently has to say about the potential for misunderstandings that could lead to sexual harassment problems?

6. Are there entries that you would change now that we've discussed them? Are there any that you are at least willing to rethink quietly on your own?

WHAT'S THE POINT?

It is possible and desirable to make a reasoned judgment as to whether certain workplace actions legally qualify as sexual harassment or are more benign offensive behavior. This demonstrates to the participants that harassing behavior needs to be identified and separated from harmless, but maybe obnoxious, actions on the basis of the reasonable woman or reasonable victim standard used by the courts in adjudicating sexual harassment cases.

Materials

✓ 50:50 Split On "Is It Reasonable?" Forms

✓ Chalkboard or pad on which to display the results

Time Required

Approximately 25 minutes

"50:50 SPLIT ON 'IS IT REASONABLE?'" FORM

Directions:

A. Mentally inventory the list, and categorize the complainant's position as Reasonable or Unreasonable. If you see shades of both in a single statement, decide what you think is best and be prepared to explain your decision.

B. You must end up with an equal number of statements in reasonable and unreasonable categories.

Descriptive Statements

A. Fred and Kathryn frequently travel on business together and have had candid discussions about almost everything, including male-female relationships. Fred can't stand to lose and persists in leaving articles (in his favor) on her desk about points they've argued. Gradually she takes offense and asks him to stop. He continues, and she accuses him of sexual harassment. Kathryn's position is (a) reasonable or (b) unreasonable.

B. Delilah solicited a personal relationship with Samson, one of her new hires. The relationship lasted a year and then cooled when he fell in love with someone else. Since she felt awkward facing him regularly, she had him transferred to another department. His opportunities for professional growth were considerably less in the new division and Samson complained of sexual harassment. Samson's position is (a) reasonable or (b) unreasonable.

C. Chad unabashedly admired the women who worked in his building. He developed a reputation as someone who undressed you with his eyes, but was generally considered harmless since he never went beyond the looking stage. His attentions were viewed differently by Julie, a new female employee who, it was later learned, had been a rape victim. She felt that his attention was threatening and told him she would file sexual harassment charges if he didn't stop. Julie's position is (a) reasonable or (b) unreasonable.

D. Lauren applied for Joel's position at the top position of the administrative ladder when he decided to leave it and return to teaching. She considered herself the top candidate for the position but underestimated the resentment of men she had left behind with the help of affirmative action. When the position was advertised nationally, the dean selected an equally qualified woman without the "baggage" he believed Lauren would bring with her. She charged harassment, accusing the school of limiting her professional growth because of previous opportunities that had accrued to her gender. Lauren's position is (a) reasonable or (b) unreasonable.

E. Hollis and Erika worked as peers in the same administrative organization. She was an attractive woman who moved effectively in a world of male associates. Hollis came to believe Erika's gender gave her advantages that he didn't have and began to resent her seemingly favored status—so much so that he dropped hints about improper relationships between Erika and clients that he had no way of proving. When she heard the rumors and asked him to stop spreading them, he refused and said that he was fighting fire with fire. Erika filed sexual harassment charges when Hollis' unwarranted stories threatened important working relationships. Erika's position is (a) reasonable or (b) unreasonable.

F. Tracy, the social director on a cruise ship, loved her work, which included rotating assignments that essentially required her to be rehired for each subsequent cruise. When it became apparent to her than she was being denied assignments to ships where she had resisted the sexual advances of senior officers, she filed sexual harassment charges against the line. Tracy's position is (a) reasonable or (b) unreasonable.

G. Prior to a managers' meeting in the company conference room, Wayne, in a moment of pique, angrily blurted out some pretty uncomplimentary comments about one of Leah's past relationships. A number of their peers overhead their conversation. Leah was embarrassed and charged Wayne with sexually harassing her. Leah's position is (a) reasonable or (b) unreasonable.

H. Pamela was a professional member of the staff making planning visits to possible franchise locations in different parts of the country. She was the only woman on the staff, and even though two of the three men with her were of equal or lower rank, her manager always asked her to coordinate arrangements for receptions and meals. At each reception or dinner, Pamela was acknowledged to those attending as the person responsible for the "lovely" arrangements. She considered this practice gender stereotyping that limited her professional potential and filed harassment charges, claiming hostile environment. Pamela's position is (a) reasonable or (b) unreasonable.

I. Matthew, a well-to-do bachelor and restaurant owner, found the wait staff at his place of business to be an excellent source of female companionship. Since he owned the place, he saw nothing wrong in juggling work schedules to favor, with lucrative shifts/nights of the week, etc., those who favored him. Some of the women who worked low-tip shifts and ended up with significantly lower incomes than the favored ones charged him with sexual harassment. The women's position is (a) reasonable or (b) unreasonable.

J. Kimberly returned from vacation to find an erotic men's magazine in the drawer of her desk. She took it as a personal affront, inquired as to who had been using her desk while she was away, and learned that it was Jerome. When confronted, he good-naturedly acknowledged that it was his magazine, said that he had left it in her drawer by accident, apologized for offending her, and thanked her for returning it. The incident seemed to pass. After several coworkers teased Kimberly about her taste in reading material, she got angry all over again and accused Jerome of harassment. Kimberly's position is (a) reasonable or (b) unreasonable.

K. Donna was recently divorced and needed a job right away. Jonathan indicated to her when he hired her that he was looking for a good-looking woman to make their trips to regional sales meetings together something memorable. He was up front about his expectations and saw to it that Donna advanced rapidly in the organization. When she secured a better position in a competing firm and left him facing charges of sexually harassing her, he was totally surprised. But she had every right to do it. Donna's position is (a) reasonable or (b) unreasonable.

L. Ava decided to compensate for her poor job performance with thinly veiled suggestions of sexual favors for her boss. When he failed to respond to her advances, she circulated a true story about how he had been fired from another company for reacting otherwise in similar circumstances and claimed she was just "doing what she had to do" to save her job. Ava's position is (a) reasonable or (b) unreasonable.

Answers (mask or remove before copying): A = (b), B = (a), C = (a), D = (b), E = (a), F = (a), G = (b), H = (b), I = (a), J = (b), K = (a), L = (b). While informed people would generally agree with these answers, some statements have aspects that could be interpreted differently, depending on the perspective of the person answering. The objective is to stimulate thinking, accent gray areas, and communicate basic guidelines rather than to provide definitive answers to legal questions.

EXERCISE 49

THIS IS REASONABLE!

Method   TRUE/FALSE

Problem   Distinguishing between behavior that legally constitutes sexual harassment and that which is crude, but may not be actionable under law, sometimes confuses modern workers and managers. Being able to use commonsense reasoning to identify behavior as sexual harassment or offensive, but not illegal, is a skill that will help workers and managers avoid unconsciously harassing others and deal with illegal behavior if it happens to them.

Objective   Demonstrate to the participants that "knowing it when they see it" will assist them in promoting reasonable operating boundaries between men and women at work. Use the exercise to develop awareness of the recognition factors, and to broaden participants' thinking to embrace the full spectrum of possibilities, including successfully determining what constitutes a reasonable response in various circumstances.

Procedure   ✓ Due to a great deal of publicity about sexual harassment, many people know the "politically correct" response to questions surrounding the issue. When you begin the exercise, acknowledge this and then emphasize that participants' answers will be anonymous and that the usefulness of the training relies on their candid responses. Ask them to express their gut feelings rather than those they think are "right" and to avoid extreme responses that do not express their true beliefs.

✓ Distribute the "This Is Reasonable!" Quiz. (A sample is provided or you may create your own.) Ask members of the group to read each statement and respond true or false.

✓ Have the respondents fold their quizzes for privacy, and ask volunteers to collect and score the results. Have them tally the number of people who marked each statement true and false. Post the results before the group and discuss them.

Discussion Questions   1. Did men and women judge the situations differently? the same? Why or why not?

2. Do you think men and women tend to view certain kinds of behavior as reasonable or unreasonable simply because they have different gender experiences throughout their lives?

3. Are there situations you found easier to classify than others? Why?

4. How do you think the ability to identify and classify offensive behavior impacts the potential for misunderstandings that could lead to sexual harassment problems?

5. Could "knowing it when you see it" help prevent sexual harassment in the first place? How?

WHAT'S THE POINT?

It is desirable to raise awareness of what constitutes sexual harassment on the job, but there is a practical necessity to distinguish between valid complaints and merely offensive behavior. Both deserve attention, but the laws must focus on serious violations, not just crudeness or bad manners. The sorting process begins on the workplace floor where employees and managers who are trained to use commonsense reasoning as one criterion defining the difference between simply objectionable but not illegal behavior and legally prohibited harassment can successfully resolve many problems without outside intervention.

Materials

✓ "This Is Reasonable!" Quiz

✓ Chalkboard or pad on which to display the results

Time Required

Approximately 20 minutes

"THIS IS REASONABLE!" QUIZ

Directions:
Read each statement and circle either True or False.

T F 1. If a woman feels her ability to do her job is severely limited because she is unable to relate professionally to her peers without their consistently interjecting comments about her sexuality, she is justified in charging sexual harassment.

T F 2. A man defends his unwelcome sexually suggestive touching of female subordinates with the comment that he is only reacting as nature intended. He claims he is not guilty of sexual harassment.

T F 3. A woman acknowledges that, in the social sphere, she's had men press a relationship with her and she's never accused them of anything more than being a nuisance, but when a man at work shows the same degree of persistence, she feels she's justified in charging him with sexual harassment.

T F 4. He said the comments about her attractiveness were nothing more than honest compliments. She found such constant "admiration" unnerving after a while and tried to avoid him in the office. When that failed, she repeatedly asked him to stop remarking on her personal appearance. Because he persisted in making remarks even after she had spoken to him, she was justified in accusing him of harassment.

T F 5. She just didn't like the way the men in the office talked about women in general. While they didn't single her out, and no individual woman appeared to be the object of their comments, she suggested that they were creating an environment hostile to her particular beliefs. She was justified in accusing them of harassment.

T F 6. He was the boss, after all, and if his preference for women who would exchange sexually tinged banter with him got them better assignments and other rewards, so be it. Women who didn't participate weren't fired; they just didn't benefit from his favors—he wasn't sexually harassing them!

Answers (mask or remove before copying): While these questions are provided more to stimulate thought and discussion than to establish legal judgments, and other interpretations are possible, informed people would generally answer: 1 = T When offensive behavior hinders job performance, harassment is probably occurring. 2 = F Control of natural urges is a reasonable expectation at work. 3 = T Unwanted pursuit at work that interferes with a woman's right to pursue her career can have sexual harassment consequences that wouldn't be present in a social situation. 4 = T He has moved beyond the reasonable point and is harassing her. 5 = F Sexual harassment laws were not intended to redress concerns of the overly sensitive. 6 = F If he has structured the distribution of rewards in his workplace on the basis of workers' gender and their willingness to banter with him sexually, he has probably created a hostile environment sexual harassment situation.

EXERCISE 50

HE'S UNREASONABLE!/SHE'S UNREASONABLE!

Method   SPONTANEOUS REACTION

Problem   Sexual harassment issues are at the top of the sensitivity list in the modern workplace, and men and women sometimes react instinctively upon hearing of (or encountering) an incident. A spontaneous reaction that is based on emotion rather than a reasoned evaluation of available facts will prevent workers and managers from protecting themselves and others from abuse. A reasoned reaction helps people to avoid inflating a situation that may be obnoxious, but relatively harmless, into something that cannot be resolved directly by those involved.

Objective   Demonstrate to the participants that when sexual-harassment-related incidents elicit spontaneous reactions, such reactions are most apt to be effective when based on a reasoned, dispassionate view of what actually occurred. Show that accurate recognition of sexual harassment aids people in limiting personal vulnerability and may prevent them from trying to make a case of offensive behavior that does not fall within the legal definitions of harassment. Use the experience to heighten awareness of whether harassment has taken place and the kinds of incidents that can occur. Cite likely differences in male/female perceptions of them, to adjust men's and women's reactions to them.

Procedure   ✓ Due to a great deal of publicity about sexual harassment, many people know the "politically correct" response to questions surrounding the issue. When you begin the exercise, acknowledge this and then emphasize that participants' answers will be anonymous and that the usefulness of the training relies on their candid responses. Ask them to express their gut feelings rather than those they think are "right" and to avoid extreme responses that do not express their true beliefs.

✓ Distribute "He's Unreasonable!/She's Unreasonable!" Reaction Form. (A sample is provided or you may create your own.) Ask members of the group to indicate their gender, read each statement, respond spontaneously with their first reaction to each item, and be prepared to defend their responses.

✓ Have the respondents fold their quizzes for privacy and ask volunteers to collect and score the results. Have them tally the number of people who marked each response for each statement. Do this for the combined group and for women and men separately. Post the results before the group and discuss them.

Discussion Questions   1. Did the men and women view many of the situations differently? the same? Why or why not?

2. How do you account for the differences?

3. Were you surprised that some of the actions, which you might have thought were grossly offensive, did not meet the reasonable person standard as harassment? Why?

4. What do you think the fact that men and women answered differently has to say about the potential for misunderstandings that could lead to sexual harassment problems?

5. Are there responses that you would change now that we've discussed them? Are there any that you are at least willing to rethink quietly on your own?

WHAT'S THE POINT?

Reacting spontaneously, men and women sometimes see different motivations, which they may immediately take to be factually correct, in potential sexual harassment incidents. The greater their awareness of what constitutes legally defined sexual harassment based on the reasonable woman or reasonable victim standard, the lower is the likelihood they will either wrongly tolerate unacceptable illegal behavior or overreact to offensive actions that fall short of harassment. Moving the genders nearer a common standard for acceptable behavior removes another obstacle to achieving equity in workplace opportunity.

Materials

✓ "He's Unreasonable!/She's Unreasonable!" Reaction Forms

✓ Chalkboard or pad on which to display the results

Time Required

Approximately 20 minutes

"HE'S UNREASONABLE!/SHE'S UNREASONABLE!" REACTION FORM

Directions:
A. Check your gender, but *do not put your name* on this anonymous form.

☐ Male   ☐ Female

B. Read each statement and immediately make a single response—your initial reaction is wanted, so don't ponder the question.

"He's Unreasonable!/She's Unreasonable!" Reaction

1. She laughed at a lot of things she really didn't consider very funny—but, hey! He's the boss and life at work is better when he's happy. She finally drew the line when he insisted that she reach into his front pants pocket each morning to get the keys to the files. It was a major factor in her sexual harassment charges against him.

    A. He's Unreasonable!   **B.** She's Unreasonable!

2. He managed an air traffic control facility staffed by several men and a woman. She good-naturedly took a lot of kidding from her colleagues, but then it turned nasty. Some of the men resented her presence because the tower "just wasn't the same" and they wanted her to quit. They directed a constant barrage of sexually explicit comments and propositions at her and made life at work miserable. She complained to her manager who suggested that she sleep with her main tormentor, get it over with, and then everything would be O.K.

    A. He's Unreasonable!   **B.** She's Unreasonable!

3. She was passed over for promotion a second time, and when the position went to a younger, more attractive woman with less time in grade, she filed hostile environment sexual harassment charges against the man who handled the selection process. There was no basis for suspecting him of any improprieties with the woman who was promoted, and he offered objective reasons for his decision.

    A. He's Unreasonable!   **B.** She's Unreasonable!

4. She didn't care for the atmosphere of the office. Men and women interacted in ways that she considered "morally loose"—they were, in her judgment, so chummy that some hanky-panky just *had* to be going on. She complained to the human resources manager who offered a reassignment, but explained that the company couldn't presume to manage the moral tone of the office as long as sexual favors were not being exchanged for favorable job treatment. She disagreed and filed hostile environment sexual harassment charges.

    A. He's Unreasonable!   **B.** She's Unreasonable!

5. He enjoyed having lunch with her and the rest of the management trainee class—she smiled and conversed with him freely in the group. When they drew the same assignment, he tried to continue the lunch dates and pressed after-hours drinks or coffee. She responded with unequivocal turn-downs which he interpreted as a "try harder" challenge that led to a final, unpleasant rebuff. He still didn't stop and she filed sexual harassment charges, stating that she was unable to do her work in peace.

    A. He's Unreasonable!   **B.** She's Unreasonable!

6. She was added to the training team at the last minute, and everyone presumed it was because an all-male team was bad for the company image. The assignment should have gone to him—he'd been preparing for it, and he knew he deserved it. He decided to confront the boss. She tacitly acknowledged that he was better qualified, but reminded him that the company has taken heavy-duty criticism on gender balance. "So even if a *minimally* qualified woman is available, well …

sorry, but that's the way it goes." He maintains he's the victim of a hostile environment in which he is made to suffer lost career opportunities because of his gender.

    A. He's Unreasonable!   **B.** She's Unreasonable!

Answers (mask or remove before copying): 1 = A Repeatedly demanding sexually demeaning obedience as a part of the workplace routine can create a hostile environment. 2 = A Being told to provide sexual favors in return for normal working conditions is *quid pro quo* harassment. 3 = B Unless sex was traded for the promotion, sexual harassment doesn't appear to be a factor. 4 = B The sexual harassment laws are not intended to protect overly sensitive people. Unless sex is impacting on careers, there is no basis for charges. 5 = A Judgment is necessary, but he is probably harassing her, as there is no indication that anything short of harassment charges would have stopped him. 6 = B Policy in this area is evolving and the decision hinges on where affirmative action crosses the line and becomes privilege based on gender.

DETERMINING EMPLOYER LIABILITY IN SEXUAL HARASSMENT CASES

Rationale

The overarching thought behind the exercises of Section 5 is: Case law is providing guidance on when the consequences of employee behavior in the workplace assume broader ramifications and the company becomes liable for the misdeeds of the individual.

Selection of Exercises

Use these thumbnail sketches of the exercises in Section 5 to choose those best suited to your purposes.

AGREE/DISAGREE

51. *The Company Knew!*—Participants anonymously score statements illustrating possible employer liability in sexual harassment incidents on an agree/disagree scale. Identifying themselves only as male or female raters, they mark each statement once with their candid opinion of company culpability in each situation. Trainers calculate averages, note extremes, and help participants accurately sort the incidents in a guided discussion that identifies boundaries and acknowledges gray areas.

DEMONSTRATION

52. *But We* Delegated *That Responsibility!*—Teams of participants are assigned workplace sexual harassment scenarios in which they demonstrate by discussion or a skit how the employer wrongly assumed that it was free from responsibility because it delegated enforcement authority to an employee. Guided discussion clarifies that *responsibility* for providing a workplace free from sexual harassment cannot be delegated.

MAKE THE CASE

53. *How Was the Company To Know?*—One group is tasked with making the case that the company is at fault in a hypothetical workplace situation where sexual harassment charges have been brought, and the other must defend it against the charges in the same situation. Participants experience both sides of the case either directly or vicariously and learn how perception colors the view of the players in sexual harassment cases in which individual and institutional responsibilities overlap.

MATCH THE ITEMS

54. *Assign the Fault*—Participants are given a series of situations and are asked to match them to possible levels of company culpability in incidents of sexual harassment. The results are tallied and trainers help participants examine their thinking and appreciate each others' positions in guided discussion.

MULTIPLE CHOICE

55. *So Whom Do You Blame?*—Participants judge the degree of employer blame in a number of sexual harassment situations by selecting multiple-choice answers. Trainers tabulate and compare the results, then aid participants in examining the strengths and weaknesses of their choices during a guided discussion.

RATE THE ACCURACY

56. *That's Hardly the Company's Fault!*—Individuals are asked to score anonymously on an accurate/inaccurate perception scale several scenarios dealing with sexual harassment in which employers claim they are not legally responsible for the wrongdoing of their employees. Identifying themselves only as male or female raters, they mark the list once with their candid opinion and once with the answer they believe is "politically correct." Trainers calculate averages, note extremes, and help participants hone their judgment in a guided discussion of their differences.

SOLVE THE RIDDLE

57. *What Do You Mean We "Fired" Her?*—Participants are asked to solve a riddle in which traditional thinking about being discharged from a position clouds their judgment and hinders their ability to find the solution. Trainers guide the discussion to reveal a more subtle way in which employees are forced from their jobs (constructive discharge) and to address its relevance to company liability.

SORT THE LISTS

58. *50:50 Split on "Can You Blame the Company?"*—Participants are asked to make forced choices on whether statements about sexual harassment fall under Blame the Company or Don't Blame the Company headings; half must be listed under each. The results are tallied and are examined during a guided discussion.

TRUE/FALSE

59. *It's the Company's Fault!*—Participants take a true/false quiz based on a series of affirmations that the company bears legal responsibility for various sexual harassment situations in the workplace. The results are tallied and the responses are examined during a guided discussion.

SPONTANEOUS REACTION

60. *You Can't Blame the Company!/Of Course You Can!*—Participants are presented with situations that have workplace sexual harassment overtones and are asked to respond with an immediate reaction as to who is to blame — the perpetrator alone, or the company along with the perpetrator. The results are tallied for men, women, and the total group, and the responses are examined during a guided discussion.

Optional Cross-References—The following chapters of *Working Together: The New Rules and Realities for Managing Men and Women at Work* (Baridon and Eyler, McGraw-Hill, 1994) are recommended if you need additional information to understand the issues and support your discussions:

Chapter 3, "Laws, Regulations, and Gender in the Workforce"

Chapter 4, "Workplace Etiquette for Men and Women"

Chapter 5, "Managing Men and Women"

EXERCISE 51

THE COMPANY KNEW!

Method   AGREE/DISAGREE

Problem   Many employers broadly assume that legal liability for sexual harassment between their employees rests solely with the harasser. They believe that as long as the company has issued written policies advocating gender fairness that make it clear that sexual harassment is wrong and will not be tolerated, it has met its legal obligations and is insulated from gender conflicts among employees. The problem arises when a worker files sexual harassment charges and claims that the company should reasonably have known harassment was occurring and taken active responsibility for correcting the problem.

Objective   Demonstrate to the participants that employers have an overarching responsibility to provide a workplace free from sexual harassment. Use the opinion survey to help individuals cultivate an appreciation for the obligations of employers in sexual harassment prevention and resolution. Show that the legal responsibility goes beyond what senior management actually knows to what it is expected to know, given its responsibilities under the law.

Procedure   ✓ Men and women may hold different views about the obligations of employers in sexual harassment situations. Because women are more likely to be the victims of harassment, they tend to have higher expectations of their employers than do men. To contrast their disparate views and increase mutual understanding, respondents are asked to indicate their gender before completing the anonymous questionnaire. Due to much publicity about this issue, many people of both genders know the "politically correct" answer but hold different personal views. To get both viewpoints, the survey asks participants to differentiate between what they honestly feel and what they believe to be the "right" response. Stress the anonymity aspect of the exercise and urge participants to respond candidly.

✓ Distribute the rating scales. (A sample is provided or you may create your own.) Ask members of the group to indicate their gender and then rate each statement candidly by circling a number on the scale. Also ask for a second rating that indicates what they *think* the politically correct (PC) answer would be. Clarify that the PC response does not have to be different from the one expressing their gut feeling. The two might be the same and they may or may not be "right." The objective is simply to react instinctively and then indicate what is perceived to be the socially acceptable response.

✓ Have the respondents fold their surveys for privacy and ask volunteers to collect and score the results. Have them calculate the average score for men, women, and the total group on each question (i.e., add up the individual scores and divide by the total number of surveys in that group for each question)—for candid and PC responses. Post the results before the group and discuss them. Note that the objective of the exercise is to examine views and develop sensitivity, not to reach definitive conclusions to the hypothetical questions.

Discussion Questions

1. Were you surprised at the answers of the opposite sex? your own gender? the group? Why or why not?
2. How do you account for the differences among the groups?
3. What messages do the results convey?
4. What are some possible implications for sexual harassment?
5. Why do you think there are differences between the candid and politically correct responses? Do you think they might be narrowed in the future? If so, why? How?

WHAT'S THE POINT?

The law is gradually refining the boundaries of employers' liability in sexual harassment incidents. If companies are to provide their employees with the protections expected under the law and protect themselves from embarrassing and potentially costly liability judgments, senior management must know and understand these boundaries. By applying their judgment on a continuous scale, participants learn to judge the proper role of the employer more accurately. As the group results are discussed, some individuals, particularly those representing management, may find this experience adjusts certain opinions nearer to the current realities, which reflect substantial employer vulnerability in sexual harassment cases.

Materials

✓ Blackboard and chalk, or markers and board or pad to display results before the group

✓ Copies of the survey for individual members of the group

✓ A pocket calculator

Time Required

Approximately 30 minutes

"THE COMPANY KNEW!" SURVEY FORM

Directions:

A. Check your gender, but *do not put your name* on this anonymous survey.

☐ Male   ☐ Female

B. Read each statement and mark it twice: (1) circle the number on the scale that best represents your candid, personal opinion; and (2) circle the number that represents what you believe to be the "politically correct" response.

1. Most people in the office knew that Candice's supervisor was making sexual demands of her and believed that if she didn't comply, she stood a good chance of losing her job. When she brought sexual harassment charges, she named her company as well as her supervisor in the complaint. Candice had a reasonable basis for including the company in her suit because it should have been aware of the problem and corrected it.

Candid opinion:

| 1 | 2 | 3 | 4 | 5 | 6 | 7 | 8 | 9 | 10 |

Agree   Disagree

Politically correct opinion:

| 1 | 2 | 3 | 4 | 5 | 6 | 7 | 8 | 9 | 10 |

Agree   Disagree

2. Suzanne included her business in a complaint against a coworker who had sexually harassed her on the job. Because the company took no steps to protect her, she felt it was to blame for what happened even though it had well publicized and vigorously enforced policies against sexual harassment. Suzanne was an unfortunate exception in an otherwise well-run program for preventing sexual harassment, so the company isn't apt to accrue blame in this case.

Candid opinion:

| 1 | 2 | 3 | 4 | 5 | 6 | 7 | 8 | 9 | 10 |

Agree   Disagree

Politically correct opinion:

| 1 | 2 | 3 | 4 | 5 | 6 | 7 | 8 | 9 | 10 |

Agree   Disagree

3. Katie was let go by XYZ Corporation when her performance declined as a result of sexual harassment by a supervisor. When she sued the corporation, its defense was that, while it regretted the harassment, her dismissal was justified because it was based on objective measures of poor job performance, whatever the cause. Since the company is being objective, it should prevail in this instance.

Candid opinion:

1	2	3	4	5	6	7	8	9	10
Agree								Disagree	

Politically correct opinion:

1	2	3	4	5	6	7	8	9	10
Agree								Disagree	

Answers (mask or remove before copying): The courts generally agree with situations one and two. If the problem was obvious to others in the job setting, as in situation one, the company should have known and corrected it. In the second illustration, it is true that a well-publicized and vigorously enforced sexual harassment policy is a good defense, and the company may escape blame since it had a well-documented track record of meeting its responsibilities. In the third situation, the courts have ruled that performance diminished by harassment is not a valid cause for dismissal.

EXERCISE 52

BUT WE DELEGATED THAT RESPONSIBILITY!

Method

DEMONSTRATION

Problem

Employers may wrongly assume that delegating authority for managing people absolves the business entity of liability for sexual harassment by subordinate employees. Since the ultimate responsibility for providing a workplace free from sexual harassment cannot be delegated, all levels of management need to understand that they cannot avoid culpability for abuses they either do not or choose not to see.

Objective

Demonstrate to the participants that management cannot remove itself from responsibility to enforce sexual harassment regulations merely by issuing complaint policies and procedures, making statements of support, and assigning the task to subordinate managers. Use the experience of articulating the employer's indefensible position to help the group gain an appreciation for why the argument is invalid within the parameters of sexual harassment laws and regulations.

Procedure

✓ Select two teams from the participants—about six members each is ideal, but the number is not critical. Include members of both sexes. Designate them Groups A and B.

✓ Separate the teams so that each is unable to listen to what the other is planning. Ask the audience not to influence the outcome by commenting or providing guidance.

✓ Give each team the scenario for its group.

✓ Give the audience both scenarios to inform the observers about what the teams are doing.

✓ After team members finish conferring, ask each team to demonstrate (through a brief skit or a spokesperson—their option) company responsibility for the harassment. First, Group A demonstrates how the company might have a poor case for avoiding responsibility by claiming it was delegated; next, Group B demonstrates how the company might make a strong case for responsibility resting with subordinates. If the spokesperson option is chosen, a male and female trainer may want to act out the skit described to give the exercise life.

✓ When both teams finish, ask each to explain its approach.

✓ If it isn't apparent, stress the importance of having a clearly articulated, vigorously enforced antiharassment policy in place.

Discussion Questions

1. Do you think that the woman in this case was sexually harassed? Why or why not?

2. Do you think her company should be absolved of blame for the actions of the alleged harasser since the relationship was a consensual one?

3. Which of the two kinds of harassment is implied in this case?

4. Do you think the woman in this case handled her problem as well as she could have? Why or why not? If not, what should she have done differently?

5. Do you think the company has a reasonable defense based on its written policies against sexual harassment? If not, what could they have done to prevent this case from ending up in court?

WHAT'S THE POINT?

Although there are situations in which diligent employer efforts to provide a harassment-free workplace are circumvented by determined subordinates, in many cases management has deliberately neglected to see and confront the problem. The purpose of this exercise is to demonstrate for workers and managers alike that a hear-no-evil, see-no-evil defense against sexual harassment rarely stands up in court. Ultimately, the employer is expected to protect its workers from sexual harassment on the job, and while actions can be delegated in an organization, responsibility cannot.

Materials

✓ Break-out areas in which Groups A and B can meet (corners of the room will do, just so the groups can confer with some degree of confidentiality)

✓ Scenarios for Groups A, B, and the audience

✓ Chalkboard or large pad to note major points in discussion

Time Required

Approximately 25 minutes

DELEGATION SCENARIO A

Situation

A senior officer for an international bank and a member of its public relations branch became involved in a sexual relationship. He was a major source of inside tips on newsworthy developments, which gave her a leg up on her competitors. She acquiesced to his sexual demands, carried on an affair with him in exchange for his "help" and was rewarded with several promotions within her own division based on her ability to get the story first. Eventually the affair ended unhappily, and when she filed sexual harassment charges, she named the bank as codefendant. She claimed that her tormentor's superiors should have been aware of the coerced liaison and had a responsibility to protect her from their subordinate's sexual demands, which he often insisted on gratifying in his private office and on company business trips.

Task for Group A

Embellish the scenario to demonstrate your point that top bank officials were indeed *culpable* in this sexual harassment case. Make the point that their claims that the company had explicit written policies against sexual harassment and could do nothing more to prevent the actions of one subordinate who chose to leverage news leaks for sex were an invalid defense. Use these scenario starters:

1. Isn't it true that he made no secret about his special interest in her, remarking that if it hadn't been for him, she'd still be at the bottom of the barrel?

2. Would the bank's travel records show it made payments for her to accompany him on business trips even though she worked in an entirely different department?

3. When she brought up the matter with her supervisor, didn't he tell her that a personal relationship between two consenting adults was none of the company's business?

DELEGATION SCENARIO B

Situation

A senior officer for an international bank and a member of its public relations branch became involved in a sexual relationship. He was a major source of inside tips on newsworthy developments, which gave her a leg up on her competitors. She acquiesced to his sexual demands, carried on an affair with him in exchange for his "help" and was rewarded with several promotions within her own division based on her ability to get the story first. Eventually the affair ended unhappily, and when she filed sexual harassment charges, she named the bank as codefendant. She claimed that her tormentor's superiors should have been aware of the coerced liaison and had a responsibility to protect her from their subordinate's sexual demands, which he often insisted on gratifying in his private office and on company business trips.

Task for Group B

Embellish the scenario to demonstrate your point that top bank officials were indeed *not culpable* in this sexual harassment case by virtue of their claims that the company had explicit written policies against sexual harassment and could do nothing more to prevent the actions of one subordinate who chose to leverage news leaks for sex. Use these scenario starters:

1. You say she never complained to a supervisor or used the bank's complaint resolution procedures until *after* the affair ended?

2. Yes, I do recall the bank acted vigorously in disciplining a middle manager for sexually harassing his secretary just last year.

3. As improbable as it may sound, top management was dumbfounded to learn what had been going on—we had no indication and assumed two professionals were doing an honest job together until she filed charges.

AUDIENCE DELEGATION SCENARIOS

Situation

A senior officer for an international bank and a member of its public relations branch became involved in a sexual relationship. He was a major source of inside tips on newsworthy developments, which gave her a leg up on her competitors. She acquiesced to his sexual demands, carried on an affair with him in exchange for his "help" and was rewarded with several promotions within her own division based on her ability to get the story first. Eventually the affair ended unhappily, and when she filed sexual harassment charges, she named the bank as codefendant. She claimed that her tormentor's superiors should have been aware of the coerced liaison and had a responsibility to protect her from their subordinate's sexual demands, which he often insisted on gratifying in his private office and on company business trips.

Task for Group A

Embellish the scenario to demonstrate your point that top bank officials were indeed *culpable* in this sexual harassment case. Make the point that their claims that the company had explicit written policies against sexual harassment and could do nothing more to prevent the actions of one subordinate who chose to leverage news leaks for sex were an invalid defense. Use these scenario starters:

1. Isn't it true that he made no secret about his special interest in her, remarking that if it hadn't been for him, she'd still be at the bottom of the barrel?

2. Would the bank's travel records show it made payments for her to accompany him on business trips even though she worked in an entirely different department?

3. When she brought up the matter with her supervisor on at least two occasions, didn't he tell her that a personal relationship between two consenting adults was none of the company's business?

Task for Group B

Embellish the scenario to demonstrate your point that top bank officials were indeed *not culpable* in this sexual harassment case by virtue of their claims that the company had explicit written policies against sexual harassment and could do nothing more to prevent the actions of one subordinate who chose to leverage news leaks for sex. Use these scenario starters:

1. You say she never complained to a supervisor or used the bank's complaint resolution procedures until *after* the affair ended?

2. Yes, I do recall the bank acted vigorously in disciplining a middle manager for sexually harassing his secretary just last year.

3. As improbable as it may sound, top management was dumbfounded to learn what had been going on—we had no indication and assumed two professionals were doing an honest job together until she filed charges.

EXERCISE 53

HOW WAS THE COMPANY TO KNOW?

Method   MAKE THE CASE

Problem   Head-in-the-sand management is common in sexual harassment cases. Upper management rightly delegates day-to-day management and counseling responsibility and authority to the subordinates designated as supervisors. Sexual harassment, however, is an institutional responsibility that cannot be delegated or ignored. Professing not to see (even if it's true) what it has a mandate to prevent from occurring is not a viable defensive argument when a company is brought into a sexual harassment dispute that took place in its domain.

Objective Provide participants with the occasion to consider sexual harassment points of view from a perspective other than their own. Have them change positions and think as advocates for an alien position. Use the experience to enlighten managers on all levels about company responsibilities for setting an example on sexual harassment, making it clear that harassing behavior will not be tolerated and will be harshly punished if it does occur. Emphasis should be placed on protecting workers who find themselves in coercive sexual harassment situations. Communicate that sexual harassment prevention is an active responsibility of the company, not one that it successfully evades by choosing not to see the problem.

Procedure

✓ Select two teams of about six each consisting of men and women.

✓ Pass out Scenarios 1 and 2 to the teams and audience.

✓ Instruct the teams to read and discuss their scenarios and come up with their strongest defense for their assigned position—whether they agree with it or not.

✓ Ask each team to have a spokesperson describe its scenario and summarize its defense for the position. Other team members are encouraged to contribute to the defense. (You may suggest a line of defense if necessary to get the discussion started.)

✓ Ask one team to challenge the other's position. (You may suggest some challenges if necessary to move the discussion forward.)

✓ Briefly note key words and phrases on a pad or blackboard—this helps people go back and elaborate on earlier points.

✓ Encourage the exchange of challenge and defense until you feel the relevant points have been made.

✓ Solicit a vote from the entire audience, which serves as the jury. The question for the jury is: Could the company have reasonably known of the sexual harassment problem and prevented it?

✓ Note that the objective is to uncover points of view that participants might not have considered. The case is deliberately ambiguous, open-ended, and subject to various interpretations and judgments (just like real life situations). Acknowledge this so you don't leave the group frustrated that a "correct" judgment was not reached.

Discussion Questions

1. Do you think it's possible for this kind of situation to exist without upper-level company knowledge?

2. Do you see legitimate arguments for each of the positions in this case? If so, what are they? What are the issues and considerations?

3. Where would you place each position on a chronology of socially progressive thinking? Caveman? American frontier? Roaring 20s? World War II? 50s? 60s? 90s? etc.?

4. Is either position out of vogue with mainstream thinking in the 90s? If so, did you realize this prior to this training exercise? Does it matter to you? Do you see any practical reasons to reconsider any of your assumptions?

WHAT'S THE POINT?

It is enlightening to be forced to advocate something you don't necessarily believe. Conscientiously doing so can give you perspectives on the opposing view that you may not have considered otherwise. Understanding (if not accepting) a position you oppose can help you deal more effectively with those who espouse it. In this exercise managers will grow more sensitive to the expectation that they act to prevent and punish harassment and not look the other way. Workers will learn that help should be expected from the harasser's supervisory chain, and that when it is not forthcoming, they have the basis for a complaint based on the failure to act.

Materials

✓ Blackboard and chalk, or markers and board or pad to display notes before the group

✓ Copies of the scenarios for the teams

Time Required

Approximately 35 minutes

"HOW WAS THE COMPANY TO KNOW?" SCENARIO 1

Directions:

Discuss the scenario as a team. Understand that *your role as a team is to defend (whether you agree with them or not) the organization and its top managers against the charges of the women alleging higher-level culpability in the sexual harassment they suffered at the hands of lower-level supervisors.* Think about the arguments people who believe in this position would use to advocate it—even if you would not. You will have a chance to say why you consider the position you articulate in this game is wrong. The team should choose a spokesperson, but everyone is encouraged to contribute to the discussion.

Situation

✓ The administrative offices of a large metropolitan corrections facility have for a decade operated a work release program in which prisoners provide support services for the regular staff. The prisoners view the assignment as a desirable break from the jail environment and are generally eager to participate. Over the years the program has deteriorated badly—it has become an opportunity to sexually exploit female prisoners by routinely parading them before supervisors who make their selections based on attractiveness.

✓ Make the case that this situation exists at the lower echelons of a large bureaucratic organization and that the organization and its top managers didn't know what was going on and should not be held responsible for the actions of a few supervisors who take advantage of their authority.

"HOW WAS THE COMPANY TO KNOW?" SCENARIO 2

Directions:

Discuss the scenario as a team. Understand that *your role as a team is to support (whether you agree with it or not) the position of the women alleging higher-level culpability in the sexual harassment they experienced at the hands of lower-level supervisors.* Think about the arguments people who believe in this position would use to defend it—even if you find it objectionable. You will have a chance later to say why you consider the position you articulate in this situation is wrong, if that is how you feel. The team should choose a spokesperson, but everyone is encouraged to contribute to the discussion.

Situation

✓ The administrative offices of a large metropolitan corrections facility have for a decade operated a work release program in which prisoners provide support services for the regular staff. The prisoners view the assignment as a desirable break from the jail environment and are generally eager to participate. Over the years the program has deteriorated badly—it has become an opportunity to sexually exploit female prisoners by routinely parading them before supervisors who make their selections based on attractiveness.

✓ Make the case that this situation exists at the lower echelons of a large bureaucratic organization, but that the organization's top managers undoubtedly knew it was going on and should be held responsible for the actions of subordinates who take advantage of their authority.

EXERCISE 54

ASSIGN THE FAULT

Method   MATCH THE ITEMS

Problem   Implementing sexual harassment policy within a business breaks down when upper-level management says the right things but looks the other way when middle management either commits or overlooks infractions among subordinates. The ability to distinguish between the fault of employees and the liability of the organization when sexual harassment occurs is important for all levels of management and the people who work for them. In this exercise participants indicate their opinions on whether the subordinate or the organization was most at fault in a number of scenarios.

Objective   Demonstrate to the participants that responsibility for sexual harassment can be assigned to both the individual committing the objectionable behavior and the organization that allowed him or her to do it. Use the experience to focus on the employer's obligation to provide a sexual-harassment-free workplace, and sketch the parameters of when an organization has done what is right and necessary to avoid liability for contributing to the problem.

Procedure   ✓ Men and women may hold different views about a company's responsibilities for preventing sexual harassment. To contrast their disparate views and increase mutual understanding, respondents are asked to indicate their genders before completing the anonymous questionnaire. Due to much publicity about the this issue, many people of both genders know the "politically correct" answer but hold different personal views. To get both viewpoints, the survey asks participants to differentiate between what they honestly feel and what they believe to be the "right" response. Stress the anonymity aspect of the exercise and urge participants to respond candidly.

✓ Distribute the "Assign The Fault" Matching Form. (A sample is provided or you may create your own.) Ask members of the group to indicate their own gender and then mark each entry candidly by circling the selection they feel indicates the best answer. Also ask for a second matching that indicates what they *think* the politically correct (PC) answer would be. Clarify that the PC response does not have to be different from the one expressing their gut feeling. The two might be the same and they may or may not be "right." The objective is simply to react instinctively and then indicate what is perceived to be the socially acceptable response.

✓ Have the respondents fold their matching forms for privacy and ask volunteers to collect the forms and tally the results. Have them tally the responses for men, women, and the total group on each item (i.e., how many men, women, and total group participants marked each item)—for candid and PC responses. Post the results before the group and discuss them.

Discussion Questions	1. Were you surprised at the answers of the opposite sex? your own gender? the group? Why or why not?
	2. How do you account for differences among the groups if there are any?
	3. What messages do the results convey?
	4. What are some possible implications for sexual harassment?
	5. Are there differences between the candid and politically correct responses? Do you think they might be narrowed in the future? If so, why? How?

WHAT'S THE POINT?

The ability to judge institutional and individual responsibility in cases of sexual harassment is an important skill for both managers and victims. A key item in the assigning of fault is distinguishing between when management should intervene to prevent or punish sexual harassment behavior and when it should mind its own business when it comes to its employees' personal lives. This exercise lets participants apply their judgment, test it against that of other individuals and the group, and refine it with the help of the trainers.

Materials

✓ Blackboard and chalk, or markers and board or pad to display results before the group

✓ Copies of the matching form for individual members of the group

Time Required

Approximately 20 minutes

"ASSIGN THE FAULT" MATCHING FORM

Directions:

A. Check your gender, but *do not put your name* on this anonymous survey.

☐ Male   ☐ Female

B. Read each statement and mark it twice: (1) circle the selection on the form that best matches your candid, personal opinion of who is at fault; and (2) circle the selection that matches what you believe to be the "politically correct" response.

1. Several women in the division have risen through the ranks much faster than is usual. It's an "open secret" that they've slept their way to the top, voluntarily entering into sexual liaisons with managers who have promotion authority and who reward subordinates in exchange for sexual favors. A group that didn't play the game and suffered when promotion time arrived filed a hostile environment sexual harassment suit, charging both the managers involved and the company. Assign the fault.

Candid opinion:	
Company at fault	Company Not at Fault

Politically correct opinion:	
Company at fault	Company Not at Fault

2. While enduring an extended period of sexual harassment from her supervisor, a woman gradually lost her effectiveness on the job and was dismissed because of poor performance. When the company was named in the sexual harassment complaint filed on her behalf, its response was that it bore no fault in the matter, but was simply reacting to poor job performance that was obvious to everyone in the shop. The company response did not mention the fact that the harassment was just as obvious. Assign the fault.

Candid opinion:	
Company at fault	Company Not at Fault

Politically correct opinion:	
Company at fault	Company Not at Fault

3. ABC Corporation was named in an action against a consultant they had hired to do periodic inspections of its field operations. Women in the business complained that they were coerced into sexual relationships by the consultant to avoid negative reports on their work. The company responded that the man was an independent contractor and not an employee of the firm. Therefore, while it acknowledged having heard about his objectionable behavior, it felt no obligation to intervene or accept responsibility for the sexual harassment he committed. Assign the fault.

Candid opinion:	
Company at fault	Company Not at Fault

Politically correct opinion:	
Company at fault	Company Not at Fault

4. An executive assistant became sexually involved with the man for whom she worked. While her compliance resulted in favorable treatment, it was a quiet arrangement that went unnoticed in an organization that had an excellent record for enforcing its sexual harassment policy. When he ended the relationship, she filed a complaint against the man and assumed that the company would automatically be held liable. Is this a correct assumption? Assign the fault.

Candid opinion:

Company at fault   Company Not at Fault

Politically correct opinion:

Company at fault   Company Not at Fault

Comments (cover or remove before copying): Each situation contains sketchy information, and answers might be different with the introduction of additional information. The examples are intended to stimulate discussion and uncover relevant points, not establish indelible criteria or provide indisputable rulings of guilt or innocence. In general, an informed person would respond: 1. At fault—The company should have known about and corrected the problem; 2. At fault—A company can't dismiss for poor performance resulting from harassment; 3. At fault—The consultant was hired by the company and could be considered its agent; 4. Not at fault—The company is not automatically liable, and they have a strong prevention program in place.

EXERCISE 55

SO WHOM DO YOU BLAME?

Method

MULTIPLE CHOICE

Problem

Implementation of a company's sexual harassment policy sometimes breaks down when management voices its commitment to preventing abuses and punishing offenders, but looks the other way when subordinates either commit or overlook infractions. When sexual harassment takes place, it is necessary to be able to distinguish between the degree of blame due subordinates and the liability of the organization. In this exercise participants indicate their opinions on whether the subordinate or the organization was most at fault.

Objective

Demonstrate to the participants that blame for sexual harassment can accrue to both the individual committing the objectionable behavior and the organization that allowed him or her to do it. Use the experience to emphasize the employer's obligation to provide a workplace free from sexual harassment, and sketch the parameters of when an organization has acted sufficiently aggressively to avoid liability for contributing to the problem.

Procedure

✓ Due to a great deal of publicity about gender conflicts, most people know the "politically correct" responses to questions about sexual harassment in the modern workplace. When you begin the exercise, acknowledge this and then emphasize that participants' answers will be anonymous and that the usefulness of the training relies on their candid responses. Ask them to express their gut feelings rather than those they think are "right" and to avoid extreme responses that do not express their true beliefs.

✓ Distribute the "So Whom Do You Blame?" Quiz. (A sample is provided or you may create your own.) Ask members of the group to indicate their gender and mark each entry candidly by selecting the multiple-choice item that indicates their belief about who is to blame for the sexual harassment problem.

✓ Have the respondents fold their quizzes for privacy and ask volunteers to collect the forms and tally the results. Have them tally the responses for men, women, and the total group on each question (i.e., how many men, women, and total group participants marked the various responses). Post the results before the group and discuss them.

Discussion Questions

1. Do you think men and women have different expectations of employers in sexual harassment matters? Why or why not?

2. How do you account for the differences among the groups answering the quiz in this exercise?

3. What messages do the quiz results convey?

4. What are some possible implications for sexual harassment?

5. Do you think gender stereotyping affected how you answered any of the questions? how your opposite-sex peers answered them? How? Why?

WHAT'S THE POINT?

Judgment and the ability to assess both institutional and individual responsibility in cases of sexual harassment are important skills for both managers and victims. Knowing where to assign blame is key in interpreting when management keeps a proper distance from employees' personal lives and when it wrongfully fails to protect them from harassment. This exercise lets participants apply their judgment, test it against that of other individuals and the group, and refine it with the help of the trainers.

Materials

✓ Blackboard and chalk, or markers and board or pad to display results before the group

✓ Copies of the "So Whom Do You Blame?" Quiz for individual members of the group

Time Required

Approximately 20 minutes

"SO WHOM DO YOU BLAME?" QUIZ

Directions:

A. Check your gender, but *do not put your name* on this anonymous quiz.

☐ Male   ☐ Female

B. Read each statement and circle the response that you think is factually correct.

1. The term "constructive discharge" defines a situation in which an employee quits because sexual harassment has gotten so bad she'd rather give up her position than endure it any longer. She's been indirectly "fired" by the employer's failure to provide a harassment-free workplace, and the company gets the blame.
   a. How ridiculous! No one "fired" her; she quit and the company had nothing to do with it.
   b. This is one of the legal grounds used in employment law to establish a company's liability for sexual harassment, because the company neglected its obligations to provide a harassment-free workplace.
   c. Constructive discharge is only a valid charge in the building trades.
   d. The company is squeaky clean if the employee quits.
   e. None of the above.

2. Having a track record of which of the following practices will help absolve a company of blame in a sexual harassment complaint?
   a. Voicing strong support for the organization's sexual harassment policy and honestly believing in it.
   b. Having a properly drawn sexual harassment policy and enforcement procedures and enforcing them vigorously when violations occur.
   c. Assigning someone to draft a sexual harassment policy and hear complaints when they are made.
   d. Not discharging employees whose performance deteriorates because of sexual harassment.
   e. All of the above.

3. Which of the following best assesses the blame in a case where some employees exchange sexual favors for privileges and rewards while those who don't participate suffer career stagnation and unfavorable treatment?
   a. An employer exercising reasonably diligent oversight should notice the differences between the groups and find out their cause.
   b. Sexual harassment was not intended to support the hurt feelings of a few employees who wear their morality on their sleeves and probably wouldn't have been promoted anyway.
   c. Agency law would add to the argument against the company, establishing that those involved in the *quid pro quo* harassment were acting on the company's behalf and it did too little to control them.
   d. a and c
   e. All of the above

4. "Apparent authority" is the power given to supervisors to make employment decisions such as hiring, firing, and promoting those who work for them. Companies that fail to both implement strong policies against sexual harassment and maintain effective complaint procedures are blamed for the acts of those to whom they give apparent authority because …
   a. The greater the apparent authority, the more power the person to whom it is delegated has to impose unwelcome sexual behavior or create/allow a hostile working environment.
   b. Apparent authority is much the same as agency law in that the employee is seen to be acting on behalf of the employer.

    c. Companies are automatically liable when they convey apparent authority.
    d. a and b
    e. All of the above.

5. The company would be to blame in which of the following situations?
    a. An employee is fired due to poor performance caused by sexual harassment on the job.
    b. An employee quits due to sexual harassment on the job and the company did too little to prevent it.
    c. One group of employees received favorable treatment because they engaged in sexual activities with supervisors while another group did not and were punished.
    d. None of the above
    e. a, b, and c

Answers (mask or remove before copying): 1 = b, 2 = e, 3 = d, 4 = d, 5 = e. NOTE: Although these answers would be accepted by most current authorities, remind the group that refinements can be added to many situations that might alter the judgment of whether harassment occurred and who was to blame for it.

EXERCISE 56

THAT'S HARDLY THE COMPANY'S FAULT!

Method   RATE THE ACCURACY

Problem   Companies often react with surprise when named in sexual harassment actions about which they have little or no knowledge. Their first reaction is that the problem is obviously between the principals and they protest that the company is not to blame for what adult employees do with their sex lives. Because such a position would leave harassed employees at the mercy of their tormentors, laws and regulations on the subject define clear areas of company responsibility. It is necessary to teach everyone involved that companies' obligations require them to allocate resources to address the problem effectively.

Objective   Demonstrate to the participants that companies are legally obligated to provide a sexual harassment-free working environment. Illustrate differences in perceptions that may exist between women and men on employers' responsibility for ameliorating disputes that arise between them on matters involving gender and workplace tensions. Use the experience to create an awareness of the employer's appropriate role and more clearly identify company resources as the place to start in resolving workplace incidents involving harassment.

Procedure   ✓ Due to a great deal of publicity about sexual harassment, most people know the "politically correct" responses to questions dealing with the issue. When you begin the exercise, acknowledge this and then emphasize that participants' answers will be anonymous and that the usefulness of the training relies on their candid responses. Ask them to express their gut feelings rather than those they think are "right" and to avoid extreme responses that do not express their true beliefs.

✓ Distribute the rating scales. (A sample is provided or you may create your own.) Ask members of the group to indicate their gender and then rate each assumption candidly by circling a number on the scale. Also ask for a second rating that indicates what they *think* the politically correct (PC) answer would be. Clarify that the PC response does not have to be different from the one expressing their gut feeling. The two might be the same and they may or may not be "right." The objective is simply to react instinctively and then indicate what is perceived to be the socially acceptable response.

✓ Have the respondents fold their surveys for privacy and ask volunteers to collect and score the results. Have them calculate the average score for men, women, and the total group for each question (i.e., add up the individual scores and divide by the total number of surveys in that group for each question)—for candid and PC responses. Post the results before the group and discuss them.

1. Were you surprised that men and women responded differently? the same? Why or why not?

2. How do you account for the differences?

3. What do you think the fact that men and women answered differently has to say about the prospects for resolving sexual harassment disputes?

4. Are your candid and PC responses different? If so, why? Will that ever change? Why or why not?

5. Are there ratings that you would change now that we've discussed them? Are there any that you are at least willing to rethink quietly on your own?

WHAT'S THE POINT?

The employer in a sexual harassment dispute is popularly seen as a passive and remote force, saying and doing what is required to comply with government mandates and avoiding embarrassing and potentially costly liability settlements. Regardless of how true this may actually be in individual cases, sexual harassment regulations are unambiguous when it comes to employer responsibilities for providing a workplace free from harassment and punishing those who violate the rules. The point of this exercise is to inform managers of their obligations as agents of their companies, and to let potential victims know that company resources should be available if they need assistance.

Materials

✓ Blackboard and chalk, or markers and board or pad to display results before the group

✓ Copies of the survey for individual members of the group

✓ A pocket calculator

Time Required

Approximately 25 minutes

"THAT'S HARDLY THE COMPANY'S FAULT!" SURVEY FORM

Directions:

A. Check your gender, but *do not put your name* on this anonymous survey.

☐ Male ☐ Female

B. In the context of workplace sexual harassment, read each scenario and judge the accuracy of perception twice: (1) circle the number on the scale that best represents your candid, personal opinion; and (2) circle the number that represents what you believe to be the "politically correct" response.

1. It began in the hiring interview when he told her she had the job but that he expected her to provide him with more than clerical services. She assumed it was just talk—she'd heard this sort of thing before—and took the position, assuming she could fend him off if he made a real approach. Her failure to meet his expectations was followed by a lengthy period of harassment, during which she couldn't do her job adequately. She sued, naming him and the company, since she had learned from others that she was the latest in a series of women he had victimized. In her thinking, it was the company's fault as well as his!

Candid opinion:

1   2   3   4   5   6   7   8   9   10

Accurate   Inaccurate

Politically correct opinion:

1   2   3   4   5   6   7   8   9   10

Accurate   Inaccurate

2. A former employee charged that the company was responsible for the actions of one of its mid-level managers who had sexually harassed her to the point where she quit rather than face him any longer. The corporate counsel maintained that the man had acted alone, and that no link between her resignation and his behavior was suggested to anyone in senior management. Since it had no prior knowledge of the problem, the company was without fault.

Candid opinion:

1   2   3   4   5   6   7   8   9   10

Accurate   Inaccurate

Politically correct opinion:

1   2   3   4   5   6   7   8   9   10

Accurate   Inaccurate

3. She was told when she joined the sales team that people there worked hard and partied harder, and that to go along was necessary if she was to enjoy continued upward mobility within the company. While she was prepared for long hours and enjoyed good times, she wasn't prepared to join a sexual intimacy pool consisting of people she hardly knew and didn't intend to know intimately. As soon as she let her feelings be known, her accounts list changed to small, marginal, geographically scattered, nonlucrative clients. When she complained to the human resources direc-

tor and raised the possibility of hostile environment charges, she was told that she had no case, since anyone joining that team was immediately apprised of its special *"esprit de corps."* That she hadn't caught on was hardly the company's fault! When she elaborated on what was expected of her, the HR rep responded coldly that this team delivers spectacular results, and senior management doesn't ask questions about their methods. Any problems she might have should be addressed to the team's manager, not the company.

Candid opinion:

| 1 | 2 | 3 | 4 | 5 | 6 | 7 | 8 | 9 | 10 |

Accurate   Inaccurate

Politically correct opinion:

| 1 | 2 | 3 | 4 | 5 | 6 | 7 | 8 | 9 | 10 |

Accurate   Inaccurate

---

4. The charges were serious enough to warrant a field visit by an investigator from the Equal Employment Opportunity Commission. Interviews with randomly selected employees at all levels revealed a generally high level of awareness of the company's policies regarding sexual harassment and the available remedies. A look at the published policies and records of complaints and their resolution showed vigorous efforts on the company's part. But the field agent noted that the complaining party in this case had not chosen to use the in-house procedures because she feared retaliation from her supervisor. The EEOC person found the company not at fault, citing that nothing in the well-documented company history on sexual harassment prevention and conflict resolution indicated that it would tolerate retaliation.

Candid opinion:

| 1 | 2 | 3 | 4 | 5 | 6 | 7 | 8 | 9 | 10 |

Accurate   Inaccurate

Politically correct opinion:

| 1 | 2 | 3 | 4 | 5 | 6 | 7 | 8 | 9 | 10 |

Accurate   Inaccurate

EXERCISE 57

WHAT DO YOU MEAN WE "FIRED" HER?

Method	SOLVE THE RIDDLE
Problem	Sometimes when men and women quit their jobs, a closer look at the circumstances reveals that they didn't resign as the term is normally used, but instead experienced a *de facto* firing, defined legally as "constructive discharge." The missed opportunities that result may have nothing to do with their qualifications or ability to meet the job's challenges. Sexual harassment is a possible reason why people "voluntarily" leave jobs in which they had every expectation of excelling.
Objective	Demonstrate to the participants that sexual harassment may have such an adverse impact on otherwise successful job aspirants that they simply cannot seize what appears to be an opportunity tailor-made for them. Making the point in a riddle presents sexual harassment in a context in which it operates in the background and not as a highly visible factor in workplace problem solving. If asked why the employee quit, many participants will probably list traditional reasons, such as personality conflicts, lacking the "right stuff" to work under pressure, unwillingness to put in long hours, etc.—with sexual harassment as an afterthought if it makes the list at all.
Procedure	✓ Pass out copies of the "What Do You Mean We 'Fired' Her?" Riddle Form to the participants. Riddles are most effective early in sexual harassment training sessions, before the group becomes predisposed to see harassment lurking in every situation. If your group jumps to the sexual harassment conclusion, use the occasion to discuss the points of the riddle, and to contrast how their reaction might have differed in the training situation and real life (i.e., they may have been less prone to see the sexual harassment problem in real life).
	✓ Ask them to work privately on solving the riddle and answering the questions that follow it. This experience will be diminished in value by allowing anyone to provide the answer before individuals ponder the puzzle on their own.
	✓ After most group members indicate they have either solved the riddle or given up, interrupt them and begin discussing the solution and its ramifications for relations between women and men at work.
Discussion Questions	1. What first occurred to you as possible reasons for Rebecca's giving up a job opportunity that she had been working toward all of her professional career? Did you think of sexual harassment as a potential reason for her departure?

235

2. Do you think Rebecca's course of action was correct? Why or why not? If not, what do you think she should have done?

3. Do you think the bank in this case bears any responsibility for Rebecca's situation? What should they have done?

4. If you could predict the future, do you think this riddle would be a useful training device before a similar audience in 20 years? Why or why not? What changes currently taking place in the work force might alter the likely reactions of future audiences?

WHAT'S THE POINT?

We are accustomed to judging employees' reasons for quitting their jobs on the basis of superficial personality problems and the like. It is important to be alert to deeper conflicts and manipulation of personal vulnerabilities that occur because of prohibited behavior like sexual harassment. This is especially true when the actions come from those normally expected to help rather than harm the workers they manage. Important to management: "Constructive discharge" can be a viable charge in sexual harassment cases where the company is faulted for the *de facto* firing of an employee because it did not protect her from harassment.

Materials

✓ "What Do You Mean We 'Fired' Her?" Riddle Forms

Time Required

Approximately 25 minutes

"WHAT DO YOU MEAN WE 'FIRED' HER?" RIDDLE FORM

Carefully read the following riddle, and privately explore your thoughts as you attempt to find the solution. Please do not discuss the riddle with others until the group addresses the solution. Answer the questions that follow.

"What Do You Mean We 'Fired' Her?" Riddle
Colleagues were surprised when Rebecca quit her job as a loan processor at a local savings bank. She had worked her way up from a clerical position, earned a degree part time, and expected to be promoted to loan officer after a pending merger with a large regional bank. Her promotion would have put her on the fast track, and she'd have been working directly for the senior lender, who was well-known in the business and had been won away from a competitor six months earlier. An intimate friend knew Rebecca had been having a devastating sexual harassment problem with the senior lender when she had been assigned to work with him in coordinating the department's merger. She put two and two together, got Rebecca the help of an employment lawyer, and in a few weeks the savings bank was facing charges that it fired her.

1. How can this be possible?
2. How could quitting her job be construed as tantamount to being fired by her employer?

Solution (cover or remove before copying): Rebecca was sexually harassed so severely that she found it necessary to quit a very promising job to avoid her tormentor, who was set to become her boss. Because her employer allowed such conditions to exist, it was legitimately accused of "constructive discharge." In the eyes of the law, the bank in effect fired her due to its neglect, even though it issued no dismissal order and had no desire to lose her services.

EXERCISE 58

50:50 SPLIT ON "CAN YOU BLAME THE COMPANY?"

Method   SORT THE LISTS

Problem   Effective implementation of a company's sexual harassment policy and enforcement procedures is hampered when management has all the right stuff on paper but turns a blind eye when subordinates either commit harassment or overlook infractions by those they supervise. Distinguishing between the fault of subordinates and the liability of the organization when sexual harassment occurs is necessary for managers and workers alike. In this exercise participants indicate their opinions on whether the organization was at fault.

Objective   Demonstrate to the participants that sexual harassment can be the fault of both the individual engaging in offending behavior and the organization that allowed him or her to do it. Use the experience to develop an awareness of the employer's obligation to provide a workplace free from sexual harassment, and demonstrate how an organization can avoid liability for contributing to the problem.

Procedure   ✓ Due to a great deal of publicity about sexual harassment, most people know the "politically correct" responses to questions about problems between the genders in the modern workplace. When you begin the exercise, acknowledge this and then emphasize that participants' answers will be anonymous and that the usefulness of the training relies on their candid responses. Ask them to express their gut feelings rather than those they think are "right" and to avoid extreme responses that do not express their true beliefs.

                        ✓ Distribute 50:50 Split on "Can You Blame the Company?" Forms. (A sample is provided or you may create your own.) Ask members of the group to place the descriptive statements under the Blame the Company and Don't Blame the Company columns. Mention that both columns must contain the same number of statements, and that the task may grow more difficult as forced choices must be made toward the end. (VARIATION: To liven up the process, instead of having participants simply read the descriptive statements, have trainers or volunteers from the group read or act them out.)

                        ✓ Have the respondents fold their surveys for privacy and ask volunteers to collect and score the results. Have them tally the responses. Post the results before the group and discuss.

Discussion Questions 1. Did you have difficulty deciding whether or not employers should be held liable for the actions of their employees? Why? What criteria did you use in making your decisions?

2. Do you think men and women tend to view employer obligations differently? If so, why?

3. Are there situations you find less offensive than others? Some that don't bother you at all? Why or why not?

4. Which situations do you consider to be the most in transition and apt to change in our lifetimes?

5. What do you think the fact that men and women answered differently has to say about the potential for misunderstandings that could lead to sexual harassment problems and make resolving them difficult?

6. Are there entries that you would change now that we've discussed them?

WHAT'S THE POINT?

The ability to assess both institutional and individual responsibility in cases of sexual harassment is an important skill for both managers and victims. Assigning blame is key to determining when management should stay out of its employees' personal lives and when it wrongfully fails to protect them from sexual harassment. This exercise lets participants apply their judgment, test it against that of other individuals and the group, and refine it with the help of the trainers.

Materials

✓ 50:50 Split on "Can You Blame the Company?" Forms

✓ Chalkboard or pad on which to display the results

Time Required

Approximately 25 minutes

50:50 SPLIT ON "CAN YOU BLAME THE COMPANY?" FORM

Directions:

A. Mentally inventory the list, and place each descriptive statement under the "Blame the Company" or "Don't Blame the Company" column. If you see shades of both in a single statement, place it where you think it fits best and be prepared to explain your decision.

B. You must end up with the same number of statements in both columns.

Descriptive Statements

A. She quit because her supervisor made her life miserable after she told him no and no one in the company did anything about it.

B. In spite of a clearly defined complaint resolution procedure and the well-publicized backing of management, she consented to an unwanted sexual relationship and no one knew there was a problem until she quit.

C. The personnel guy in charge of temporary help created a virtual harem for himself by requesting particular women by name because they were willing to satisfy more than his word processing and filing needs. When someone finally complained, the folks on up the line in top management chuckled to themselves—they had watched with some grudging admiration as the young man "got the job done." But it was his neck, not the company's—right?

D. At the coffee bar after work, several young managers were speculating about how a smart woman could easily set herself up for a nice monetary settlement from the company by having an affair with the right guy and then screaming sexual harassment. From what they understand, even a well-run company with a good track record on protecting rights and punishing offenders is automatically liable in such cases—right?

E. He was a former top executive who had taken early retirement to side-step sexual harassment charges. The company hired him as an independent consultant, and soon he was up to his old tricks—harassing a woman in the department where he's assigned. The woman brought charges against him and the company. "Not to worry, " said company executives. "After all, he's an independent contractor now and fully responsible for his own actions"—right?

F. It was a bitter case that cost the company a lot of good will among its employees and the community, but now it was taking a favorable turn in the eyes of management. The head of human resources had been targeted for the failure of the sexual harassment prevention program. It looked like he'd be the scapegoat and the company would walk away from the problem unscathed. After all, responsibility for the program had been delegated to him. The company was on solid ground and had nothing else to fear—right?

G. Quietly and with no fanfare the woman and her recently hired administrative assistant were having a mutually consensual sexual relationship. Within the firm the only concern was for appearances if they failed to keep the liaison discreet or allowed it to interfere with business. When the relationship hit the skids and the young man decided to charge his former lover and the company with sexual harassment, the corporate counsel was comfortable that the company had nothing to worry about since its records contained successful complaint resolutions based on well-publicized complaint procedures that this man hadn't even attempted to use. A voluntary relationship, no attempt to articulate a problem before placing charges—the company lawyer's right, it's not apt to be faulted!

H. The company said she was let go for a well-documented failure to perform her duties satisfactorily, and her after-the-fact charges (she didn't use the complaint procedure) that her supervisor sexually harassed her to the point where she couldn't do her job didn't stand up to scrutiny in the view of corporate counsel. None of her colleagues corroborated her story, and the man she named was an exemplary employee with an excellent reputation on the job and in the community. The company has nothing to worry about—right?

I. He ran the department like his own fiefdom for twenty years and upper management stayed out of his affairs—quite literally—until last year. His series of sexual liaisons with coworkers was almost legendary in the firm, but up until now, victims who filed complaints left quietly after being paid off and coerced into signing confidentiality agreements. A woman who was hired eight months ago encountered his same old behavior, used the newly effective complaint procedure and promptly got satisfaction, but decided to pursue her case in court anyway. Based on the company's history, it could still have to pay her a costly settlement—how will it end up?

J. The women did not claim that anyone requested sexual favors or exposed them to sexually offensive language or actions, yet they charged that they were losing out on advancement opportunities because other women were trading on their sexuality, if not sexual favors, for favorable treatment that benefited their careers. The company's view was: "That's life. It's natural to reward those whose company you find stimulating!" Could this be a problem for the company?

Blame the Company	Don't Blame the Company
A.	A.
B.	B.
C.	C.
D.	D.
E.	E.

Answers (cover or remove before copying): A = B, B = DB, C = B, D = DB, E = B, F = B, G = DB, H = DB, I = DB, J = B. While informed people would generally agree with these answers, some statements have aspects that could be interpreted differently, depending on the perspective of the person answering. The objective is to stimulate thinking and communicate basic guidelines rather than to provide definitive answers to legal questions.

EXERCISE 59

IT'S THE COMPANY'S FAULT!

Method   TRUE/FALSE

Problem   Implementing sexual harassment policy breaks down when the organization's upper-level management says the right things but looks the other way when middle management either commits or overlooks infractions among subordinates. The ability to distinguish between the fault of employees and the liability of the organization when sexual harassment occurs is important for all levels of management and the people who work for them. In this exercise participants indicate their opinions on whether the subordinate or the organization was most at fault in a number of scenarios.

Objective   Demonstrate to the participants that responsibility for sexual harassment can be assigned to both the individual committing the objectionable behavior and the organization that allowed him or her to do it. Use the experience to focus on the employer's obligation to provide a sexual-harassment-free workplace, and sketch the parameters of when an organization has done what is right and necessary to avoid liability for contributing to the problem.

Procedure   ✓ Due to a great deal of publicity about sexual harassment, many people know the "politically correct" response to questions surrounding the issue. When you begin the exercise, acknowledge this and then emphasize that participants' answers will be anonymous and that the usefulness of the training relies on their candid responses. Ask them to express their gut feelings rather than those they think are "right" and to avoid extreme responses that do not express their true beliefs.

✓ Distribute "It's The Company's Fault!" Quiz. (A sample is provided or you may create your own.) Ask members of the group to read each statement and respond true or false.

✓ Have the respondents fold their quizzes for privacy and ask volunteers to collect and score the results. Have them tally the number of people who marked each statement true and false. Post the results before the group and discuss them.

Discussion Questions   1. Did men and women judge the situations differently? the same? Why or why not?

2. Do you think men and women tend to view particular types of behavior in a certain way simply because they have different gender experiences throughout their lives?

3. Are there situations you found easier to classify than others? Why?

242

4. How do you think the ability to identify and classify offensive behavior and assign blame impacts potential misunderstandings that could lead to difficulty in resolving sexual harassment disputes?

5. Could knowing what employers are obligated to do help prevent sexual harassment in the first place? How?

WHAT'S THE POINT?

The ability to judge institutional and individual responsibility in cases of sexual harassment is an important skill for both managers and victims. A key item in assigning fault is distinguishing between when management should intervene to prevent or punish sexual harassment behavior and when it should mind its own business when it comes to its employees' personal lives. This exercise lets participants apply their judgment, test it against that of other individuals and the group, and refine it with the help of the trainers.

Materials

✓ "It's the Company's Fault!" Quiz

✓ Chalkboard or pad on which to display the results

Time Required

Approximately 20 minutes

"IT'S THE COMPANY'S FAULT!" QUIZ

Directions:

Read each statement and circle either True or False.

T F 1. She quit because the sexual harassment was so bad she preferred to give up her work than face it. No one in the company seemed to notice, much less do anything about it. The company shares substantial responsibility for the problem.

T F 2. They didn't get the good assignments and promotions they deserved because others were getting all the goodies in exchange for sexual favors. This situation involves substantial liability for the company.

T F 3. A first-rate sexual harassment program was in place and everyone acknowledged that it worked extremely well. Still she felt reluctant to use the remedies provided for fear her tormentor would find out and retaliate. The company will bear substantial liability.

T F 4. If her company fired her because she wasn't performing her duties satisfactorily, but it was common knowledge that her decline in productivity coincided with protracted sexual harassment, the company will share responsibility in a harassment suit.

T F 5. Her romance with the company CEO was at an end, and now she was determined to exact a high financial price from the executive committee she felt had resented their relationship from the outset. The courts will likely rule in her favor in a sexual harassment suit.

T F 6. He had the power to coerce her into an unwanted relationship because he was the gatekeeper for her retention and advancement—there were no real checks on his authority and he took full advantage of it. The firm will be liable for allowing this situation to exist.

Answers (mask or remove before copying): Although these questions are provided more to stimulate thought and discussion than to establish legal judgments, and other interpretations are possible, informed people would generally answer: 1 = T This might be a case for "constructive discharge" where she was indirectly "fired" by a company that didn't protect her; 2 = T The company cannot allow favorable or unfavorable treatment in exchange for sexual favors; 3 = F The company did all it could reasonably have been expected to do; 4 = T The company can't dismiss her due to poor job performance resulting from sexual harassment they should have prevented; 5 = F No indication of sexual harassment—she can't use it just to punish the company for personal considerations; 6 = T Common-law agency principles and "apparent authority" would likely be used to show the company gave power and, irresponsibly, failed to control it.

EXERCISE 60

YOU CAN'T BLAME THE COMPANY!/ OF COURSE YOU CAN!

Method   SPONTANEOUS REACTION

Problem   Implementing sexual harassment policy sometimes breaks down when company management voices its commitment to preventing abuses and punishing offenders, but looks the other way when subordinates either commit or overlook infractions by others. It is necessary to be able to distinguish between the degree of blame due subordinates and the liability of the organization when sexual harassment takes place. In this exercise participants indicate their opinions on whether the subordinate or the organization was most at fault.

Objective   Demonstrate to the participants that blame for sexual harassment can accrue to both the individual committing the objectionable behavior and the organization that allowed him or her to do it. Use the experience to emphasize the employer's obligation to provide a workplace free from sexual harassment, and sketch the parameters of when an organization has acted sufficiently aggressively to avoid liability for contributing to the problem.

Procedure   ✓ Due to a great deal of publicity about sexual harassment, many people know the "politically correct" response to questions surrounding the issue. When you begin the exercise, acknowledge this and then emphasize that participants' answers will be anonymous and that the usefulness of the training relies on their candid responses. Ask them to express their gut feelings rather than those they think are "right" and to avoid extreme responses that do not express their true beliefs.

✓ Distribute "You Can't Blame The Company!/Of Course You Can!" Reaction Form. (A sample is provided or you may create your own.) Ask members of the group to indicate their gender, read each statement, and respond spontaneously with their first reaction to each item and be prepared to defend their responses.

✓ Have the respondents fold their quizzes for privacy and ask volunteers to collect and score the results. Have them tally the number of people who marked each response for each statement. Do this for the combined group and for women and men separately. Post the results before the group and discuss them.

Discussion Questions 1. Did the men and women view many of the situations differently? the same? Why or why not?

2. How do you account for the differences?

3. Were you surprised that some of the actions, which you might have thought were grossly offensive, did not qualify as harassment? Why?

4. What do you think the fact that men and women answered differently has to say about the potential for misunderstandings that could lead to sexual harassment problems?

5. Are there responses that you would change now that we've discussed them? Are there any that you are at least willing to rethink quietly on your own?

WHAT'S THE POINT?

Judgment and the ability to assess both institutional and individual responsibility in cases of sexual harassment are important skills for both managers and victims. Knowing where to assign blame is key in interpreting when management keeps a proper distance from employees' personal lives and when it wrongfully fails to protect them from harassment. This exercise lets participants apply their judgment, test it against other individuals and the group, and refine it with the help of the trainers. Those representing management are sensitized to company responsibilities and encouraged to take proper initiatives on its behalf.

Materials

✓ "You Can't Blame the Company!/Of Course You Can!" Reaction Forms

✓ Chalkboard or pad on which to display the results

Time Required

Approximately 20 minutes

"YOU CAN'T BLAME THE COMPANY!/
OF COURSE YOU CAN!" REACTION FORM

Directions:

A. Check your gender, but *do not put your name* on this anonymous form.

☐ Male   ☐ Female

B. Read each statement and immediately make a single response—your initial reaction is wanted, so don't ponder the question.

You Can't Blame the Company!/Of Course You Can! Reaction

1. XYZ Corporation once ran a glitzy training program on sexual harassment, plugged its name into a computer-software-generated personnel policy manual that addressed the topic, distributed it to all employees, and announced that harassment would not be tolerated. However, a long-standing affair between an executive and her upwardly mobile assistant was common knowledge and his favorable treatment was widely resented. When people complained to human resources about sexual harassment, they were told to "try and work things out" with no offers of further help if that didn't work. When a frustrated employee finally made a serious harassment complaint to an outside agency and it was investigated, the likely finding was …

    A. You Can't Blame the Company!   **B.** Of Course You Can!

2. The Jackson Companies conducted an elaborate task analysis study that resulted in published objective performance criteria. Failure to meet stipulated levels of job performance was grounds for dismissal. Cassandra, formerly an outstanding production worker, slipped noticeably, was counseled by her supervisor, failed to improve, and was dismissed. But there was more to her story. She revealed in a later complaint that the deterioration in her performance was due to intense sexual harassment by her supervisor (the same one who counseled her on her declining productivity). Considering the guy's reputation, the problem could hardly have been a mystery to the next level of management. The company insisted her dismissal was based on a thoroughly objective assessment of her performance and denied knowing about the harassment, which was secondary to her not getting the job done anyhow. The judge ultimately ruled …

    A. You Can't Blame the Company!   **B.** Of Course You Can!

3. Diana worked uneventfully in a mid-level professional position at a large nonprofit organization for many years. It was generally assumed she would retire from there in another ten years. When she abruptly resigned, many people were surprised, but others knew that her new boss of six months had been sexually harassing her and a number of other women since his first day on the job. An extremely private person, she was profoundly embarrassed and found it impossible to discuss the matter with anyone, so she left her job rather than pursue an existing complaint resolution channel within the organization. Lawyers representing her later alleged that she had been "constructively discharged"—let down so badly by the company that it might as well have fired her.

    A. You Can't Blame the Company!   **B.** Of Course You Can!

4. The executive committee of Worthmore, Inc., a socially conscious, consumer-oriented firm that prides itself on enlightened personnel policies, was shocked to find a sex-for-promotions scandal unfolding in its marketing department. Worse, it learned that papers would soon be filed by a group of nonparticipating workers, naming the company as a defendant in a civil suit claiming that hostile environment sexual harassment unfairly limited their career progress. Disturbed as they were by the prospect of adverse publicity engendered by a court case, the executive committee took comfort in their belief that because the company had clearly delegated responsibility for

preventing such things to the department head, culpability stopped with him. Therefore, they might be embarrassed, but at least the company would not have to come up with a financial settlement. What was the likely opinion of the court?

    A. You Can't Blame the Company!   **B.** Of Course You Can!

5. Rita is a frumpy, middle-aged manager in a government agency where most of the work is top secret and many of the employees have been there for decades. Because of the nature of the organization, her complaints about sexist treatment dating from early in her career stopped with the "old boys" who ran the place. They waved her away every time she complained, saying that since no one was making improper sexual demands of Rita, she really had no basis for grousing about being referred to as "the girl," having to make coffee, buy presents for her boss's wife, etc. A contemporary legal review of the matter would likely find …

    A. You Can't Blame the Company!   **B.** Of Course You Can!

6. Carlos was notorious for having sexual liaisons with women who worked for him. He had complete power over their careers, and if they didn't "play," they found themselves relegated to bottom-of-the-barrel positions that were going nowhere. Management had heard things but was content to stay out of his way as long as his shop ran efficiently. Eventually his excesses drew a legal challenge and, to its surprise, the company was named as well. According to the employment lawyer making the case, the firm was guilty of extending "apparent authority" (giving Carlos the power to make employment decisions as though the firm were making them) and not controlling its use. The ruling was …

    A. You Can't Blame the Company!   **B.** Of Course You Can!

Answers (mask or remove before copying): 1 = B To provide a shield, corporate policy and practices must be effective;. 2 = B Objective proof of nonperformance will not fly as a defense if the poor work stems from harassment that the company had responsibility for preventing; 3 = B The company is guilty of constructive discharge unless it can demonstrate that it has effective complaint resolution policies and procedures that this particular employee just did not use; 4 = B Responsibility for providing a harassment-free environment cannot be delegated; 5 = B Even in the absence of sexual activity or language, gender is an unacceptable basis for discriminating, and using it to do so creates an illegal work environment; 6 = B A supervisor's authority almost certainly derives from his or her employer, who generally shares liability for the supervisor's actions.

CONCLUSION

If you have used the exercises in actual training sessions or merely reviewed them in preparation for future sessions, you can sense that sexual harassment is not always a black-and-white issue that lends itself to simple yes/no, guilty/not guilty answers. Of course, some situations *are* that simple—behavior has been so blatant that there is no question as to who is right and who is wrong. The fix here is clear, if not easy. Company policy describes behavior that will not be tolerated, and how to punish it when it occurs. Let potential victims know you won't bury your head in the sand and pretend you don't know that bad things are happening to them, and assure them you will respond when they sound the alarm for help, and sexual harassment horror shows will not likely occur on your watch.

But many more cases of sexual harassment involve shades of gray and the scenarios posed in these workbook exercises have as one of their goals the clarifying of boundaries in the fog of complex human behavior that envelops gender conflicts in the workplace. The task of ameliorating less severe but more pervasive tensions between the sexes among relatively normal people of reasonably good will is a massive one. And this is where you, the trainer, can be most effective. Managers and their subordinates need the facts from you—what does the law require from the employee? the manager? the company? How can they stay out of trouble? What is at the heart of gender conflicts? What are the myths and realities about gender differences and what do they mean? They also need controlled, safe experiences that will give them a visceral appreciation ("ah ha!" learning) of lessons already learned by others. They need to develop a sense of accurate boundaries, a skill best learned by experiencing workplace situations—even those contrived for training. Through prudent use of these exercises, you can help the participants avoid potential embarrassment and possibly even costly litigation.

So be clear and unapologetic about your objectives and avoid the trap of advocating values. Settle for describing workplace behavior standards that are clearly expected, and leave the personal value judgments to the individuals themselves. The exercises you conduct are designed to meet combined objectives: (1) they are occasions to communicate facts about the nature of sexual harassment, what it is, what it isn't, how to "know it when you see it," the legal obligations of business to prevent and protect, etc.; and (2) they are the arena in which you help your charges "feel" the problems, "sense" the boundaries required by law, and "accept" group norms as desirable benchmarks for future workplace behavior.

Also by the authors

Working Together: The New Rules and Realities for Managing Men and Women at Work, Andrea P. Baridon and David R. Eyler

More Than Friends, Less Than Lovers: Managing Sexual Attraction in Working Relationships, David R. Eyler and Andrea P. Baridon